Caroline Sutherland.

Active Participation -218

Group membership 165.

D0222367

COMMUNICATION AND PERSUASION

Communication and Persuasion

PSYCHOLOGICAL STUDIES OF OPINION CHANGE

by Carl I. Hovland

Irving L. Janis

and Harold H. Kelley

DEPARTMENT OF PSYCHOLOGY, YALE UNIVERSITY

GREENWOOD PRESS, PUBLISHERS
WESTPORT, CONNECTICUT

Library of Congress Cataloging in Publication Data

Hovland, Carl Iver, 1912–
 Communication and persuasion.

 Reprint. Originally published: New Haven : Yale
University Press, c1953.
 Includes bibliographies and index.
 1. Communication. 2. Persuasion (Rhetoric)
I. Janis, Irving Lester, 1918– . II. Kelley,
Harold H. III. Title.
[P90.H69 1981]   001.51   81-20104
ISBN 0-313-23348-9 (lib. bdg.)   AACR2

Reprinted with the permission of Yale University Press.

Reprinted in 1982 by Greenwood Press,
A division of Congressional Information Service, Inc.
88 Post Road West, Westport, Connecticut 06881

Printed in the United States of America

10 9 8 7 6 5 4 3 2 1

Preface

A GREAT deal of descriptive information has accumulated concerning persuasive communications—such as educational programs, publicity campaigns, advertising, and propaganda—and their effects on behavior and opinion. Most of this information comes from studies which focus on practical questions posed by communicators who make use of mass media. But for purposes of developing scientific propositions which specify the conditions under which the effectiveness of one or another type of persuasive communication is increased or decreased, the available evidence is extremely limited. Although applied research can be useful in suggesting tentative hypotheses and in posing theoretical problems for further analysis, the practical emphasis often results in the neglect of significant and provocative issues which do not appear to have immediate application. Hence basic research is greatly needed to supplement the findings derived from investigations of a practical nature. Such research, involving psychological experiments in a communication setting, can contribute to our understanding of the processes of memory, thought, motivation, and social influence. The material communicated can be controlled with much the same precision possible in laboratory research, but motivational and emotional factors can be permitted to operate more naturalistically than in the laboratory.

A program of research of this type, on the experimental modification of attitudes and opinions through communication, was set up by the authors under a grant from the Rockefeller Foundation. It is a great pleasure to record here our appreciation of the Foundation's support and encouragement.

The program was set up as a cooperative research and study group rather than as a .centralized, hierarchically organized project. Approximately 30 individuals have contributed to the work and many are at present continuing to investigate various problems discussed in this volume. Each individual in the group is encouraged to design and pursue a phase of the research in line with his own interests and in directions of promising opportunities. Over-all coordination of the research is achieved through frequent conferences and seminars. Most of the studies involve collaboration among a number of individuals with complementary skills and training. The majority of the participants are psychologists interested in personality, social relations, and higher thought processes. The group also includes representatives from sociology and anthropology. It is to be hoped that as the program develops political scientists and economists interested in the formation and modification of values will also participate.

The three authors of this book approach the problems of communication with quite different types of background and training. This diversity may occasionally result in some lack of uniformity in the terminology and theoretical principles applied in the various chapters. Initial differences were progressively reduced through continual conferences and debate at each stage of the planning and writing. As a result of this close collaboration it is difficult to allocate credit for the individual chapters, or to define seniority of authorship. Accordingly the authors are merely listed in alphabetical order. General responsibility for Chapters 4 and 8 was assumed by C. I. Hovland, for Chapters 3, 6, and 7 by I. L. Janis, and for Chapters 2 and 5 by H. H. Kelley. All three authors shared responsibility for Chapters 1 and 9.

The authors owe a considerable intellectual debt to all of the other participants in the program who contributed not only to the specific research reported but also to the formulation of problems through criticisms and suggestions during conferences and seminars. The individuals whose research will be discussed include at the faculty level Leonard W. Doob, Arthur I. Gladstone, Floyd G. Lounsbury, Arthur A. Lumsdaine, Fred D. Sheffield, Muzafer Sherif, and Edmund H. Volkart. Graduate student fellows and assistants whose research will be discussed include Elaine Bell, Daniel Berlyne, Seymour Feshbach, Marvin Herz, Herbert Kelman, Bert King, Kenneth Kurtz, Wallace Mandell, Harry C. Milholland, Jr., Marvin Schwartz, Walter Weiss, and Christine Lipps Woodruff. Others who have contributed to the program in the past or have work under way at present include Russell Clark, Enid Hobart, Harriet Linton, Rosalind Lorwin Feierabend, Anna Muhlbauer, Dean Pruitt, Eva Rosenbaum, Gerald Wiener, Hardy Wilcoxon, Jepson Wulff, and Norman Zide.

Several summer conferences on various fields of research were particularly helpful to us in outlining areas needing research. Participants in these planning conferences included Arthur A. Lumsdaine, Theodore M. Newcomb, and Edmund H. Volkart.

It is a pleasure to acknowledge our especial indebtedness to Fred Sheffield for his important contributions in numerous research planning conferences and for his critical reading of the first draft of the present volume. We also wish to record our thanks to a number of individuals who made suggestions after reading individual chapters: Robert P. Abelson, Solomon E. Asch, Daniel Bell, James W. Carper, Irvin L. Child, George Mahl, Neal E. Miller, Theodore M. Newcomb, and Muzafer Sherif. Herbert Kelman made valuable comments concerning a number of chapters and also assisted in preparing summaries of the experiments which were useful in writing the final chapter. Mrs. Rosalind Lorwin Feierabend provided editorial assistance in the revisions of the first and last chapters. Gerald Wiener not only helped in the routine chores of library work but also made several valuable suggestions concerning theoretical points. The library assistance provided by James Nora and Robert H. Peters is also gratefully acknowledged. Our special appreciation goes to Mrs. Lorraine S. Coe and Mrs. Alice M. Myers for assuming responsibility for the considerable task of typing the various drafts of the manuscript. Miss Jane Olejarczyk and Mrs. Susan Henry gave essential aid in this task at various critical points. We also wish to thank Sherman Tatz for taking time while in the midst of graduate work to prepare drawings for the figures.

The writers are deeply grateful to Leonard W. Doob, who served informally as editor of the volume and made a number of important suggestions concerning organization. We also wish to acknowledge the helpful cooperation of the entire staff of the Yale University Press, and particularly that of Miss Roberta Yerkes who provided advice, counsel, and suggestions in the later stages of preparation of the manuscript.

C. I. Hovland
I. L. Janis
H. H. Kelley

New Haven, Conn.
July, 1953

Contents

PREFACE v

1. INTRODUCTION 1

2. CREDIBILITY OF THE COMMUNICATOR 19

3. FEAR-AROUSING APPEALS 56

4. ORGANIZATION OF PERSUASIVE ARGUMENTS 99

5. GROUP MEMBERSHIP AND RESISTANCE TO INFLUENCE 134

6. PERSONALITY AND SUSCEPTIBILITY TO PERSUASION 174

7. ACQUIRING CONVICTION THROUGH ACTIVE PARTICIPATION 215

8. RETENTION OF OPINION CHANGE 241

9. SUMMARY AND EMERGING PROBLEMS 269

INDEX 303

Figures

Figure 1. Degree of opinion change as related to agreement or disagreement between communicator's avowed intention and audience's initial opinions.   26

Figure 2. Differential effectiveness, immediate and delayed, of high vs. low credibility communicators.   40

Figure 3. Hypothetical generalization gradients for communicator expertness.   52

Figure 4. Effects of a one-sided vs. a two-sided presentation on beliefs.   107

Figure 5. Comparison of a one-sided vs. a two-sided presentation for groups exposed and not exposed to subsequent counterpropaganda.   110

Figure 6. Effect of serial position.   118

Figure 7. Opinion change in response to counternorm communication for Scouts with various degrees of valuation of membership.   142

Figure 8. Effect of counternorm communication on high and low valuation members.   143

Figure 9. The effects on mean attitude scores of variations in salience of Catholic membership for high school students.   159

Figure 10. Retention over three-day interval of opinion changes produced under conditions of high and low salience.   162

Figure 11. Personal adjustment factors related to high persuasibility.   188

Figure 12. Personal adjustment factors related to low persuasibility.   198

Figure 13. Forgetting curve for a single presentation of meaningful prose material.   245

Figure 14. Retention curves obtained with three different methods of measuring retention.   249

Figure 15. Retention of opinion change.   255

Figure 16. Retention of opinion with and without reinstatement of source.   257

Figure 17. Effects of content and prestige factors on degree of belief immediately after the communication and three weeks later, with and without reinstatement of the communicator.   258

Tables

Table 1. Effects of high and low credibility sources on evaluations of fairness and justifiability of identical communications   29

Table 2. Net changes of opinion in direction of communication for sources classified by experimenters as of high or low credibility   30

Table 3. Audience evaluations of the same talk on juvenile delinquency when delivered by positive, neutral, and negative communicators   32

Table 4. Immediate effects of different communicators on opinion scores   33

Table 5. Evaluations of identical communications when presented by suspect and nonsuspect communicators   34

Table 6. Content analysis of the three forms of a dental hygiene communication   69

Table 7. Per cent of subjects reporting feelings of worry or concern evoked during the dental hygiene communication   70

Table 8. Effect of threat appeals: percentage who reported feeling worried about decayed teeth and diseased gums   71

Table 9. Effect of the illustrated talk on conformity to dental hygiene recommendations   80

Table 10. Effect of the illustrated talk on reactions to subsequent counterpropaganda   81

Table 11. Per cent of subjects changing opinion on "Devaluation" from before to after communication   102

Table 12. Opinion change under public and private conditions, for various degrees of valuation of membership   146

Table 13. Comparison of active participants with passive controls: changes in opinion estimates following exposure to persuasive communications   221

Table 14. Effect of role playing on opinion changes following exposure to a communication concerning the prospects of military service for college students   225

Table 15. Mean scores on three measures of the quality of essays written by conformists under three different incentive conditions   227

Table 16. Mean number of correct and incorrect recall responses by verbalization and control groups   232

Table 17. Per cent of initial attitude change produced by films, remaining at various time intervals   242

Table 18. Retention of opinion change after a counteracting news event   262

CHAPTER 1: *Introduction*

DURING recent years the study of the effectiveness of communication has become a subject of major interest in human relations research. In part this may be ascribed to the important role of mass communications in the economic, political, and social organizations of modern society. The growing interdependence of ever larger numbers of people along with advances in the techniques of transmitting communication have led to a high degree of reliance upon mass media to convey information to various types of public and thereby mold their convictions. Executives in many organizations feel the need to improve their communication systems in order to achieve widespread acceptance of the standards and values necessary to the success of their enterprises. In the sphere of international relations, numerous practical communication problems are posed by the "cold war," particularly for government policy makers who wish to increase our "influence" on the people of foreign countries and to counteract potentially disruptive foreign propaganda. Also, a major concern of agencies such as UNESCO is in developing mass educational programs that will be effective in breaking down psychological barriers which prevent mutual understanding between nations. A similar need has long been apparent to leaders within our own country who have worked to counteract racial, ethnic, and religious prejudices interfering with the consistent operation of democratic values.

All of these problems converge upon the area of scientific inquiry concerned with understanding the ways in which words and symbols influence people. Research in this area is of great practical importance not only to those who make use of mass media but also to specialists in human relations who rely upon such face-to-face situations as small group conferences or psychotherapeutic interviews. Ultimately, an increase in scientific knowledge in this field may be expected to have even broader social application, affecting preventative psychiatry, child rearing, and education in its broadest aspects.

While research on communication and persuasion is of considerable practical concern, perhaps its greatest attraction for the scientist

1

is that it involves central theoretical problems in individual and social psychology. Study of the way in which opinions and beliefs are affected by communication symbols provides an excellent means for examining the role of the higher mental processes in assimilating the numerous and often contradictory influences impinging upon the individual in everyday life.

To explore this area, a program of coordinated systematic research on variables determining the effects of persuasive communication was begun by the writers several years ago, designated the Yale Communication Research Program. The present volume is a report of this research, delineating the major problems which have been explored, summarizing experiments which have been completed, and discussing the theoretical formulations developed in the course of the work. It is, in a sense, a progress report on the preliminary phases of a long-term research program to investigate the principles involved in persuasive communication.

THE COMMUNICATION RESEARCH PROGRAM

The program may best be described in terms of three of its principal characteristics. The first, already implied, is that it is primarily concerned with theoretical issues and basic research. It is thus to be contrasted with the greater part of research in this area which is of an applied or "action oriented" nature. Practical problems are investigated only to the extent that there is clear indication they will contribute to the formulation of important theoretical issues. It is to be expected, however, that theoretically oriented research will ultimately provide the answers to practical problems, whether it be increasing the effectiveness of persuasive communications or educating the public to resist specious propaganda. As Kurt Lewin once said: "Nothing is so practical as a good theory."

A second characteristic of the research program is that it draws upon theoretical developments from diverse sources, both within psychology and in related fields. It is clear that the problems of communication and opinion change cut across the various scientific disciplines as currently defined. Thus while the primary emphasis of the present program is on a psychological analysis of social influence, hypotheses are derived from several other social science areas. The fact that our hypotheses are derived from diverse theoretical systems makes it, of course, very difficult to develop a single, comprehensive treatment. It is hoped that more intensive work over the next decades will help to reduce the gaps between the various formulations and to integrate the contributions of anthropology, sociology, political science, psychiatry, and psychology into a general theory of communication.

One theory most useful to our work has been the "learning theory" developed by Hull [5] and subsequently adapted to complex forms of social behavior by Miller and Dollard [9], Mowrer [10], and others. The implications of this formulation for responses to symbols are particularly relevant to the study of communication.

For an analysis of the role of learning in the changing of opinions through communication the problem of motivation is of central importance. The motives with which the communication specialists will deal are generally learned, or acquired, motives. In considering these, the hypotheses of Freud and other psychoanalysts are of considerable relevance, and are accordingly drawn upon in analyzing the influence of symbols upon an individual's motivational state.

Another source of theoretical concepts comes from research on the effects of group membership. In considering the factors influencing acquired motivations, one immediately sees that some of the major sources of gratification are to be found in the groups to which the individual belongs. The theoretical formulations of Lewin [7] and his co-workers (e.g., Festinger [2]) have been especially fruitful in analysis of the factors affecting the extent to which membership in groups serves to maintain opinions and attitudes of members, in the presence of powerful pressures to change. Similarly, the concept of "reference group" and the attendant theoretical developments of Sherif [12], Newcomb [11], and Merton and Kitt [8] have provided some provocative leads as to the effects of group awareness and group affiliation.

A final characteristic of the research program lies in its emphasis upon testing propositions by controlled experiment. In the majority of the studies reported the results are obtained from experimental designs in which specially constructed communications are presented under conditions where the effects of the various factors influencing opinion change can be isolated.

The data obtained in the present research program supplement those derived from other researches in this area, which typically base their generalizations on survey and correlational methods. Sometimes the relationships derived from comparing the opinion questionnaire responses of various subgroups shed considerable light on causal factors, but frequently it is impossible to draw valid inferences from such data. An example of the difficulty involved in deriving adequate generalizations from correlational data is provided by the research showing a high correlation between amount of information concerning an ethnic or national group and a favorable attitude toward the group. This result is sometimes interpreted to mean that there is a dynamic relationship between the two variables, and that increasing an individual's information about a group will also tend to make his attitude toward the group more favorable. But the crucial test of this implied cause-and-effect relationship is to determine whether or not the transmission of information actually does change attitudes. To carry out such a test requires a controlled analytical experiment in which the independent factor (amount of information communicated) is varied and the dependent factor (amount of attitude change) is assessed. When studies of this type have been carried out it has been found that the generalization does not necessarily hold [4].

Controlled analytical experiments differ not only from static correlational studies but also from evaluative studies which employ experimental techniques, where the only interest is in ascertaining whether or not a particular communication has an effect. Much of the research during the 1920's and 30's was of this type. Studies were designed to determine whether or not mass communications had any effect at all upon attitude or else to compare the relative merits of two particular communications, each differing from the other in numerous respects. This type of research sometimes has practical value, but provides little insight into the causal factors responsible for differences in the effectiveness of communications. During recent years there has been increased emphasis on the isolation of basic factors related to general theoretical formulations. The present research program represents a continuation of this approach. In most of the studies an attempt has been made to devise controlled experiments which vary systematically the basic factors derived from theoretical analysis.

Mainly because of the greater possibility of rigorous experimental control, the communications employed in most of the present studies are of the one-way variety: a fixed communication is presented to a "captive" audience and interaction among the recipients of the communication is restricted. It is the belief of the authors, however, that most of the basic principles derived from studying one-way communications will prove applicable also to the type of persuasion involved in group discussions and in psychotherapy, even though additional propositions concerning face-to-face interaction effects will also be required.

It is presumptuous, of course, to expect all problems to be amenable to investigation in this fashion. Nor can all propositions concerning communication and opinion change be submitted to experimental test at the present time. Extensive case-study analysis and opinion surveys are sometimes essential to define an issue more sharply or to ascertain whether the conditions which are theoretically required for a particular outcome are actually present. Moreover, in studying such factors as personality predispositions, which do not lend themselves readily to experimental manipulation, only the nature of the communication can be experimentally controlled.

Even when a controlled analytical experiment shows a given factor to be significantly related to communication effectiveness, the question still remains as to the generality of the relationship. For example, experimental results may show that a communication designed to induce people to volunteer for civilian defense activities is more effective when fear-arousing appeals precede rather than follow the action recommendation. Would the outcome be the same in the case of a different topic? Or a different type of communicator? Or another medium? Or a different type of audience? Or a different type of recommended action? The solution to these problems lies, of course, in replication with strategic variations. The first experiment to test a general hypothesis is capable only of showing that the hypothesis holds true under the conditions represented in the experiment. It is necessary to carry out further investigations of the same hypothesis under carefully selected conditions, assigning different values to the supposedly irrelevant factors. Only in this way can one ultimately determine whether or not the hypothesis is a valid generalization and, if so, whether it requires specification of limiting conditions. Experiments of the type reported in the present volume usually provide only tentative generalizations which will have to be tested through later verification and replication.

WORKING ASSUMPTIONS

In this volume we shall not attempt to present a systematic theory of persuasive communication. Nevertheless, in order to understand our choice of variables for study and our interpretations of the results, the reader may find it helpful to know the general framework within which the research was conducted and the working definitions which were found most useful. Accordingly a brief discussion of the authors' point of view concerning the nature of opinion change and the types of variables involved in persuasive communication will be presented.

NATURE OF OPINION CHANGE

"Opinion" will be used in a very general sense to describe interpretations, expectations, and evaluations—such as beliefs about the intentions of other people, anticipations concerning future events, and appraisals of the rewarding or punishing consequences of alternative courses of action. Operationally speaking, *opinions are viewed as verbal "answers" that an individual gives in response to stimulus situations in which some general "question" is raised.* Consider, for example, a person's opinion concerning the imminence of another world war. We would say that an individual has a consistent opinion on this issue if in general he gives the same answer whenever the pertinent question is raised. The stimulus situations in which the question is posed may be extremely varied. Sometimes the individual is asked directly to tell what he thinks about the issue, perhaps at a formal group meeting or in an informal discussion with a friend. At other times the individual may pose the question to himself, if, for example, he is faced with the problem of deciding whether or not to join a military reserve organization.

The foregoing working definition makes it necessary to comment on the differentiations between "opinion" and "fact" and between "opinion" and "attitude." Both facts and opinions represent "answers" to "questions," and as Hovland, Lumsdaine, and Sheffield [4] point out, it is impossible to draw a sharp distinction between the two. But at one end of a continuum are statements typically regarded as matters of opinion, which are difficult to verify—for example, inferences as to the motives of political leaders, the causes of inflation, or predictions concerning future inventions. At the opposite end are statements which are universally regarded as "incontrovertible" facts. Ordinarily when we speak of persuasive communications we are referring to those which deal with issues that cannot be resolved by direct observation and which present conclusions about which there are differences of opinion.

Both "opinion" and "attitude" refer to implicit responses, and, in theoretical terms, are intervening variables. The relationship between the two is an intimate one. But while the term "opinion" will be used to designate a broad class of anticipations and expectations, the term "attitude" will be used exclusively for those implicit responses which are oriented toward approaching or avoiding a given object, person, group, or symbol. This may be interpreted as meaning that attitudes possess "drive value" (Doob [1]). Another distinguishing factor is the extent to which the two can be verbalized. Opinions are considered to be verbalizable, while attitudes are sometimes "unconscious," e.g., avoidance tendencies mediated by nonverbal processes, such as those involved in conditioned fear.

An important implication of this view is that there will be a high degree of mutual interaction between attitudes and opinions. Changes in general approach and avoidance orientations ("attitudes") may affect one's expectations ("opinions") on a number of related issues. Conversely, and of greater importance for our purpose, changes in opinion may modify one's general attitudes. On one hand, a change in an individual's general attitude of hatred toward a political figure may affect his opinion concerning the man's motives. On the other hand, a change in opinion about the politician's motives may change one's attitude of opposition toward him. Our assumption is that there are many attitudes which are mediated by verbal beliefs, expectations, and judgments and that one of the main ways in which communications give rise to changes in attitudes is by changing such verbal responses.

When we say that opinions are "verbalizable" and are "implicit responses" we mean that they are verbal "answers" that one covertly expresses to himself in inner speech. They are thus distinguishable from *overt* verbal responses, which are the answers expressed to others when the question is accompanied by additional stimuli which either demand or instigate verbalization of the answer. Typically the overt and covert responses are identical. But it sometimes happens, of course, that a person will think one answer to himself and give a different answer to others. In such instances the overt verbalizations would be regarded as inadequate indicators of his opinion—it would be said that he is "dissimulating," "distorting," or "lying." If one accepts this usage, the term "opinion" is then restricted to implicit verbal responses. This would seem a useful definition of opinion since overt responses are apt to vary with the external constraints that are present at the moment when an overt response is demanded, whereas implicit responses may be more consistent. Furthermore, implicit responses will affect the individual's decisions, appraisals, and actions whenever the external constraints are not present. Correspondingly, "opinion change" is defined in terms of a change in the *implicit* verbal response. If, for example, an individual should merely change his overt response while the inner one remains unmodified, we would not call this a change in opinion but would say rather that the individual had learned to conceal or to avoid expressing his true opinion.

The above discussion of opinion change immediately raises an important methodological problem: how can one observe changes in implicit verbal responses? Actually, in order to investigate implicit verbal responses, it is necessary to elicit overt verbal responses. The assumption is made that under certain conditions overt verbalizations will be approximately the same as implicit verbal responses; the methodological problem is to set up these conditions. Various techniques are commonly employed for this purpose. In the case of those opinions which involve shame, guilt, or other disturbances that would motivate conscious or unconscious distortion (e.g., preferences relating to perverse sexual practices or hostile evaluations of authority figures) special interview techniques are necessary, such as those used in psychoanalysis, in which the individual learns to give free associations in a permissive interpersonal setting. With opinions which are usually expressed more freely, less complicated techniques are used. Here, opinion questionnaires, designed and administered in such a fashion as to minimize the tendency to suppress or distort, are frequently employed.

In the experiments on persuasion reported in this volume, the topics typically have been chosen to arouse little motivation for either suppression or distortion. In order further to minimize such tendencies standard methodological precautions have been taken: careful attention has been given to question wording, test administrators are clearly designated as research workers who are dissociated from persons having authority over the respondents, subjects are informed that differences of opinion are to be expected, and usually assurances are given that answers will remain anonymous. Under these conditions, it seems fairly safe to assume that the individual's overt verbal responses will correspond fairly well to his implicit verbal responses.

A related methodological problem arises in connection with the "significance" or generality of an observed opinion change: will the individual respond differently to stimuli other than the specific symbols used in the questionnaire? Will responses other than those required in answering the questionnaire be affected? These questions are often raised indirectly in the form of the more general query: how does one know that the observed change represents a *real* change in *opinion* (and not just a change in response to a questionnaire item)? This problem is one for which satisfactory solutions are difficult to obtain and further methodological investigation is required. Nevertheless, for present research purposes an attempt is made to meet the need for assessing the degree of generality by using a series of questionnaire items which consider the same general issue from a variety of points of view, and by selecting questions involving patterns of verbal stimuli most similar to those found in everyday situations. As a supplement to check-list measures of opinion, free answer questions are sometimes included so that the respondent's own phrasing may be used as a check on the generality of response.

Ultimately, of course, the justification for the use of questionnaire methods derives from their utility in enabling the investigator to observe consistent relationships between communication stimuli and changes in verbal response. The interpretations of these relationships and the generality of the hypotheses which they support can be validated in part by their compatibility with observations from other sources, including intensive interviews of individuals exposed to psychotherapy or to mass communications, and behavioral data such as those derived from studies of buying, contributing, and voting.

NATURE OF PERSUASIVE COMMUNICATION

We assume that opinions, like other habits, will tend to persist unless the individual undergoes some new learning experiences. Exposure to a persuasive communication which successfully induces the individual to accept a new opinion constitutes a learning experience in which a new verbal habit is acquired. That is to say, when presented with a given question, the individual now thinks of and prefers the new answer suggested by the communication to the old one held prior to exposure to the communication.

What are the factors in the communication situation responsible for this change and how do they operate so as to replace the original verbal response by a new one? Without attempting to give a full theoretical account of this learning process, we shall present a tentative summary of the main factors in communication situations which are assumed to be responsible for producing opinion changes.

One key element in the persuasion situation is, of course, the "recommended opinion" presented in the communication. This element may be conceptualized as a compound stimulus which raises the critical question and gives a new answer. For example, imagine the communicator's conclusion to be that "It will be at least ten years before the United States will engage in a war with Russia." We assume that in presenting this idea the communication contains words which operate as effective stimuli in posing the question, "How long before the United States will be at war with Russia?" At the same time the conclusion states a specific answer, "At least ten years." In the course of a lengthy communication this conclusion may be asserted dozens of times or perhaps only once. Even when a communicator does not give an explicit statement of his conclusion, the indirect verbal statements he presents must operate implicitly to pose a question and suggest an answer; otherwise we would not regard the communication as capable of inducing a new opinion.

When exposed to the recommended opinion, a member of the audience is assumed to react with at least two distinct responses. He thinks of his own answer to the question, and also of the answer suggested by the communicator. The first response results from the previously established verbal habit constituting the individual's original opinion; the second response is assumed to result from a general aspect of verbal behavior, namely, the acquired tendency to repeat to oneself communications to which one is attending. Hence, a major effect of persuasive communication lies in stimulating the individual to think both of his initial opinion and of the new opinion recommended in the communication.

Merely thinking about the new opinion along with the old would not, in itself, lead to opinion change. The individual could *memorize* the content of the conclusion while his opinion remained unchanged. Practice, which is so important for memorizing verbal material in educational or training situations, is not sufficient for bringing about the *acceptance* of a new opinion. We assume that acceptance is contingent upon *incentives,* and that in order to change an opinion it is necessary to create a greater incentive for making the new implicit response than for making the old one. A major basis for acceptance of a given opinion is provided by arguments or reasons which, according to the individual's own thinking habits, constitute "rational" or "logical" support for the conclusions. In addition to supporting reasons, there are likely to be other special incentives involving anticipated rewards and punishments which motivate the individual to accept or reject a given opinion. Discussion of the nature of these incentives will be postponed until later chapters.

It is assumed that there are three main classes of stimuli present in the communication situation which are capable of producing the shifts in incentive described above. One·set of stimuli has to do with the observable characteristics of the perceived source of the communication. Another involves the setting in which the person is exposed to the communication, including, for example, the way in which other members of the audience respond during the presentation. Communication stimuli also include important content elements, referred to as "arguments" and "appeals." Whether or not stimuli of these various types operate successfully as incentives depends upon the predispositions of the individual. A successful communication is one in which these various stimuli are both adapted to the level of verbal skill of the individual and capable of stimulating his motives so as to foster acceptance of the recommended opinion.

ORGANIZATION OF THE VOLUME

From the foregoing discussion of opinion and opinion change the reader may be able to predict the topics discussed in this volume. Implicit throughout has been a definition of communication which may be more formally stated as the process by which an individual (the communicator) transmits stimuli (usually verbal) to modify the behavior of other individuals (the audience). This definition specifies the research task as consisting in the analysis of four factors: 1) the *communicator* who transmits the communication; 2) the *stimuli* transmitted by the communicator; 3) the *audience* responding to the communication; 4) the *responses* made by the audience to the communication [3]. These topics parallel closely the well-known formula of *who* says *what* to *whom* with *what effect* [13].

In the subsequent chapters of this book selected topics within each of the four categories will be considered. The topics covered are those for which results are available from studies done in our research program. Topics not treated in our research, but which are sometimes included in the preceding descriptive formula, are those pertaining to the nature of the *medium* and the *situation* in which the communication is given. It will also be noted that all of the studies are concerned with the problems encountered when an audience is available to a communicator and do not deal with the prior problem of securing or enlarging the audience.

To indicate the general context within which the specific researches were conducted, each chapter contains a "Background" section. Following the presentation of "Research Evidence" bearing on each topic, there is an "Implications" section containing discussion of related aspects of the problem and suggestions for further research. In discussing our own results and those of prior investigators we shall attempt to indicate some of the general theoretical problems within the field. But such discussions do not by any means constitute a systematic theory of persuasion or opinion change. Rather they serve to indicate some of the issues which must be considered in constructing a general science of communication.

The major topics to be treated are presented under the following headings:

1. The Communicator

An important factor influencing the effectiveness of a communication is the person or group perceived as originating the communication—and the cues provided as to the trustworthiness, intentions, and affiliations of this source. In extreme instances, merely perceiving a particular source as advocating the new opinion will be sufficient to induce acceptance. This is generally referred to as "prestige suggestion." In most of the persuasive communications of daily life, however, the communication includes auxiliary contents, such as appeals and arguments, which operate as incentives for inducing opinion change. In such instances, the nature of the source may affect the way in which the audience responds to these auxiliary incentives. The aspects of the problem with which our investigations have been concerned are the effects of variations in the trustworthiness and expertness of the communicator on the recipients' evaluation of the presentation and on their acceptance of the position advocated by the communicator. These topics will be dealt with in Chapter 2.

2. Content of the Communication

A. Motivating appeals. This class of stimuli consists of communication contents which arouse emotional states or which are capable of providing strong incentives for acceptance of the new opinion and/or rejection of the original opinions held by the audience. Theoretical problems concerning the use of one major class of incentives—fear-arousing appeals—will be discussed in relation to available research findings in Chapter 3.

B. Organization of persuasive arguments. The types of arguments employed and their manner of organization will influence what the audience thinks about during exposure to a communication and hence may have a marked effect on its acceptance or rejection. The type of argument and the order of presentation may either facilitate or interfere with rehearsal of both new and old opinions. A number of selected problems concerning the organization of arguments are examined in Chapter 4: implicit as compared with explicit statement of the conclusion, presentation of one side versus two sides of an issue, and primacy versus recency effects produced by different orderings of the arguments.

3. Audience Predispositions

A. Group conformity motives. The influence exerted by a communicator and by what he says is often dependent upon the individual's adherence to group norms or standards. Thus, one of the important sets of audience predispositions concerns the conformity motives which stem from membership in, or affiliation with, various social groups. Predispositional factors underlying resistance to communications which advocate nonconformity will be discussed in Chapter 5, focusing particularly upon the individual's valuation of group membership. The effects of certain situational stimuli upon the strength of group conformity motives are also considered.

B. Individual personality factors. Some individuals are likely to be highly responsive to persuasion while others are more resistant. These individual differences in susceptibility to persuasion may arise from differences in abilities (e.g., capacity for comprehending the meaning of what others say) or in motives (e.g., strong desire to avoid considering adverse consequences stressed by communicator). Chapter 6 will discuss hypotheses and evidence concerning the relationship of persuasibility to general intellectual ability and to various personality factors which reflect motivational tendencies.

4. Responses

A. Overt expression of the new opinion. If a persuasive communication is effective, there is often a change in the individual's overt verbal behavior such that he regularly expresses the new opinion whenever a pertinent situation arises. As mentioned earlier, however, a person may sometimes be induced to conform verbally, thus overtly expressing the recommended opinion, but without inner conviction. Nevertheless, even when only superficial conformity occurs (e.g., by inducing the individual to play a social role), the overt expression of the new opinion may have some effect on inner acceptance. In Chapter 7 a series of studies on this aspect of opinion change will be described, together with various hypotheses concerning the ways in which the effects of overt verbalization are mediated.

B. Retention of opinion change. When the recipients of a communication consistently express the new opinion, especially where there are no external constraints making for overt conformity, the inference is that the communication has produced acceptance of the new opinion. But there are a number of problems concerning the degree to which such opinions are subsequently retained. For example, powerful sources of interference may arise from subsequent exposure to competing communications which foster rejection of the opinions recommended in the first communication. Even with no subsequent counterpressure, an individual may forget the incentive material learned from the communication, so that after a short period he fails to recall those ideas favoring continued acceptance. On the other hand, the individual may initially show great resistance during the communication but subsequently appear to accept it "spontaneously." Various factors which facilitate or interfere with the persistence of opinion change are discussed in Chapter 8.

CHARACTERISTICS OF COMMUNICATION LEARNING

In the foregoing discussion, we have assumed that the effectiveness of persuasive communications is a matter of learning. To some extent, we would expect to find that there are common principles which apply equally to the learning of new opinions, of various verbal and motor skills, and of other habits. But it is necessary to recognize that the *type* of learning and the *conditions* of learning are ordinarily quite different in the case of producing opinion change through persuasive communication than in the case of other learning situations.

In his preface to Klapper's recent book [6] Lazarsfeld has emphasized the difficulties involved in taking results from laboratory studies
of human learning and applying them to the presentation of persuasive communications via mass media, where the audience may "leave
the field" if uninterested. He characterizes the mass communication
situation as one equivalent to "a learning experiment where people
walk in and out as they please, where some of the most valuable effects
are achieved with people who come in by mere accident, where the
motivation to learn is often very low and where the possible rewards
for learning are obvious neither to the experimenter nor to the subject . . ." (Klapper, Foreword, pp. 6 and 7).

The utilizer of mass communications often has an antecedent problem with which our research has not been concerned, that of attracting
an audience in the first place. But even when persuasive arguments
are presented to a relatively "captive" audience—for example, to
delegates at a political convention—there are still a number of unique
features which make the learning situation different from academic
teaching or from skill instruction in which new verbal habits are
acquired:

1. When formal instruction is given, the audience ordinarily is set
to learn, and voluntarily accepts the status of students in relation to
an instructor. This is generally not the case with persuasive communications in everyday life.

2. In many situations of verbal learning, as in courses on science,
a major goal is to teach a large number of facts and propositions. In
order to attain this objective, a great deal of practice is necessary before the individual can memorize and retain all of the information
which he is expected to learn. In the case of persuasive communications, however, the recommended opinion generally consists of a single statement which is within the memory span of most individuals
and in many instances a single communication is sufficient to induce
opinion change. During exposure to the communication, the audience may rehearse the recommended opinion several times, but sometimes only once is sufficient for the simple task of memorizing the
recommended conclusion. The main problem for the communicator,
of course, is to induce the audience to accept. Thus, routine practice
plays a smaller role in this type of learning. On the other hand, while

one-trial learning may be within the repertoire of the learner, the communicator must often provide the special kind of practice necessary for "transfer of training," so that the learner will apply the new opinion in the many different situations in which it is subsequently relevant.

3. The retention of verbally mediated skills or of memorized verbal material sometimes suffers interference from the subsequent practice of new responses to the same stimuli. Generally speaking, however, it seldom happens that, following formal instruction, the individual is exposed to competing instruction designed to break down the new verbal habits which he has just acquired. In the case of persuasive communications dealing with controversial opinions, on the other hand, this type of interference occurs fairly frequently. Shortly after being exposed to one communication, the audience is likely to be exposed to additional communications presenting completely different points of view and designed to create completely different opinions. Hence, the long-run effectiveness of a persuasive communication depends not only upon its success in inducing a momentary shift in opinion but also upon the sustained resistance it can create with respect to subsequent competing pressures.

From the above discussion it is apparent that there may be many special factors which are important to changing opinion but are of relatively little importance in formal verbal instruction. Search for some of these factors is one of the objectives of the present research. We shall return to this problem in the concluding chapter.

Before a comprehensive theory of communications can be constructed, it will be necessary to identify and understand the major communication variables. To this end, attention must be devoted to laying the necessary groundwork of empirical propositions concerning the relationships between communication stimuli, audience predispositions, and opinion change. The present volume represents the outcome of a continuing research project which aims at isolating key variables and providing an initial framework for subsequent theory building. To further the latter objective, we shall not only include hypotheses and experimental results but also point out some of the implications for developing in the future a general theory of communication and persuasion.

References

1. Doob, L. W. The behavior of attitudes. *Psychol. Rev.*, 1947, *54*, 135–156.
2. Festinger, L. Informal social communication. *Psychol. Rev.*, 1950, *57*, 271–282.
3. Hovland, C. I. Social communication. *Proc. Am. Philos. Soc.*, 1948, *92*, 371–375.
4. Hovland, C. I., Lumsdaine, A. A., and Sheffield, F. D. *Experiments on mass communication*. Princeton Univ. Press, 1949.
5. Hull, C. L. *Principles of behavior*. New York, Appleton-Century, 1943.
6. Klapper, J. T. *The effects of mass media*. New York, Columbia Univ. Bureau of Applied Social Research, 1949. (Mimeo.)
7. Lewin, K. *Field theory in social science*, D. Cartwright, ed. New York, Harper, 1951.
8. Merton, R. K., and Kitt, Alice S. Contributions to the theory of reference group behavior. In R. K. Merton and P. F. Lazarsfeld, eds. *Continuities in social research*. Glencoe, Ill., Free Press, 1950.
9. Miller, N. E., and Dollard, J. *Social learning and imitation*. New Haven, Yale Univ. Press, 1941.
10. Mowrer, O. H. *Learning theory and personality dynamics*. New York, Ronald Press, 1950.
11. Newcomb, T. M. *Social psychology*. New York, Dryden Press, 1950.
12. Sherif, M. *An outline of social psychology*. New York, Harper, 1948.
13. Smith, B. L., Lasswell, H. D., and Casey, R. D. *Propaganda, communication, and public opinion*. Princeton Univ. Press, 1946.

CHAPTER 2: *Credibility of the Communicator*

THE effectiveness of a communication is commonly assumed to depend to a considerable extent upon who delivers it. Governmental agencies take great pains to have their statements presented to Congress by the most acceptable advocates. Backyard gossips liberally sprinkle the names of respectable sources throughout their rumors. The debater, the author of scientific articles, and the news columnist all bolster their contentions with quotations from figures with prestige.

Approval of a statement by highly respected persons or organizations may have much the same positive effect as if they originate it. The organizer of a publicity campaign acquires a list of important persons who, by allowing their names to be displayed on the letterheads of the campaign literature, tacitly approve the campaign's objectives. The impact of a message probably depends also upon the particular publication or channel through which it is transmitted. The credibility of an advertisement seems to be related to some extent to the reputation of the particular magazine in which it appears ([27] p. 660).

The examples above suggest the importance of persons, groups, or media which can be subsumed under the general category of "sources." Differences in effectiveness may sometimes depend upon whether the source is perceived as a speaker who originates the message, an endorser who is cited in the message, or the channel through which the message is transmitted. However, the same basic factors and principles probably underlie the operation of each of the many types of sources, so an analysis of the psychological processes mediating the reactions to one kind of source may be expected to be applicable to other types. In this chapter we shall deal primarily with situations in which the effects are attributable to a single clear-cut source, which is usually an individual speaker who communicates directly to the audience and gives his own views on an issue. We shall refer to this kind of source as a "communicator."

In terms of the analysis of opinion change presented in the preced-

19

ing chapter, a communicator can affect the change process in a variety
of ways. For example, if he is a striking personality and an effective
speaker who holds the attention of an audience, he can increase the
likelihood of attentive consideration of the new opinion. If he is
personally admired or a member of a high status group, his words
may raise the incentive value of the advocated opinion by suggesting
that approval, from himself or from the group, will follow its adoption. When acceptance is sought by using arguments in support of
the advocated view, the perceived expertness and trustworthiness of
the communicator may determine the credence given them.

We shall assume that these various effects of the communicator are
mediated by attitudes toward him which are held by members of the
audience. Any of a number of different attitudes may underlie the
influence exerted by a given communicator. Some may have to do with
feelings of affection and admiration and stem in part from desires to
be like him. Others may involve awe and fear of the communicator,
based on perceptions of his power to reward or punish according to
one's adherence to his recommendations or demands. Still other important attitudes are those of trust and confidence. These are related to perceptions of the communicator's credibility, including beliefs about his knowledge, intelligence, and sincerity.

These and other attitudes which affect communicator influence
are learned by each individual in a variety of influence situations.
Through his experiences of accepting and rejecting social influences,
the individual acquires expectations about the validity of various
sources of information and learns that following the suggestions of
certain persons is highly rewarding whereas accepting what certain
others recommend is less so. The products of this learning, which constitute a complex set of attitudes toward various persons as sources of
influence, generalize to a wide variety of other persons, groups, and
agencies and thereby affect the individual's reactions to communications which he perceives to emanate from them.

If the conditions of learning these attitudes are variable (as they
almost inevitably are), the communicator characteristics relevant to
the amount of influence exerted cannot be expected to fall into neat
categories; they are probably specific as to time and cultural setting.
For example, the specific attributes of persons who are viewed as

powerful or credible can be expected to differ from culture to culture. There is also likely to be some degree of variability within a given culture, particularly as different subject matters are considered. However certain kinds of attitudes, such as those related to affection, the communicator's power, and his credibility, are probably important in all societies. Moreover, the general principles concerning the antecedents and consequences of such attitudes may be expected to have a high degree of generality, at least within our own culture.

The limited area chosen for investigation in our research program concerns the factors related to *credibility* of the source. Analysis of this area in the present chapter will focus on two problems. How do differences in the credibility of the communicator affect 1) the way in which the content and presentation are perceived and evaluated? 2) the degree to which attitudes and beliefs are modified? In analyzing the findings bearing on these questions, we shall briefly consider possible psychological processes underlying the observed effects and the changes that occur with the passage of time.

BACKGROUND

An individual's tendency to accept a conclusion advocated by a given communicator will depend in part upon how well informed and intelligent he believes the communicator to be. However, a recipient may believe that a communicator is capable of transmitting valid statements, but still be inclined to reject the communication if he suspects the communicator is motivated to make nonvalid assertions. It seems necessary, therefore, to make a distinction between 1) the extent to which a communicator is perceived to be a source of valid assertions (his "expertness") and 2) the degree of confidence in the communicator's intent to communicate the assertions he considers most valid (his "trustworthiness"). In any given case, the weight given a communicator's assertions by his audience will depend upon both of these factors, and this resultant value can be referred to as the "credibility" of the communicator. In this section we shall review some of the background material bearing upon the two components of credibility: expertness and trustworthiness.

A variety of characteristics of the communicator may evoke attitudes related to expertness. For example, the age of a communicator may sometimes be regarded as an indication of the extent of his experience. A position of leadership in a group may be taken as an indication of ability to predict social reactions. In certain matters persons similar to the recipient of influence may be considered more expert than persons different from him. An individual is likely to feel that persons with status, values, interests, and needs similar to his own see things as he does and judge them from the same point of view. Because of this, their assertions about matters of which the individual is ignorant but where he feels the viewpoint makes a difference (e.g., about the satisfaction of a given job or the attractiveness of some personality) will tend to carry special credibility. Hence the research on the factors of age, leadership, and similarity of social background may involve the expertness factor to some extent.[1] *

Few systematic investigations have been made of the effects of variations in expertness on opinion change, but suggestive results come from a number of studies. Typical findings are those of Bowden, Caldwell, and West [7], concerning attitudes toward various solutions of the economic problem of an appropriate monetary standard for the United States. Using subjects from a broad age range, they determined the amount of agreement with statements when attributed to men in different professions (e.g., lawyers, engineers, educators). The statements were approved most frequently when attributed to educators and businessmen, and least frequently when attributed to ministers. A study by Kulp [24] provides evidence that for graduate students in education the social and political opinions of professional educators and social scientists are somewhat more influential than the opinions of lay citizens. While other factors may have been involved, it seems likely that the results of these studies are partly attributable to differences in perceived expertness of the various sources.

With respect to the second component of credibility, there have

---

* At various points in the text additional comments about pertinent research evidence or elaborations of theoretical points are necessary. In order to avoid interrupting the main presentation, this additional material is covered separately in a series of Notes, referred to by superscripts in the text and presented at the end of each chapter. Note 1 (pp. 49 f.) contains additional discussion of the factors of age, leadership, and similarity.

been numerous speculations about the characteristics of communicators which evoke attitudes of trust or distrust and about the consequences of these attitudes for acceptance of communications. One of the most general hypotheses is that when a person is perceived as having a definite *intention* to persuade others, the likelihood is increased that he will be perceived as having something to gain and, hence, as less worthy of trust. As Lazarsfeld, Berelson, and Gaudet ([25] pp. 152–153) have pointed out, casual and nonpurposive conversations probably derive part of their effectiveness from the fact that the recipient of a remark does not have the critical and defensive mental set that he typically carries into situations where he knows others are out to influence him. Remarks such as those overheard in subways and other crowded public places would be especially effective in this respect because under such circumstances it is quite apparent that the speaker has no intention to persuade the bystanders. This phenomenon seems to be exploited in some of the techniques currently used in commercial advertising.

A specific set of cues as to the motives or intentions of the communicator has to do with symbols of his social role. Persons in some occupations and offices (e.g., radio announcers, publicity agents, salesmen) are known to be under special pressures to communicate certain things and not others. For other roles, for example that of the newspaper reporter, the pressures may be perceived to operate in the direction of giving all the facts as accurately as he can ascertain them. That publicity men assume greater credibility will be accorded news stories as compared with advertisements is manifested by their repeated attempts to obtain publicity for their clients in the news columns ([13] pp. 323–324).

Suggestive evidence on the importance of the communicator's being considered sincere rather than "just another salesman" is provided by Merton's analysis of Kate Smith's war bond selling campaign during which she broadcast continuously for eighteen hours [30]. It appears that one of the main reasons for her phenomenal success was the high degree of sincerity attributed to her by the audience: ". . . *she really means* anything she ever says" (p. 83). Even though she appeared frequently on commercially sponsored programs and engaged in much the same promotional activities as other radio stars, the public felt that in carrying out the bond drive she was interested only in the national welfare and did not care about the personal publicity she would obtain. One of the most interesting suggestions of Merton's analysis is that the marathon effort itself may have contributed to her reputation as a sincere, unselfish person. Even among the persons who regularly listened to her programs (as well as among nonlisteners), more of those who heard the marathon were convinced of her selflessness in promoting the bonds than of those who failed to hear it. "Above all," Merton says, "*the presumed stress and strain of the eighteen-hour series of broadcasts served to validate Smith's sincerity*" (p. 90).

The possible effects on opinion change of attitudes of trust or distrust toward communicators are suggested by some correlational data from Hovland, Lumsdaine, and Sheffield ([*18*] pp. 100–103). The basic data involve audience reactions to the War Department's orientation films. The pertinent attitudes were not specifically directed toward the communicator but consisted rather of general judgments as to the purposes for which the film was being presented. After viewing "The Battle of Britain" the soldiers were asked this open-ended question: "What did you think was the reason for showing this movie to you and the other men?" On the basis of their answers, the men were classified as to whether they considered the film's purpose to be "propagandistic" (in the sense of having a manipulative intent) or "informational." A comparison of the two groups in terms of the opinion changes produced by the film revealed it to be less effective with men who judged its intent to be manipulative than with men considering it informational. This correlation may merely indicate a general attitude toward the content of the film which is reflected in both opinion change and judgments of the film. But another possible interpretation is that there exists a tendency to reject communications which are perceived as being manipulative in intent.

The material just considered suggests that attitudes related to the expertness and trustworthiness of a communicator may affect his influence. Evidence from systematic research can contribute much to determining the conditions under which this phenomenon occurs and, in addition, can answer questions as to the specific processes involved. In the next section we shall consider the available evidence from the point of view of the two following problems:

First, do variations in the characteristics of a communicator with respect to expertness and trustworthiness affect recipients' evaluations of his presentation and of the arguments and appeals he uses? This problem becomes particularly important when a communication is constructed so as to derive much of its effectiveness from persuasive arguments and motivating appeals. Sometimes a communication presents only a conclusion, without supporting argumentation, and its acceptance appears to be increased merely by attributing it to a prestigeful or respected source. A large proportion of past experimental investigations of communicator effects—the studies of "prestige suggestion"—have concentrated upon this particular phenomenon [2, 24, 26, 36]. Presumably, the observed effects are mediated by an increased incentive value of the recommended opinion brought about through implicit promises of approval from the communicator or the group he represents, or through implicit assurances, by virtue of the authoritativeness of the source, that the opinion has adequate justification in fact and logic. But when a communication includes explicit supporting evidence and arguments, the question arises as to whether they are judged to be any more relevant, sound, or logical when presented by a highly credible source than by a less credible one. In brief, to what extent is the effectiveness of the supporting argumentation dependent upon attitudes toward the communicator?

Second, how do variations in the communicator characteristics related to expertness and trustworthiness affect the amount of opinion change produced by a communication? This, of course, is the crucial problem for persuasive communications. It is necessary to investigate opinion change independently of the kinds of changes specified above. As we shall see, the characteristics of the communicator may affect evaluations of the presentation without necessarily affecting the degree to which the conclusion is accepted.

RESEARCH EVIDENCE

As noted earlier, it has been suggested that perceptions of the communicator's intentions to persuade his audience may affect judgments of his credibility. A study by Ewing [15] deals with a special aspect of this problem—the degree of agreement between a communicator's announced intentions and the audience's initial bias. The results suggest that this variable affects the amount of opinion change produced and that this effect may be mediated by different evaluations of the presentation. Two groups of subjects were given the same communication which, as compared with the subjects' initial opinions, was unfavorable toward Henry Ford. In the introduction and throughout his presentation the propagandist made explicit statements about his intention: in one group he claimed that his purpose was to make people feel more favorable toward Ford and in the other group to make them feel less favorable.

The results on opinion change, presented in Figure 1, show that more change in the direction of the communication was produced in the first group where the intent of the propagandist was represented as being in agreement with the subjects' initial bias.

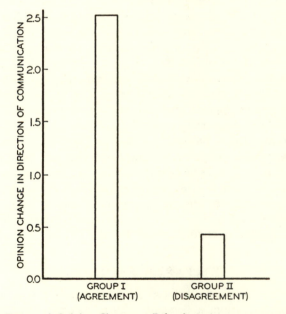

FIGURE 1. Degree of Opinion Change as Related to Agreement or Disagreement between Communicator's Avowed Intention and Audience's Initial Opinions. *Data from Ewing [15]*.

In general, Ewing's results support the hypothesis that when a communication comes from an unknown or ambiguous source, acceptance will be increased if, at the beginning, the communicator explicitly claims that his own position is in accord with that held by the audience. His results suggest that this effect occurs even when the communication advocates a view directly opposed to the audience's initial opinions. This outcome would not be expected, of course, when the content of the communication obviously and repeatedly belies the communicator's statement of his intent.

Ewing presents further analysis of his data which suggests that this result may be influenced by how favorably the recipients react to the communication in terms of its bias, logic, etc. Apparently these evaluations depend not only upon the content but upon the amount of conflict between the initial bias of the recipient and the avowed intention of the communicator. If a communicator presents material in support of a conclusion somewhat different from his avowed position, this may sometimes be taken to indicate great objectivity in his thinking and form the basis for confidence in his arguments.

An experimental variation in source credibility through the use of communicators differing in trustworthiness was produced in the study by Hovland and Weiss [20] of retention effects (cf. pp. 254–256). The general procedure consisted of presenting an identical communication to two groups, in one case from a source of high credibility and in the other from one of low credibility. Opinion questionnaires were administered before, immediately after, and a month after the communication. Four different topics were selected, each presented to some subjects by a source of high credibility and to other subjects by one of low credibility. Affirmative and negative versions of each topic were employed.

Each of the subjects (college students in an advanced undergraduate course) received a booklet containing one article on each of the four topics with the name of the source given at the end of each article.

The four topics and the sources used in the experiment were as follows:

	High Credibility Source	Low Credibility Source
A. *Antihistamine Drugs:* Should the antihistamine drugs continue to be sold without a doctor's prescription?	*New England Journal of Biology and Medicine*	Magazine A (A mass circulation monthly pictorial magazine)
B. *Atomic Submarines:* Can a practicable atomic-powered submarine be built at the present time?	Robert J. Oppenheimer	*Pravda*
C. *The Steel Shortage:* Is the steel industry to blame for the current shortage of steel?	*Bulletin of National Resources Planning Board*	Writer A (An antilabor, anti-New Deal, "rightist" newspaper columnist)
D. *The Future of Movie Theaters:* As a result of TV, will there be a decrease in the number of movie theaters in operation by 1955?	*Fortune* magazine	Writer B (A woman movie-gossip columnist)

A questionnaire administered before the communication obtained judgments from the subjects as to the trustworthiness of a long list of sources, including the specific ones used. An analysis of these judgments revealed very definitely that the sources used with the communications differed greatly in their credibility. The four high credibility sources were judged to be trustworthy by 81 to 95 per cent of the subjects; the low credibility sources were judged trustworthy by 1 to 21 per cent.

Evaluations of presentation. The differences in initial attitudes toward the sources definitely affected audience evaluations of the presentation, which were obtained immediately after exposure to the communication. The data summarizing audience evaluations of the four presentations are given in Table 1. Even though the communications being judged were identical as to content, it can be seen that the presentations were considered to be "less fair" and the conclusions to be "less justified" when the source was of low rather than of high credibility. Although responses to these questions may have involved reactions to the entire communication situation rather than just eval-

TABLE 1. *Effects of High and Low Credibility Sources on Evaluations of Fairness and Justifiability of Identical Communications*

A. Per cent considering author "fair" in his presentation

Topic	High Credibility Source		Low Credibility Source	
	N *	Per Cent	N	Per Cent
Antihistamines	31	64.5	27	59.3
Atomic Submarines	25	96.0	36	69.4
Steel Shortage	37	24.3	26	19.2
Future of Movies	29	93.1	33	63.7
Mean		65.6		54.9

B. Per cent considering author's conclusion "justified" by the facts

Topic	High Credibility Source		Low Credibility Source	
	N	Per Cent	N	Per Cent
Antihistamines	31	67.7	27	51.8
Atomic Submarines	25	80.0	36	44.4
Steel Shortage	37	32.4	26	26.9
Future of Movies	29	58.6	33	42.4
Mean		58.2		41.8

* N = number of cases used.

From Hovland and Weiss [20]

uations of the arguments and conclusions per se, they do indicate that judgments of content characteristics, such as how well the facts in a given communication justify the conclusion, are significantly affected by variations in the source.

Opinion change. Opinion change in the direction advocated by the communication occurred significantly more often when it originated from a high credibility source than when from a low one. Table 2 presents the results on opinion change shown immediately after the communication. The expected difference is obtained on three of the four topics, the exception being the one having to do with the future of movie theaters.

When data were obtained on opinion changes shown four weeks after having read the articles, the differential effectiveness of sources with high and low credibility had disappeared; there were no significant differences between them. This resulted from decreased acceptance of the point of view advocated by the high credibility sources and increased acceptance of the position of the low credibility sources. The former result could be attributed to forgetting of the content,

TABLE 2. *Net Changes of Opinion in Direction of Communication for Sources Classified by Experimenters as of High or Low Credibility* *

Net percentage of cases in which subjects changed
opinion in direction of communication

Topic	High Credibility Sources		Low Credibility Sources	
	N	Per Cent	N	Per Cent
Antihistamines	31	22.6	30	13.3
Atomic Submarines	25	36.0	36	0.0
Steel Shortage	35	22.9	26	−3.8
Future of Movies	31	12.9	30	16.7
Mean		23.0		6.6
Difference			16.4	
p			<.01	

* Net changes = positive changes *minus* negative changes. Cf. [*18*] pp. 302–305 for a discussion of the use of this measure.

From Hovland and Weiss [*20*]

decreased awareness of the communicator's credibility, or both. The increase in opinion change shown by the low credibility group, however, suggests that the negative effects of the "untrustworthy" source wore off and permitted the arguments presented in the communication to produce a delayed positive effect. According to this explanation, the effect of the source is maximal at the time of the communication but decreases with the passage of time more rapidly than the effects of the content. This is one of the mechanisms that can account for an increased adherence to the communicator's conclusion after a lapse of time. (Cf. pp. 254–259).

This explanation suggests that in the present experiment there was relatively independent retention of the source and content, with the sustained effects apparently determined primarily by retention of the content. The phenomenon would be expected to occur when the communication contains not only the source's opinion but supporting evidence and arguments. This expectation is based upon the assumption that these supporting aspects of the communication can be evaluated on their own merits and without regard to the source. They will not initially evoke evaluative responses involving the source to the degree that the purely "opinion" aspects of the message will. Subsequently they will more frequently occur without accompanying responses which label the source and bring it to mind.

Under other conditions, however, one may expect the source and the content to be closely associated in memory. For example, when the communication presents a message that only one or a few persons could have originated, retention of the content will tend to be accompanied by retention of the source. If a person hears a radio talk by a cabinet member about policy decisions made in the President's Cabinet, he is likely to recall the source when he recalls the assertion. On the other hand, if the assertion could have emanated from a variety of sources, retention of the two will tend to be independent.

The preceding hypotheses may be specific cases of a more general proposition: the stronger the perceptual response to the source during initial exposure to the communication, the more likely it is that the source will be evoked when, on subsequent occasions, any aspect of the communication situation is present. Strong responses to a communicator would presumably occur when the communication situation highlights his uniqueness as a source or when the situation forces the audience to consider his characteristics in evaluating the assertion. Other factors may operate in the same manner; e.g., when the communicator's manner of speaking elicits a strong emotional response to him, the audience will be especially likely to remember who presented the message. A systematic exploration of these factors awaits further investigation.

Another study involving variations in source credibility was conducted by Kelman and Hovland [23]. During regular class periods students taking senior work in a summer high school were requested to listen to a recording of an educational radio program ostensibly to judge its educational value. In the course of this program a guest speaker was introduced who proceeded to give a talk favoring extreme leniency in the treatment of juvenile delinquents. Three different versions of the introduction to the speaker were used. In a *positive* version he was identified as a judge in a juvenile court—a highly trained, well-informed, and experienced authority on criminology and delinquency; sincere, honest, and with the public interest at heart. In a *neutral* version he was identified as a member of the studio audience, chosen at random. No information about him was given.[2] In a *negative* version he was also presented as selected from the studio audience, but it came out in the introductory interview that he had been a delinquent as a youth and was currently involved in some shady transactions, being out on bail after arrest on a charge of dope peddling. During the interview he openly expressed low regard for the law and great disrespect for his parents, even though they had provided well for him. Many of his statements showed that he was self-centered and that his favoring leniency was motivated by self-interest.

The basic opinion data were obtained by an adaptation of the Wang-Thurstone scale on attitudes toward the treatment of criminals. The scale was administered immediately after the communication and three weeks later. Before the communication, a special set of attitude items bearing on the same issue had been used to insure the comparability of the ten classes involved in the experiment.

Evaluations of presentation. Audience reactions to the presentation were obtained directly after the communication. The results are summarized in Table 3. With identical content, audience judgments concerning the fairness of the presentation were much more favorable when it was given by the positive communicator than by the negative one. The judgments for the neutral communicator were intermediate but more similar to those for the positive one.

TABLE 3. *Audience Evaluations of the Same Talk on Juvenile Delinquency When Delivered by Positive, Neutral, and Negative Communicators*

	NATURE OF THE SOURCE		
Judgment	Positive N = 110	Neutral N = 60	Negative N = 102
Per cent judging him as giving a "completely fair" or "fair" presentation . . .	73%	63%	29%

For positive vs. negative, $p < .001$

From Kelman and Hovland [23]

Opinion change. The opinion results closely parallel the evaluations of the presentation. In Table 4 it can be seen that the group hearing the communication from the positive source favored more lenient treatment (as indicated by a higher score) than those hearing it from the negative source. The fact that the opinion scores produced by the neutral source are more similar to those of the positive source, taken in conjunction with the pattern of evaluations described above, suggests that attitudes toward fairness and trustworthiness played a greater role on this issue than did attitudes related to expertness.

TABLE 4. *Immediate Effects of Different Communicators on Opinion Scores* *

Group	N	Mean †
Positive communicator	97	46.7
Neutral communicator	56	45.7
Negative communicator	91	42.8

* A high score represents the position of leniency advocated in the communication.

† $t_{pos.-neg.} = 4.11$ $p < .001$
  $t_{pos.-neutr.} = 0.79$ $p = .21$
  $t_{neutr.-neg.} = 2.36$ $p < .01$

From Kelman and Hovland [23]

Three weeks after the communication, an alternative form of the attitude scale was administered. The differences among the experimental groups were no longer present. As in the case of the experiment by Hovland and Weiss, there had been a decrease in acceptance of the communication for those having had the positive communicator and a slight increase for those having had the negative communicator. (For further results of this study including those pertaining to the effects of "reinstating" the source, cf. Chapter 8, pp. 256 to 259.)

A study by Hovland and Mandell [19] concerns primarily the variable of trustworthiness. A communication on the topic "Devaluation of Currency" was given to college students in introductory psychology classes. On the basis of a general discussion of the American monetary system and the description of some historical examples, the communication led up to a conclusion favoring the devaluation of our currency, which for some subjects was stated explicitly and for others was not. (For a discussion of conclusion drawing cf. pp. 100–105.) An introduction was used which elicited either 1) suspicion of the communicator's motives or 2) belief in his impartiality. For subjects in the suspicion variation, the speaker was introduced as the head of a large importing firm. Since it was explicitly stated in the communication that importers would profit from devaluation, it was expected that this introduction would give the audience the impression that the speaker had something to gain by having his conclusion accepted. In the second (nonsuspicion) variation, the communicator was introduced as an economist from a leading American university.

The subjects were asked to give their opinions on the issue before and after the speech. At the latter time they were also asked to give their reactions to the program and speaker.

Evaluations of presentation. The results of two of the questions on evaluations of the presentation are shown in Table 5. They indicate that the suspicion-arousing introduction was successful in leading the

TABLE 5. *Evaluations of Identical Communications When Presented by Suspect and Nonsuspect Communicators*

A. Question: "Do you think this radio program did a good or a poor job of giving the facts on devaluation of currency?"

	Nonsuspect Communicator (N = 113)		Suspect Communicator (N = 122)
Per cent of subjects answering			
"A very good job"	41.1		21.1
Difference		20.0	
p		<.001	

B. Question: "Do you feel that the speaker was fair and honest about America's devaluating its currency or did the facts seem too one-sided?"

	Nonsuspect Communicator (N = 113)		Suspect Communicator (N = 122)
Per cent of subjects saying communicator gave a "fair and honest" picture	52.7		36.7
Difference		16.0	
p		<.01	

From Hovland and Mandell [19]

audience to view the "motivated" speaker as having done a poorer job and as having been less "fair and honest" in his presentation than the "impartial" communicator. This is true despite the fact that the content and conclusion of the speech were identical for the two. Thus it appears that cues as to the communicator's motives influenced judgments of his presentation and content.

Opinion change. The results indicate that the communication produced no greater net change in opinions when emanating from the nonsuspect communicator than when from the suspect one ($p = .23$ using a one-tailed test [22]). Thus, even though the experimental variation produced large differences in the subjects' evaluations of the two presentations, the subsequent differences in opinion change are quite small. This finding highlights the necessity of assessing various communicators in terms of their effectiveness in producing changes in opinion rather than relying merely on audience evaluation of the presentation of the content. In this experiment, sizable variations in judgments of the impartiality of the presentation made little difference in the amount of opinion change produced. Further research is needed to determine the conditions under which this outcome will occur in contrast to that obtained in the preceding experiments.

In summary, the research evidence indicates that the reactions to a communication are significantly affected by cues as to the communicator's intentions, expertness, and trustworthiness. The very same presentation tends to be judged more favorably when made by a communicator of high credibility than by one of low credibility. Furthermore, in the case of two of the three studies on credibility, the immediate acceptance of the recommended opinion was greater when presented by a highly credible communicator.

From the results, it is not possible to disentangle the effects of the two main components of credibility—trustworthiness and expertness—but it appears that both are important variables. In the Hovland and Mandell study where the suspect source differed from the nonsuspect one primarily in characteristics relevant to trustworthiness (motives, intentions), a marked effect occurred on judgments of the fairness of the presentation, but there was little effect on amount of opinion change. The small effect on opinions may be attributable to a special combination of factors such that the content of the speech and the qualifications of the speaker were more important than his personal motives. On the other hand, in the Kelman and Hovland investigation, it appears that variations in attitudes related to fairness and trustworthiness were responsible for the sizable differences in amount of opinion change.

It may be noted in passing that even with untrustworthy sources the over-all effect was usually in the direction favored by the communication. The negative communicator tended merely to produce *less* positive change than the positive source. Presumably, the arguments contained in the communications produced large enough positive effects to counteract negative effects due to the communicator. Negative or boomerang effects might be expected where no arguments are contained in a communication delivered by a negative source or when the audience members anticipate that his conclusions will consistently be in opposition to their best interests.

Bases of Differential Effects

The fact that identical communications are evaluated differently by subjects exposed to sources of different credibility is subject to several interpretations. Judgments about content and style are often merely specific symptoms of general approach or avoidance reactions to the entire communication situation. On the basis of psychological studies of the manner in which expectations influence perceptions and of the phenomenon of "halo effect" in judgmental behavior, these broad effects of different labeling of the communicator come as no surprise. They do, however, raise some question as to the processes which mediate or make possible the differential opinion changes. For example, do persons initially negative toward the source listen less closely to the communication? Or do they, perhaps, distort the meaning of what is said, and hence judge it to have been less well presented? The more general problem here is essentially this: At what point in the process of attending to, perceiving, interpreting, learning, and believing the content of the communication do attitudes toward the source have their effect?

In accounting for the different amounts of opinion change produced by communicators of high versus low credibility, one obvious possibility would be that people tend not to expose themselves to communications from sources toward whom they have negative attitudes. However, the present experiments all involve captive audiences, typically college classes, whose members could hardly avoid being exposed to the communication. Under these conditions there remain two different explanations for the lesser effectiveness of unfavorable (e.g., low credibility) communicators in bringing about opinion change:

1. Because of their unfavorable attitudes, members of the audience do not pay close attention to the content and/or do not attempt to comprehend the exact meaning of what is said. The former could result from thinking about the communicator, while the latter might result from "reading into" the content various implications that correspond to the assumed intent of the communicator. As a result, they *learn* the material less well than when it is presented by a favorable source and, failing to learn it, are unable to adhere to the recommended conclusions.

2. Because of their unfavorable attitudes, members of the audience are not motivated to *accept* or believe what the communicator says and recommends.

With respect to choosing between these two explanations, the foregoing studies present recall data which indicate the extent to which the materials presented by the various communicators were learned. In the study of high versus low credibility sources, on a variety of topics, Hovland and Weiss found no significant difference in the number of fact quiz items answered correctly immediately after the communication. In the study of suspect versus nonsuspect sources, Hovland and Mandell administered a fact quiz on the economics of devaluation immediately after the communication. There was no difference between the two source versions in the number of items answered correctly.

In the Kelman and Hovland study, recall for items on the communication was determined at the delayed after-test. Here again there was no significant difference between the positive and negative sources. An interesting incidental finding was that recall was significantly better when the communication was given by the neutral source than by either the positive or negative source. The authors suggest that affective responses may adversely influence the amount of material learned and recalled, and that both the positive and negative communicators were responded to with greater affect than the neutral one. An emotional reaction to the communicator may focus attention upon him to the detriment of attending to his conclusions and learning his arguments.[3] This result indicates, as we would expect, that there are some instances in which the communicator affects the degree to which the content is acquired.

In summary, the present studies of various sources in general reveal little difference between the most and least credible sources in the degree to which the content of their communications is *learned*. In most instances, the differences were certainly not large enough to account for the differential opinion changes produced by high and low credibility communicators. Thus, persons exposed to a low credibility communicator evidently learned as much of what was said as did persons exposed to a high credibility source, but the former accepted the recommendations much less than did the latter. These findings, together with those from Weiss's investigation (p. 252), indicate that some recipients learned what was said without believing the communicator or modifying their attitudes accordingly. Change of opinion obviously requires not only learning what the new point of view is but also becoming motivated to accept it.

In some instances where there is strong resistance to the content and an opportunity to avoid exposure to it, the recipient may, of course, neither learn the content nor accept it. Not only were the captive audiences of the present experiments in classroom situations where they are generally set to pay close attention, but the communications were generally highly structured and permitted relatively little misinterpretation. Although under these conditions subjects apparently are motivated to learn and remember most of the assertions in the communications, there are large differences among experimental treatments in the degree to which the arguments are accepted and incorporated as changes in opinions. This strongly suggests that a critical aspect of opinion change is the degree to which recipients become motivated to accept the assertions contained in the communication. The evidence is quite clear that acceptance or rejection depends in part upon attitudinal reactions toward the source of the communication.

Why is acceptance likely to be heightened by increasing the credibility of the communicator? Our principle assumption is that the individual is motivated to accept conclusions and recommendations which he anticipates will be substantiated by further experiences or will lead to reward, social approval, and avoidance of punishment. These anticipations are increased when a recommendation is presented by a person who is believed to be informed, insightful, and willing to express his true beliefs and knowledge, and are decreased when cues of low credibility are present. Thus the motives of the audience to accept recommendations are higher the more credible the person making them. It should also be noted that the strength of these motives probably depends upon the situation in which the recipient of the communication finds himself and upon his corresponding dependence upon others for information and advice. The motivation to seek and accept advice from credible sources seems to be increased considerably when the person is in a situation which requires finer discriminations than he is capable of or which demands specialized information not at his disposal (Cf. [*12*]).

Are the Effects of High Credibility Sources Enduring?

We have noted that in terms of immediate opinion change high credibility sources tend to be somewhat more effective than low credibility sources. However, delayed after-tests in the experiments by Hovland and Weiss [*20*] and Kelman and Hovland [*23*] indicated that this differential effectiveness had disappeared after an interval of about three weeks. These results are summarized in Figure 2. In both studies there was a highly significant difference between high and low communicators on the immediate after-test, but in both instances this difference had virtually disappeared several weeks later.

These results raise important questions about the long-term significance of the credibility of the communicator. Unfortunately, little other evidence is available on the degree to which communicator effects are sustained.[4] The main implication of the present results is that the credibility of the communicator may, under certain circumstances mentioned earlier (pp. 29–31), be important only with respect to the amount of *immediate* opinion change produced. Under circumstances where there is a very close association between the source and content of a communication, however, the effect of the communicator may be more enduring. The immediate effects reported here may have considerable practical significance if the purpose of the communication is to elicit some type of immediate action and if subsequent behavior is of little concern. Furthermore, if the immediate action involves some type of formal or informal commitment, lasting effects may be obtained.

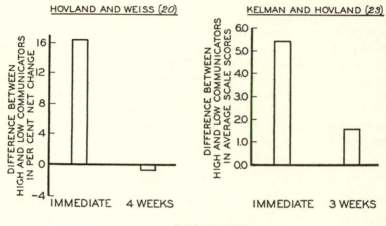

FIGURE 2. Differential Effectiveness, Immediate and Delayed, of High vs. Low Credibility Communicators.

The problems posed by the retention data must be considered in relation to other factors affecting retention. These will be discussed more fully in Chapter 8.

IMPLICATIONS FOR FURTHER RESEARCH

The findings in the preceding section indicated that the delivery of a communication by a communicator of high credibility increases the amount of opinion change measured immediately after exposure, and that a communicator of low credibility may bring about a decrease in opinion change. What are the limiting conditions under which such effects are obtained?

Let us begin with cases of the type where the source has been found to *augment* acceptance. Typically a source of high credibility delivers a communication containing arguments and assertions which, because of their lack of compellingness, their inadequate substantiation, or incompatibility with pre-existing opinions, the recipient has little tendency to accept. There are certain variations from this situation in which it is fairly obvious that the credibility of the source will have little or no effect on opinion change. For example, if the message is fully accepted on its own merits, the highly credible source can have no added effect on acceptance; if the credibility of the source is negligible (e.g., the source is trustworthy but completely uninformed), the message may be accepted to no greater degree than if it were reacted to in terms of its intrinsic qualities. In general, it appears that source credibility has maximal effects on acceptance when the source and content are such that there would be considerable discrepancy between the attitudinal responses to each of them alone—in this particular case, when the communicator would produce a considerable tendency to accept whatever he says and the communication, in and of itself, would produce little or no tendency toward acceptance.

There are important variations of the typical case which would seem on theoretical grounds to represent limiting conditions for the generalization that positive communicators increase acceptance for their messages. The first to be considered consists of a highly reliable communicator giving a communication which, on its own merits, would be strongly rejected.

With respect to this first situation, the following hypothesis is suggested: Under conditions where positive attitudes toward the source are very strong (e.g., he is considered as highly credible) and where the tendency to reject the conclusions and arguments in the communication is very strong, *there is a tendency to dissociate the source and the content*. We may also speculate as to the various forms this dissociation may take. At the time of exposure, it may consist either in denying the source's responsibility for the communication or in reinterpreting the content and conclusion of the message. In effect, the individual can conclude either that "someone else gave this communication" or that "this communicator meant something else when he gave it." Dissociation may also occur in the form of not recalling who said what, as is suggested by the retention data described in the preceding section. In any event, the importance of dissociation for the effectiveness of persuasive communications is that it reduces or eliminates the direct influence of the source on acceptance of the content. To the extent that the recipient is able to dissociate source and message, *the acceptance of the message will be independent of the source.*

Phenomena which appear to be related to these dissociation effects have been noted in the literature and in the present research. In several reports, it appears that where a communication was highly incompatible with the audience's preconception of the alleged source, denial was made that the suggested source was really responsible for the assertion. For example, Lewis [26] had college students judge political slogans as to their social significance, compellingness to action, intelligence of their authors, etc. Subsequently, some of the subjects (those who were in sympathy with the Communist party) were given evaluations of the slogans allegedly made by Earl Browder, at that time leader of the party in the United States. The purpose was to see whether this communication, which was in considerable disagreement with the subjects' previous judgments, would affect their evaluations of the slogans. Several of the subjects suspected a hoax and refused to believe that the evaluations had been made by Browder. Another subject suggested that Browder had been misquoted by newspapermen. A similar phenomenon was observed in Birch's study [6]. Another phenomenon of this type consists in attributing special motives to the communicator or assuming that his delivery of the communication can be discounted because of unusual circumstances. This defines the communication as a special act not to be taken at face value. For instance, confronted with contradictory evaluations supposedly coming from Franklin Roosevelt, one of Lewis' subjects, who respected Roosevelt, stated: "Roosevelt's ranking seems to me to be slightly off. Perhaps it was before he became social-conscious" ([26] p. 246). Other subjects felt Roosevelt was trying to be objective or was deliberately using special criteria in making his judgments. Asch ([4] pp. 427–428) provides other examples in which an incongruity between source and content is resolved by making highly specific interpretations of the source's motives for communication.

The reinterpretation of the message is related to a phenomenon which has been emphasized by Asch. It has frequently been assumed, at least implicitly, that communication-induced changes in opinion indicate re-evaluation of the same objects or statements judged initially. Asch has challenged this assumption and argued strongly that these processes involve *"a change in the object of judgment, rather than in the judgment of the object"* (Asch [2] p. 458; italics his). The example most often cited to illustrate change in the object of judgment appears in Asch's study [2] of college students' judgments of professions as influenced by evaluations allegedly made by 500 other students. When told that the other students had judged the profession of politics highest with respect to intelligence, social usefulness, etc., the subjects markedly raised their valuation of politicians. In subsequent interviews they reported having shifted their conception of politics from that of local ward politics to that of national politics and statesmanship. Thus, they apparently reinterpreted what it was that the 500 students were evaluating. Similar examples found in studies by Lewis [26] and Luchins [28] also indicate that the type of change emphasized by Asch may occur at least under some conditions.

The effects noted by these investigators suggest what happens when subjects dissociate the original source and content: they are likely to deny that the source actually was responsible for the communication or to reinterpret the "real" meaning they believe the message to have. For example, if the message given by a highly respected source is repugnant to the audience's values, the source may be thought to be someone else capable of originating such ideas, or the message will be interpreted so as to be congruent with the actual respected source. These specific tendencies, as well as some of the other effects discussed here, can be derived from Heider's logical analysis of "attitudes and cognitive organization" [16]. He suggests that we tend to maintain the same attitude toward persons as toward their possessions and actions. As applied to the problem of source credibility, the implications would be as follows: When we attribute high credibility to a person but dislike what he communicates, our attitudes related to him are in an "unbalanced" state. This tends to be resolved in any of three ways: 1) change in attitudes toward the communication (which would include either accepting it or reinterpreting it), 2) change in attitudes toward the communicator, and 3) change in perception of the communicator's role in originating the communication.

These changes tend to be of such a nature as to restore a state of balance or congruence among the various attitudes related to the communicator and his actions.

Dissociation of source and content may also occur following exposure to the communication and may take the form of forgetting that the particular communicator gave the specific content. Some of the results on retention from the experiment by Hovland and Weiss [20] bear on this hypothesis. High credibility sources initially produced greater acceptance of the conclusion than low credibility ones. With the passage of time, this difference disappeared. However, the subjects were able, when asked, to recall both the original source and content. The authors suggest that with the passage of time there is a decrease in tendency to "associate spontaneously" the content with the source. Some results from Kelman and Hovland [23] on reinstatement of source (cf. Ch. 8), suggest that subjects can be made to re-establish the association of source and content, with a resulting reappearance of the original differences in the degree to which the communications of high and low credibility sources are accepted. The results are generally consistent with the hypotheses that dissociation between source and content can occur following the communication and that to the degree that dissociation does occur the effect of the source on acceptance is attenuated.

We have already speculated as to the conditions under which dissociation through time of source and content are likely to occur. The central hypothesis is that dissociation will occur to a lesser degree the more vivid and intimate the relation between source and content at the time of the initial exposure. A vivid and intimate relation would occur, for example, if a particular source is one of the few persons who could possess the "inside" information contained in the communication or if, in evaluating new or unexpected information of great importance, the recipient must rely heavily on evaluations of the source.

Several hypotheses may also be mentioned which specify the conditions under which denial of the source's responsibility for the message or reinterpretation of the content will occur. One would expect a greater tendency for denial of the source to occur the more ambiguous the evidence is as to his responsibility. The evidence will be most clear-cut when the source appears personally and presents the communication directly. It will be more ambiguous when the speech is recorded, printed, or filmed, and even more so when the source is quoted by someone else. We may also hypothesize that reinterpretation of the content will occur more frequently when there is some ambiguity as to the question raised and the conclusion suggested in the communication. This would be true for complicated issues which have many sides and where the conclusion is qualified in several ways.

When source and content are such that they tend to elicit radically different reactions from the audience, a problem arises as to whether a contrast effect occurs. Consider, for example, a communicator who is viewed as highly expert and of whom stimulating and insightful ideas are expected. If he makes a banal or trivial statement, he may seriously violate the audience's high expectations. If a listener cannot readily dissociate him from the statement (via the processes described above) the statement may seem much less acceptable than if it had been presented by a source for whom expectations were not so high. This raises the possibility of a special situation in which there is an inverse relation between credibility of source and acceptance of his conclusions.

Interesting problems also arise when highly objectionable content is presented by communicators of only moderate credibility. For example, let us consider the instance where the content is unsubstantiated and runs counter to the audience's loyalties. In this case the recipient is likely to remain uninfluenced by the content and, instead, change his evaluation of the communicator. In other words, attitudes toward a communicator are not maintained without reference to what he says and does. In this regard, Duncker [*14*] and Asch [*3*] have pointed out that the prestige of a source is too often viewed as something that can be "tacked on" to any assertion and that is equally effective no matter what is being said. The hypothesis which requires investigation is that under these conditions, where the assertion is repulsive to the audience and the source is only mildly respected, there is a tendency to change one's attitude toward the communicator in the direction of attributing less credibility to him or otherwise becoming more negative toward him. This result is more probable the less positive are the initial attitudes toward him. (It may be noted that this type of change is one of those suggested by Heider's analysis mentioned above.)

Examples of changes in attitudes toward the communicator as a result of objectionable content are infrequent in the literature. In two studies involving length judgments, some of the subjects began to doubt the source's eyesight after hearing assertions greatly at variance with reality [5, 28]. In another case [26], initially negative attitudes toward the source seem to have been strengthened by the "absurdity" of the assertion. The paucity of examples of this type can be attributed to the fact that most investigators in this field have been primarily interested in changing attitudes on the issues discussed in the communication. As a result, the typical investigation has used highly prestigeful sources toward whom initial attitudes are fairly strong and stable, and has not included measures of attitudes toward the communicators, so that even if changes in these attitudes occurred, they would not have been detected.

The preceding discussion has been limited to situations where the credibility of the source might be expected to heighten acceptance. What of situations where material is presented by low credibility sources? Dissociation effects and changes in attitudes toward the communicator might also be expected to occur here. For example, if arguments are presented by a communicator whose motives are open to suspicion, acceptance would ordinarily be lowered; but if the arguments are well substantiated and very impressive, the content may be dissociated from the source in the manner described above. If the initial negative attitudes toward the source are not very strong, they may be improved by the favorable presentation. This does not mean that the positive and negative communicators act upon the process of opinion change in exactly the same way. For example, inattentiveness will be more marked with communicators of low credibility, so that even though their message might be quite convincing it may never receive an adequate hearing. The positive communicator who gives an unacceptable message will probably have the audience's attention, at least during the initial part of his presentation. However, certain generalizations about dissociation phenomena and changes in attitudes toward communicators probably apply to both positive and negative, high and low credibility communicators.

The foregoing analysis suggests some of the possible limiting conditions under which the relationship between source credibility and acceptance may be eliminated or greatly attenuated. It also indicates some of the effects other than variations in acceptance (e.g., dissociation of source and content, change in attitude toward source) which can arise out of situations where, for example, unacceptable content is presented by a positive source. In order to understand these various effects and the conditions under which they occur, one is led to a fact which is obvious but has rarely been incorporated into investigations of communicator effects: Attitudes toward the communicator and the cues which elicit them operate in interaction with many other factors of the communication situation. These other factors include such variables as initial attitudes toward the content, cues as to the source's responsibility for the content, the congruence between what is said and prior knowledge about the source's position on the issue, the complexity of the question raised in the communication, the ambiguity of the proposed answer, and the vividness of the source.

Another broad set of factors includes the characteristics of the situation in which the communication occurs. While the individual has attitudes of reliance and trust toward various kinds of communicators, the extent to which these attitudes are evoked at any given time depends to some degree upon the kind of situation in which he finds himself. For example, in a situation where he is confronted with a problem whose solution he believes requires highly technical information, an individual will be especially susceptible to influence from persons who are perceived to be experts. In like manner, when involved in a conflict with a socially disapproved impulse, an individual may seek reassuring advice from older persons who resemble his parents and are in positions of authority with respect to dominant moral values. When the problem is one of gaining social acceptance, the most effective communicators probably will be those group leaders and officials viewed as most able to predict majority reactions. In these and other ways the nature of the problem situation which exists at the time of receiving a communication will affect a person's responsiveness to specific kinds of communicators.[5] We should also note the possible influence of attitudes toward the communicator which are unrelated to credibility, such as affection, admiration, awe, and fear. The existence of these attitudes may make changes in attitudes toward the source less probable. For example, a person may less readily deny the expertness of a communicator for whom he has great affection, even though that communicator transmits objectionable material.

All of these various factors in the communication situation interact with attitudes toward the communicator's credibility and determine the degree to which the fact of the source's being reliable will heighten acceptance or whether the other outcomes we have suggested will occur. Unfortunately, evidence bearing on the kinds of hypotheses considered here is almost nonexistent. What is needed is investigations using modern experimental designs which will permit systematic analysis of the interaction among these variables. As theory in this area develops, we can expect additional hypotheses as to the limiting conditions for the differential effects on opinion change of various types of sources. Some of these will undoubtedly shed further light upon the persistence of source effects. The evaluation of such hypotheses through the use of experimental procedures promises to be a very fruitful area for future research.

Notes

1. That older persons tend to be more influential than younger ones is suggested by a variety of investigations. Some of the relevant findings come from research aimed at identifying the persons within a community from whom advice is sought [*31, 38*]. Such characteristics as education, income, and participation in local organizations do not differentiate those frequently sought for advice and those little sought. However, there is some tendency for persons to seek advice from those somewhat older than themselves.

Several studies involve simultaneous variations in the ages of recipients and communicator. Duncker [*14*] found young children more likely to be influenced by the food preference of an older child than vice versa. Berenda [*5*] found a similar relation in a length-judging situation where a single child was exposed to the unanimous and wrong answers of eight classmates. The younger children were influenced more than the older ones. However, her evidence on age is complicated by changes in the social relationships with increased age and by age differences in ability to make the necessary judgments in the absence of social influence. Both Duncker and Berenda find that adults had surprisingly little influence in these situations. We take this to indicate the operation of other important factors which are unrelated or inversely related to the age difference between influencer and recipient (e.g., desire to retain the approval of other members of one's peer group, similarity of influencer to recipient in status and interests). Age appears as an important variable in a number of other studies of influence but usually as a characteristic of the recipients rather than of the communicator.

As a special case of the expertness factor, leaders of groups might be expected to be more influential in matters pertaining to the group norms than rank-and-file members. Recent research by Chowdhry and Newcomb [*11*] indicates that leaders are superior to other group members in their ability to estimate the consensus of opinion within the group on matters related to the common interests and goals. (That this is not true for all intragroup issues is indicated by Hites and Campbell [*17*] who find no superiority for leaders.) Such superiority could form the basis for acquiring confidence in leaders' assertions about how various events will be received by the members or about future decisions of the group. Relatively little existing evidence is directly pertinent to this generalization. Other studies demonstrate the influence of opinions attributed to national leaders and the heads of churches and political parties [*9, 26, 36*], but it is likely that subjects in these studies possess not only attitudes of trust toward these persons but attitudes of affection and respect.

In their analysis of the special properties of direct face-to-face influence, Lazarsfeld, Berelson, and Gaudet suggest that one of the advantages of personal contacts may be that the individual tends to encounter persons similar to himself ([25] p. 155). Redl [33] discusses the importance of similarity as a factor in the infectious spread of influence among the members of a face-to-face group, a phenomenon frequently observed among delinquent adolescents and referred to as "behavioral contagion." When several persons are in similar conflicts between their "undesirable" impulses and internalized social prohibitions, the act of one of them, whether it be in the direction of expressing the impulses or in reaffirming conformity to the prohibitions, serves to evoke the same act in the others. In short, the conflict resolution found by one person is imitated by others who have similar conflicts. This is, perhaps, a specific instance of the more general tendency when confronted with a problem to imitate the solutions found by others in the same dilemma. Perhaps the term "expert" should be broadened to include persons who have found adequate solutions to the problem an individual faces, even though in other respects they may be no more experienced than he and may be very much like him. This may account for some of the instances noted by Duncker [14] and Berenda [5] where peers or slightly older children were found to be more influential than adults.

2. A difficult problem is raised in this investigation by the attempt to establish a "neutral" source to serve as a base line from which to measure positive and negative effects. Kelman and Hovland recognize that the source they define as "neutral" may not be completely neutral, but there seems to be no way of telling whether he is or not. Presumably, a neutral source is one that would *not* modify the effectiveness of a communication from what it would be purely on the merits of the arguments and material contained therein. It is difficult to conceive of an operation to provide an indication of the effectiveness of a communication purely on its own merits since all of our methods for presenting communications necessarily involve some kind of source. Perhaps the closest we ever approach neutrality is when an experimenter, representing himself to be completely unbiased in the matter, presents a set of arguments "which have been suggested" by vague and indefinite persons. Under these circumstances, where the source of a message is ambiguous, if the arguments are contrary to strong initial biases the resultant change may consist of a negative labeling of the source and hostile attitudes toward it. These attitudes, however, would be outcomes of the communication and not attitudes pertaining to the neutrality of the source as initially presented.

3. Kelman's and Hovland's explanation of their result is reminiscent of earlier discussions of the importance in prestige suggestion of an emotional relation between the influencer and influencee. Murphy, Murphy, and Newcomb refer to contradictory ideas and habits which ordinarily inhibit the individual's conformity to verbal suggestions. They go on to say: "The fixation of attention upon the experimenter whom one respects (or perhaps sometimes fears) seems sufficient to block these ordinarily available counter-suggestions" ([32] p. 178). A major differ

ence lies in the fact that whereas these authors use emotional constriction of attention as an explanation of heightened susceptibility to influence, Kelman and Hovland suggest that it may interfere with learning what the communicator says. It seems probable that an emotional reaction to the communicator may have a double-barreled effect. On the one hand, it may have a facilitating effect where it serves to focus attention on what he says and to exclude irrelevant influences in the environment. On the other hand, when the focusing is upon the communicator per se—upon his person, dress, style of speaking, mannerisms, and so on—an emotional reaction may interfere with the acquisition of his content and hence with his effectiveness as a communicator.

4. Results from Kulp [24] are often cited as indicating the persistence of the effects of prestigeful sources over a considerable period (eight weeks). Unfortunately the absence of a control group at the time of the delayed after-test leaves some uncertainty as to whether the results do indicate genuine retention of the original effects. Assuming they do, a possible explanation for the greater permanency of prestige effects in Kulp's study is his method of introducing prestige. Subjects were asked to indicate their agreement or disagreement with opinion items, using test blanks that were already marked with responses attributed to certain prestige groups. This procedure may create a condition where the "source" becomes closely associated with the test items themselves, so that on subsequent occasions they "reinstate" the prestigeful source. Note should also be taken of another important difference between Kulp's procedure and that generally used in the present studies on source credibility: the latter not merely involve the "conclusion" or opinion of the source but also include arguments and evidence in support of the conclusion. This type of supporting content may be retained in a different manner than conclusions alone; for example, arguments and evidence may be dissociated from the source more readily.

5. The problem situation confronting a person can affect his reactions to communicators in various ways. As indicated earlier, the individual's responses to various communicators depend, at least in part, on the degree to which he generalizes from earlier experiences in which he has acquired expectations about the expertness, trustworthiness, and so forth of certain sources. The effects of the communication situation upon reactions to various sources may be examined in terms of how it influences this process of generalization.

In learning studies on stimulus generalization, it has been shown that the learned response to a given stimulus is elicited by other similar cues, but that it tends to appear less frequently and less strongly the more different from the original stimulus are the others ([21] pp. 183–203). To describe these results, a gradient of generalization may be drawn. The solid line in Figure 3 suggests how such a generalization gradient might apply in the case of communicator expertness. On the ordinate is represented the strength of tendency to accept communications given by any specific source and on the abscissa are the cues as to the various

sources' expertness. At the left end of the abscissa would be a source identical
with or very similar to one whom the person had learned to regard as extremely
expert. Moving to the right, one would encounter sources presenting cues in-
creasingly different from those associated with high expertness and, as indicated

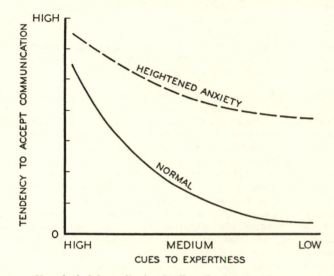

FIGURE 3. Hypothetical Generalization Gradients for Communicator Expertness. *Mod-
eled after Rosenbaum's empirical curves for manual habits* [35].

by the gradient, there would be a decreasing tendency to accept the sources' recommendations.

Any factor which affects the shape or height of this generalization curve will
affect the person's responsiveness to various communicators. We shall consider
here only the manner in which the communication situation can produce such
effects by changing the individual's *motivation*. Animal experiments [8, 34] have
shown that increasing the level of drive produces a general elevation of the generalization curve. An experiment with humans by Rosenbaum [35] suggests that
heightened anxiety elevates the gradient and also flattens it out. The dotted line
in Figure 3 shows how this effect of anxiety might appear in the case of communicator expertness. From a comparison of the two curves in Figure 3, it would
be expected that if the person is in a situation which raises his anxiety level his
responses to various communicators will be affected in three ways: 1) The tendencies to accept communications from sources differing in expertness will be more
nearly equal; in other words, the person will appear to discriminate less sharply
between sources of different degrees of expertness. 2) The tendency to accept com-

munications will be heightened for all sources normally having an effect, this being most marked for those at the low end of the scale. 3) Certain sources at the low end who normally elicit no acceptance whatever will tend, under heightened anxiety conditions, to exert some influence.

These three effects require systematic investigation. For the present, we may note that the literature on social influence contains certain hypotheses and evidence which are consistent with the assumption that such effects can be produced by situational factors. One such hypothesis is that times of stress and uncertainty are especially propitious for the spread of rumors and acceptance of new leaders [*1, 10*]. One of the possible factors contributing to this phenomenon may be the tendency, under conditions of high anxiety, to accept recommendations from persons who normally would produce little or no acceptance. A related hypothesis concerns the "problematic" nature of the situation confronting the individual at the time of receiving a communication. If faced with an important problem which is quite difficult to solve, the individual's anxiety level is likely to be heightened. As a consequence, he might be less sensitive to differences among sources of advice with respect to their credibility [*12*]. In a difficult situation, any person's advice may be welcomed: there is less tendency to question whether the garage man is a master mechanic or whether the doctor is a qualified specialist.

Other hypotheses have to do with the amount of evidence or support a person can muster for a given belief or judgment. An individual generally desires to feel that his judgments are "correct" or valid. This feeling is usually derived from checking his judgments against evidence obtained directly from the physical world or against other person's opinions. In circumstances where these kinds of evidence are absent, the individual becomes highly motivated to obtain some sort of validation for his beliefs. Accordingly, we might expect him to make less fine discriminations among persons with respect to their credibility and to be responsive to the opinions of persons who had previously carried little weight with him. This effect of heightened motivation on the generalization gradients may account in part for the heightened susceptibility to social influence observed in situations where the stimulus situation is quite ambiguous or unstructured or where social support for initial opinions is lacking ([*4*] pp. 450–501; [*29*]; [*37*] pp. 43–50).

References

1. Allport, G. W., and Postman, L. *The psychology of rumor.* New York, Holt, 1947.
2. Asch, S. E. Studies in the principles of judgments and attitudes: II. Determination of judgments by group and ego standards. *J. Soc. Psychol.*, 1940, *12*, 433–465.
3. Asch, S. E. The doctrine of suggestion, prestige and imitation in social psychology. *Psychol. Rev.*, 1948, *55*, 250–276.
4. Asch, S. E. *Social psychology.* New York, Prentice-Hall, 1952.
5. Berenda, Ruth W. *The influence of the group on the judgments of children.* New York, Columbia Univ., King's Crown Press, 1950.
6. Birch, H. G. The effect of socially disapproved labeling upon a well-structured attitude. *J. Abnorm. Soc. Psychol.*, 1945, *40*, 301–310.
7. Bowden, A. O., Caldwell, F. F., and West, G. A. A study in prestige. *Am. J. Sociol.*, 1934, *40*, 193–204.
8. Brown, J. S. The generalization of approach responses as a function of stimulus intensity and strength of motivation. *J. Comp. Psychol.*, 1942, *33*, 209–226.
9. Burtt, H. E., and Falkenburg, D. R., Jr. The influence of majority and expert opinion on religious attitudes. *J. Soc. Psychol.*, 1941, *14*, 269–278.
10. Cantril, H. *The psychology of social movements.* New York, John Wiley, 1941.
11. Chowdhry, Kalma, and Newcomb, T. M. The relative abilities of leaders and non-leaders to estimate opinions of their own groups. *J. Abnorm. Soc. Psychol.*, 1952, *47*, 51–57.
12. Coffin, T. E. Some conditions of suggestion and suggestibility. *Psychol. Monogr.*, 1941, *53*, No. 4.
13. Doob, L. W. *Public opinion and propaganda.* New York, Holt, 1948.
14. Duncker, K. Experimental modification of children's food preferences through social suggestion. *J. Abnorm. Soc. Psychol.*, 1938, *33*, 489–507.
15. Ewing, T. N. A study of certain factors involved in changes of opinion. *J. Soc. Psychol.*, 1942, *16*, 63–88.
16. Heider, F. Attitudes and cognitive organization. *J. Psychol.*, 1946, *21*, 107–112.
17. Hites, R. W., and Campbell, D. T. A test of the ability of fraternity leaders to estimate group opinion. *J. Soc. Psychol.*, 1950, *32*, 95–100.
18. Hovland, C. I., Lumsdaine, A. A., and Sheffield, F. D. *Experiments on mass communication.* Princeton Univ. Press, 1949.
19. Hovland, C. I., and Mandell, W. An experimental comparison of conclusion-drawing by the communicator and by the audience. *J. Abnorm. Soc. Psychol.*, 1952, *47*, 581–588.
20. Hovland, C. I., and Weiss, W. The influence of source credibility on communication effectiveness. *Publ. Opin. Quart.*, 1951, *15*, 635–650.
21. Hull, C. L. *Principles of behavior.* New York, Appleton-Century, 1943.

22. Jones, L. V. Tests of hypotheses: one-sided vs. two-sided alternatives. *Psychol. Bull.*, 1952, *49*, 43–46.
23. Kelman, H. C., and Hovland, C. I. "Reinstatement" of the communicator in delayed measurement of opinion change. *J. Abnorm. Soc. Psychol.*, 1953, *48*, 327–335.
24. Kulp, D. H., II. Prestige, as measured by single-experience changes and their permanency. *J. Educ. Res.*, 1934, 27, 663–672.
25. Lazarsfeld, P. F., Berelson, B., and Gaudet, Hazel. *The people's choice; how the voter makes up his mind in a presidential campaign.* New York, Duell, Sloan & Pearce, 1944.
26. Lewis, Helen B. Studies in the principles of judgments and attitudes: IV. The operation of "prestige suggestion." *J. Soc. Psychol.*, 1941, *14*, 229–256.
27. Lucas, D. B., and Britt, S. H. *Advertising psychology and research.* New York, McGraw-Hill, 1950.
28. Luchins, A. S. On agreement with another's judgments. *J. Abnorm. Soc. Psychol.*, 1944, *39*, 97–111.
29. Luchins, A. S. Social influences on perception of complex drawings. *J. Soc. Psychol.*, 1945, *21*, 257–273.
30. Merton, R. K. *Mass persuasion; the social psychology of a war bond drive.* New York, Harper, 1946.
31. Merton, R. K. Patterns of influence: A study of interpersonal influence and of communications behavior in a local community. In P. F. Lazarsfeld and F. N. Stanton, eds., *Communications research, 1948–1949.* New York, Harper, 1949. Pp. 180–219.
32. Murphy, G., Murphy, Lois B., and Newcomb, T. M. *Experimental social psychology* (rev. ed.). New York, Harper, 1937.
33. Redl, F. Group emotion and leadership. *Psychiatry*, 1942, *5*, 573–596.
34. Rosenbaum, G. Temporal gradients of response strength with two levels of motivation. *J. Exp. Psychol.*, 1951, *41*, 261–267.
35. Rosenbaum, G. Stimulus generalization as a function of level of experimentally induced anxiety. *J. Exp. Psychol.*, 1953, *45*, 35–43.
36. Saadi, M., and Farnsworth, P. R. The degrees of acceptance of dogmatic statements and preferences for their supposed makers. *J. Abnorm. Soc. Psychol.*, 1934, *29*, 143–150.
37. Sherif, M., and Cantril, H. *The psychology of ego-involvements.* New York, John Wiley, 1947.
38. Stewart, F. A. A sociometric study of influence in Southtown. *Sociometry*, 1947, *10*, 11–31.

CHAPTER 3: *Fear-arousing Appeals*

IN THIS chapter attention will be focused on content stimuli which operate as "appeals" that arouse motives to accept the opinions recommended in persuasive communications. In the formation and modification of beliefs and attitudes, as in other types of human learning, motivational factors are generally assumed to play a prominent role. Basic preferences and aversions are acquired from life experiences in which the individual's needs are satisfied or fail to gain satisfaction. Early in each individual's development, personal values and ideals, as well as a wide variety of specific attitudes and beliefs, are transmitted through direct parental rewards which satisfy strong motives such as the need for esteem, for love, and for avoiding punishment. Later on, the child develops new and more differentiated attitudes from family and peer group experiences in which socially acquired motives are satisfied by signs of approval that often are purely verbal. As the child grows older, he becomes more and more responsive to verbal symbols which designate future rewards and punishments. In adult life, new political, social, and ethical beliefs are developed through a complex patterning of incentives provided by the symbols contained in direct interpersonal communications and in communications presented via mass media.

Political scientists and sociologists as well as social psychologists frequently emphasize the importance of motives in relation to public opinion formation and social change. But despite widespread agreement on this point, social science research has provided little precise information on the conditions under which motivational factors facilitate or interfere with opinion change. Only a few experimental studies have been carried out in which the effects of persuasive communications were investigated in relation to the use of content appeals which arouse different kinds of motives.[1]

This chapter will deal primarily with the effects of one class of "emotional" appeals—referred to as "threat" appeals—for which preliminary evidence is available from studies carried out as part of our research program. The primary purpose of the studies was to investigate factors which determine the degree to which threat appeals are effective or ineffective in producing opinion change. Before examining the evidence, we shall indicate the theoretical considerations which were taken into account in designing the studies and which form the general setting for our research in this area. First, we shall consider briefly a number of problems concerning the nature of the effects produced by motivating appeals in general, and then, at somewhat greater length, a set of specific assumptions about the psychological mechanisms that are likely to mediate the effectiveness of appeals which arouse emotional tension.

BACKGROUND

Diverse Effects of Motivating Appeals

Probably the best known experiments on motivating appeals are those which compare the effects of "emotional" and "rational" appeals. Several investigators have reported experimental data which indicate that communications containing "emotional" appeals were comparatively more effective than communications which relied exclusively on "rational" argumentation (e.g., Hartmann [*13*], Menafee and Granneberg [*26*]). Other experimental findings, however, fail to confirm the superiority of "emotional" appeals and even suggest the possibility that such appeals can sometimes be less effective than "rational" ones (e.g., Knower [*22*]).

Some of the problems of interpreting results in this field of research can be well illustrated by considering the outcome of the well-known experiment by Hartmann [*13*]. In this study the effects of two different types of political propaganda were investigated in a community situation, election returns being used as a behavioral index of communication effectiveness. Two leaflets which urged the recipients to vote for the Socialist party were distributed in different sections of the same city. The emotional leaflet used highly sentimentalized language to play up various threats (war, economic depression, etc.), and emphasized the satisfactions to be derived if the Socialist program were put into effect. The rational leaflet presented a series of programmatic statements and emphasized that a voter who agrees with the majority of the statements should support the Socialist party in order to attain his goals. In one set of election wards every family received the emotional leaflet while in another set of wards every family received the rational leaflet. A third set of wards was used as a control group. The outcome was determined by analyzing the Socialist party vote in terms of per cent increase over the vote received in an election campaign that had been held one year earlier. All wards were found to have increased in Socialist party votes but the greatest increase occurred in the wards which received the emotional appeal. (The Socialist vote increased by 50 per cent in the "emotional" wards, by 35 per cent in the "rational" wards and by only 24 per cent in the control wards.) The evidence indicates that while both forms of propaganda were effective the emotional leaflet had a relatively greater effect than the rational leaflet.

"Emotional" appeals of the sort used in Hartmann's study are sometimes discussed as if they were the only motivational devices employed in persuasive communications. Actually, of course, "rational" appeals may also have a marked effect on motives. For example, the challenging questions raised in the rational leaflet may have markedly increased the recipient's motivation to think about the issues and to take account of the alleged benefits to be gained from voting for the Socialist party. Presumably, either of the two types of appeals is capable of bringing about some *change* in the existing motives that are already operative at the time of exposure to a communication. The questions which ultimately need to be answered from research data have to do with describing the nature of such changes produced by each type of appeal and explaining how they bring about an increase (or decrease) in the effectiveness of persuasive communications.

One of the major difficulties that arises when one attempts to answer such questions from studies which compare different types of appeals is that one cannot clearly identify the effective content stimuli. In such studies, the classification of different contents as "emotional" or "rational" appeals has not been based on clear-cut operational definitions. Most investigators seem to use the term "emotional appeal" to refer to any set of assertions which is presumed to have the effect of arousing affective reactions in an audience. But the question of which types of content actually do elicit emotional responses is an empirical one that requires systematic investigation. An adequate classification scheme for separating "emotional" appeals from other types of appeals would seem to require, first, the use of some form of content analysis technique for classifying assertions according to their semantic meanings (cf. Lasswell and Leites, et al. [24]) and second, controlled experimentation to differentiate those contents which evoke one or another type of emotional reaction from those which evoke other reactions.

Once the effective content stimuli can be adequately specified, a second major question arises: in what way does the use of a given type of appeal facilitate (or interfere with) the over-all effectiveness of a communication? When motives are aroused by the appeals contained in a persuasive communication, there are at least three different aspects of audience responsiveness which might be differentially affected:

1. attention to the verbal content of the communication;

2. comprehension of the message of the communication;

3. acceptance of the conclusions advocated by the communication.

Increased incentive to pay attention, to comprehend, or to accept the communication could account for the effectiveness of any given motivating appeal.[2] Accordingly, it is essential to differentiate these effects in order to arrive at systematic knowledge concerning the ways in which motivating appeals bring about opinion change.

Attention effects might have played some part in the outcome of Hartmann's study. For instance, under conditions where people are free to choose whether or not to expose themselves to a printed communication, an emotional appeal may produce a greater incentive to read it all the way through. Or perhaps the dominant motivational impact is more *attentive* reading, which may involve a more intense mental rehearsal of the communication. Attention effects of this kind may have been partly responsible for the outcome of Hartmann's experiment, inasmuch as he reports that postelection interviews showed that more people remembered having received the emotional leaflet than the rational leaflet.

A second type of effect to be considered involves the motivation to comprehend the message of the communication. In order for opinion changes to result from a verbal communication, it is probably not sufficient merely to attend to the specific meanings conveyed by the content. Somehow, the implications must be thought over and interpreted in relation to one's own goals, values, and potential behavior. It seems quite possible that an "emotional" appeal could have the effect of increasing the incentive to try out new ideas or to consider the implications of what is being said. Hence such an appeal may sometimes influence the way in which the content is understood and interpreted.

Although attention and comprehension may be affected to some degree, it seems likely that the effectiveness of an "emotional" appeal would usually involve increasing the audience's motivation to accept the conclusion. In the case of Hartmann's experiment, one cannot tell in what way, if any, the "emotional" appeal induced greater willingness to accept the recommendations urged by the leaflet. Was positive affect toward the Socialist program stimulated by the sentimentalized statements about the bright future that it could provide for one's sons and daughters? Or did the predominant reaction consist of heightened emotional tension, evoked by the threats of unemployment and economic deprivation that were also depicted in the emotional leaflet? Specific information about the occurrence of such reactions is needed if research on "emotional" appeals is to contribute to our understanding of the psychological processes which mediate acceptance.

THEORETICAL ASSUMPTIONS

Among the various types of assertions that are likely to have a motivating effect on an audience are those which predict, explicitly or implicitly, that by adopting the communicator's recommendations one can avoid social disapproval or avert some form of physical danger or deprivation. We use the term "threat appeal" to refer to those contents of a persuasive communication which allude to or describe *unfavorable consequences* that are alleged to result from failure to adopt and adhere to the communicator's conclusions. Such appeals are likely to stimulate at least a mild degree of emotional tension. Occasionally the dire consequences are emphasized to the point where the audience becomes extremely apprehensive and upset.

The use of threat appeals which arouse fear is a prominent feature of many mass communications. For example, in their publicity campaigns, health authorities sometimes try to persuade people to visit tumor detection clinics by dramatizing medical facts in such a way as to induce fear of cancer; government spokesmen, from time to time, attempt to elicit public support for national defense activities by arousing apprehensiveness about dangers that could result from being unprepared. When appeals of this sort are used, what are the main factors that determine whether or not they will be successful? The discussion which follows will be oriented primarily toward answering this question. We shall begin with a theoretical analysis of the way in which content stimuli which evoke emotional tension can contribute to the over-all effectiveness of a persuasive communication. A set of theoretical assumptions will be presented concerning the special type of reinforcement that is likely to occur in learning situations where fear or other strong emotions are aroused and then alleviated. The implications of these assumptions will be examined in relation to specific hypotheses bearing on the conditions under which threat appeals are effective or ineffective in producing opinion changes.

Considerable clinical and experimental evidence has accumulated during the past few decades in support of the general assumption that any intensely disturbing emotion, such as fear, guilt, shame, anger, or disgust, has the functional properties of a drive (cf. Mowrer [29] and Miller [28]). The motivating power of unpleasant emotional states has been especially emphasized in psychoanalytic accounts of defense mechanisms, such as rationalization and denial. Freud [7, 8] and other psychoanalysts cite many examples of ideological beliefs that people accept and cling to, despite contradictory evidence, because the beliefs have the effect of alleviating anxiety or guilt. Recent discussions of behavior theory have explicitly postulated that beliefs, attitudes, and verbal thought sequences can be reinforced by the reduction of strong emotional reactions. (Cf. Mowrer [29], Dollard and Miller [4], Brown and Farber [3]). The concept of fear as a learned drive, on which these theoretical analyses are based, has been summarized as follows by Dollard and Miller: "When fear is learned as a response to a new situation, it serves as a drive to motivate trial-and-error behavior. A reduction in the strength of the fear reinforces the learning of any

new response that accompanies it" ([*4*] p. 78). We shall assume that
the same principle applies in the case of persuasive communications
which strongly arouse fear or other unpleasant emotions. The specific
assumptions can be briefly schematized as follows: While a person is
paying attention to a communication, certain contents are presented
(notably those evoking anticipation of a threat to the self) which induce unpleasant emotional reactions. Under these conditions the individual becomes highly motivated to try out various responses, both
symbolic and overt, until the unpleasant emotional state is alleviated.
The variable responses that are tried out are determined mainly by
past learning experiences in which similar emotional states were successfully eliminated or reduced. The prepotency of one response or
thought sequence over another is also influenced by environmental
cues—including those presented in the communication at the time
emotional tension is aroused. Whatever response terminates or greatly
reduces the intensity of the emotional state is reinforced and therefore
tends to become a habitual response. Thus it is assumed that a threat
appeal is most likely to induce an audience to accept the communicator's conclusion if *a*) the emotional tension aroused during the communication is sufficiently intense to constitute a drive state; and *b*)
silent rehearsal of the recommended belief or attitude is immediately
followed by reduction of tension.

When a communication arouses emotional tension by depicting potential dangers or deprivations, the most effective reassurances are
likely to be statements which elicit anticipations of escaping from or
averting the threat. We shall use the term "reassurance" to refer to
those verbal statements—resolutions, plans, judgments, evaluations,
etc.—which successfully reduce emotional tension. One main type of
reassurance consists of imagining oneself as engaging in one or another form of *activity* which will avert the threat. Because of past experiences during which emotional tension was successfully alleviated
by *doing something* to ward off danger, thoughts of this sort are likely
to be prepotent over other types of thoughts when an ego-involving
threat is anticipated.

The above theoretical assumptions focus directly upon the effects
of content stimuli which evoke anticipations of threat and, of course,

do not pertain to those "emotional" appeals which elicit sympathy, affection, elation, or other "positive" emotions.[3] Nevertheless the assumptions concerning threat appeals may have implications that apply to many different types of persuasive communications. "Scare propaganda," which is deliberately designed to frighten people into accepting the propagandist's ideas, is the most obvious type of communication that is likely to involve the arousal of emotional tension. But there are numerous other techniques of persuasion, in addition to those that make use of fear appeals, which can be conceptualized as attempts to augment the effectiveness of a communication by inducing emotional tension. For example, many religious and moral leaders arouse emotional reactions of guilt by calling attention to ubiquitous weaknesses or by depicting the "shameful" consequences of giving in to common temptations. Such appeals may induce greater acceptance of the communicator's admonitions concerning ways and means of avoiding moral transgressions. The arousal and alleviation of emotional tension may also be involved in many instances where persuasive communications produce aggression or other unintended (boomerang) effects. Incidental findings from an experiment by Feshbach [6] confirm the widely accepted hypothesis that when a communicator arouses anger or resentment by making statements which are regarded as offensive, the audience tends to develop unfavorable attitudes not only toward the communicator but also toward the groups, enterprises, and goals with which he is identified. Thus an adequate understanding of the psychological effects of appeals which arouse emotional tension may help to illuminate many different aspects of successful and unsuccessful communication.

Not all threat appeals are successful in facilitating acceptance of the reassuring recommendations advocated by the communicator. The theoretical assumptions concerning such appeals require further elaboration in order to discern their implications for the central problems with which the present discussion is primarily concerned: Under what conditions are threat appeals effective in producing acceptance of a communicator's recommendations? What are the main factors that influence the degree to which an audience will accept the conclusions advocated by a communication which arouses emotional tension?

The following schematic account is intended to provide a hypothetical model of what happens when a person is influenced by a highly effective threat appeal:

1. The individual is first exposed to relatively neutral content cues, such as those which define the topic of the communication. These cues are accompanied or followed by threat statements which are interpreted as referring to a genuine danger and which evoke anticipations that include self-reference: "This might happen to me." As these anticipations are mentally rehearsed, the individual experiences a marked increase in emotional tension.

2. While in a state of high emotional tension, the individual is exposed to other statements in the communication which make assertions about ways of averting the threat (e.g., the threat can or should be warded off by performing the recommended action or by adopting the recommended attitude). As the reassuring recommendation is mentally rehearsed, emotional tension subsides. The reduction of emotional tension operates as a *reinforcement* of the reassuring recommendation, and this verbal response will tend to occur on subsequent occasions, when similar symbol stimuli are present.

3. The chain of responses evoked during exposure to the communication can be represented as follows:

Content cues (C) → *Emotional reaction (E)* → *Reassuring recommendation (R)*.

This sequence of responses will tend to become a habitual chain, such that whenever a topic or subject matter similar to that of the original communication comes to the focus of attention, the person will again experience emotional tension and will tend to think of the reassuring recommendation.

The reduction of emotional tension would account for the reinforcement of the last element (R) in the chain, but other learning processes may be involved in the acquisition of the emotional reaction (E). The pairing of emotion-producing statements with neutral subject matter cues may produce some degree of emotional conditioning, as a result of which the formerly neutral cues become conditioned stimuli which tend to elicit the emotional reaction. The acquisition of this component of the habit chain could be interpreted as an instance of simple Pavlovian conditioning; but it may prove to be the result of more complex mechanisms of verbal learning, involving the mediation of anticipations of threat which become associated with the subject matter of the communication. In any case, we shall assume that two separate habits are acquired when a threat appeal succeeds in producing acceptance of the communicator's reassuring recommendations: 1) $C \rightarrow E$; and 2) $(C + E) \rightarrow R$. One of the main implications of this assumption is that a threat appeal may succeed in building up or strengthening the first component in the habit chain $(C \rightarrow E)$ without necessarily reinforcing the reassuring recommendations (R). (Later on we shall discuss the factors which are likely to produce this type of unsuccessful outcome.)

In order to illustrate the meaning of the theoretical assumptions, consider the typical example of a communication that promotes a civil defense program by playing up the threat of atomic war. In the context of discussing various topics pertaining to civil defense and the prospects of a future war, fear or anxiety is strongly aroused by presenting threat appeals (e.g., statements about the enemy's capabilities, the potential magnitude of an A-bomb attack, the way the individual and his family may be affected by the impact of an atomic explosion, etc.). At a time when the anxiety level of the individuals in the audience has been considerably raised, the communicator presents his recommendations regarding the civil defense program which elicit thoughts about averting the threat. The recommendations will be strongly reinforced if immediately followed by a marked decrease in anxiety. The above sequence might occur many times in the course of a single communication session. Subsequently, when the recipients of the communication think about the possibility of a future atomic war, the same chain of responses will tend to be evoked: thoughts about a future atomic war (C) will lead to a momentary increase in the level of emotional tension (E) which, in turn, will be followed by anxiety-reducing thoughts about the protective value of the civil defense program (R). If the communication is successful, this habit chain will tend to persist, unless modified by subsequent learning experiences.[4] But the communication may not succeed in building up the complete habit chain. Even though it may have the effect of creating anxiety about the A-bomb threat, it may fail to produce increased acceptance of the recommended civil defense program.

From the above discussion, it becomes apparent that there are two main sets of factors which influence the effectiveness of threat appeals: 1) factors which make for successful arousal of emotional tension (E) and 2) factors which make for successful rehearsal and reinforcement of the communicator's reassuring recommendations (R). In the sections which follow, these two sets of factors will be discussed in turn. First, emotional tension will be considered as the *dependent* variable, for the purpose of examining the conditions under which emotional tension can be sufficiently aroused so as to function as a drive state. Then, in the succeeding sections, emotional tension will be treated as the *independent* variable; we shall examine the conditions under which the arousal of emotional tension leads to learning and acceptance of the communicator's conclusions and to other effects, all of which will be treated as dependent variables.

RESEARCH EVIDENCE

FACTORS INFLUENCING THE AROUSAL OF EMOTIONAL TENSION

We shall first examine hypotheses about communication factors which appear to influence the intensity of emotional arousal. The factors on which some experimental evidence is available can be conveniently classified into three general categories: 1) content of the appeal, 2) source of the communication, and 3) antecedent communication experiences.

Content Factors

Hypotheses. Obviously, the content of the threat appeal must be such that it presents cues to which the individual has previously learned to react emotionally. If a state of affairs is depicted (with the intention of conveying a threat) that happens to be meaningless to the audience, in the sense that they have never previously experienced it or heard about it, the anticipations evoked by the rehearsal of the communicator's sentences will fail to arouse emotional tension. The "meaningfulness" of a threat appeal will vary, however, depending upon the degree to which the communication spells out its implications. For example, the mere announcement that there will be an influx of refugees from another country may elicit very little emotional reaction unless it is accompanied by statements to the effect that the newcomers will be competing for scarce supplies and for scarce jobs. By appropriately elaborating his predictions about a potential threat situation, a communicator can call attention to goals and values that are threatened. It would be expected that the less familiar the potential threat the more elaboration is required in order to elicit emotional tension.

Even when a relatively familiar threat situation is called to their attention, many individuals may experience little emotional reaction because they have learned to minimize the threat. There are numerous ways in which familiar threats are likely to be minimized (cf. Janis [*15*] pp. 233–242). For example, a potential threat that is depicted in the communication may be spontaneously perceived by the audience as improbable ("most likely it won't ever really happen") or as temporarily remote ("it might happen but there's no need to bother about it now"). The threat may also be discounted as unimportant ("even if it happens, it won't be so bad") or as inapplicable to oneself ("others may suffer but I won't be affected"). In order to raise the level of emotional tension, a threat appeal may require supplementary elaborations that will counteract the various types of minimization which are likely to occur spontaneously among the audience.

Clinical observations suggest that many people tend to ignore meaningful threats until there are clear signs of imminent danger [*9, 10, 15, 25*]. Most often this seems to be due to spontaneous anticipations of being personally exempt from the potential danger. Expectations of personal exemption are sometimes based on empirically sound considerations but frequently they are unrealistic rationalizations. Even under threatening wartime conditions, soldiers who knew they were about to face the dangers of combat and civilians who realized that their city was apt to be heavily bombed managed to maintain a strong sense of "personal invulnerability" (cf. Grinker and Spiegel [*10*], pp. 130 ff.; and Janis [*15*], pp. 171 ff.). Probably there are similar tendencies on the part of most people when exposed to communications which evoke anticipations of familiar threats to personal values. If so, it would be expected that the level of emotion aroused by a threat appeal will depend upon the degree to which the content breaks down the audience's expectations of being personally exempt from the threat that is depicted.

Experimental evidence. Illustrative evidence concerning content factors which influence the level of emotional tension was obtained from a study by Janis and Feshbach [*18*] on the effects of fear-arousing communications. The evidence concerning opinion changes will be discussed later in this chapter; for the present, we shall consider only some of the incidental findings which bear on immediate emotional reactions.

The experiment was designed to investigate the effects of three different intensities of "fear appeal" in a standard communication on dental hygiene. A 15-minute illustrated lecture was prepared in three different forms, all of which contained the same essential information about causes of tooth decay and the same series of recommendations concerning oral hygiene. The three forms of the illustrated talk differed only with respect to the amount of threat material presented. Form 1 contained a "strong" appeal, emphasizing the painful consequences of tooth decay, diseased gums, and other dangers that can result from improper dental hygiene. Form 2 presented a "moderate" appeal in which the dangers were described in a milder and more factual manner. Form 3 presented a "minimal" appeal which rarely alluded to the consequences of tooth neglect. In Form 3 most of the threat material was replaced by relatively neutral information not relevant to any of the specific recommendations made. In all other respects, however, Form 3 was identical with Forms 1 and 2.

The major differences in content among the three forms of the communication are summarized in Table 6, which is based on a systematic content analysis of the three recorded lectures. The data in this table show how often each type of threat was mentioned. The main difference between the strong appeal and the moderate appeal was not so much in the total frequency of threat references as in the severity of the threatening consequences which were elaborated. The minimal appeal, however, differed markedly from the other two in that it contained relatively few threat references, almost all of which were restricted to terms like "cavities" or "tooth decay."

TABLE 6. *Content Analysis of the Three Forms of a Dental Hygiene Communication: References to Consequences of Improper Care of the Teeth*

Type of Reference	Form 1 (Strong Appeal)	Form 2 (Moderate Appeal)	Form 3 (Minimal Appeal)
1. Pain from toothaches	11	1	0
2. Cancer, paralysis, blindness, or other secondary diseases	6	0	0
3. Having teeth *pulled,* cavities *drilled,* or other painful dental work	9	1	0
4. Having cavities *filled* or having to *go to the dentist*	0	5	1
5. Mouth infections: sore, swollen, inflamed gums	18	16	2
6. Ugly or discolored teeth	4	2	0
7. "Decayed" teeth	14	12	6
8. "Cavities"	9	12	9
Total references to unfavorable consequences	71	49	18

From Janis and Feshbach [18]

The fear appeals were designed to stimulate emotional reactions in order to motivate the audience to conform to a set of recommendations. The main technique was that of emphasizing the potential dangers that can ensue from nonconformity. For example, the strong appeal contained such statements as the following: "If you ever develop an infection of this kind from improper care of your teeth, it will be an extremely serious matter because these infections are *really dangerous*. They can spread to your eyes, or your heart, or your joints and cause secondary infections which may lead to diseases such as arthritis, paralysis, kidney damage, or total blindness." In playing up the threat of pain, disease, and body damage, the material introduced into the strong appeal was probably representative of the more extreme forms of fear appeals currently to be found in persuasive communications presented via the press, radio, television, and other mass media.

One of the unique characteristics of the strong appeal was the use of *personalized* threat references explicitly directed to the audience, i.e., statements to the effect that "this can happen to you." The moderate appeal, on the other hand, described the dangerous consequences of improper oral hygiene in impersonal language. In the minimal appeal, the limited discussion of unfavorable consequences also used an impersonal style.

The elaborations of the threats in the fear appeals did not rely exclusively upon verbal material to convey the threatening consequences of nonconformity. In the strong appeal the slides used to illustrate the lecture included a series of highly realistic photographs which vividly portrayed tooth decay and mouth infections. The moderate appeal included photographs with milder examples of oral pathology. And the minimal appeal substituted X-ray pictures, diagrams of cavities, and photographs of completely healthy teeth for the photographs of oral pathology.

The entire freshman class of a large Connecticut high school was divided on a random basis into four equivalent groups. Each of the three forms of the communication was given to a separate experimental group as part of their standard instruction on hygiene. The fourth group was used as a control group and was exposed to a similar communication on a completely different topic (the structure and functioning of the human eye).

Evidence is presented in Table 7 that the three forms of the illustrated talk differed with respect to the amount of emotional tension

TABLE 7. *Per Cent of Subjects Reporting Feelings of Worry or Concern Evoked during the Dental Hygiene Communication*

	Experimental Groups		
Questionnaire Responses	Exposed to Strong Appeal (N = 50)	Exposed to Moderate Appeal (N = 50)	Exposed to Minimal Appeal (N = 50)
1. Felt worried—a "few times" or "many times"—about own mouth condition	74	60	48
2. Felt "somewhat" or "very" worried about improper care of own teeth	66	36	34
3. Thought about condition of own teeth "most of the time"	42	34	22

From Janis and Feshbach [18]

evoked during the communication. Immediately after exposure to the communication, the students were asked three questions about the feelings they had just experienced "while the illustrated talk was being given." Their responses indicated that the fear stimuli were successful in arousing affective reactions. The differences between the strong group and the minimal group were statistically significant ($p <$ .05, based on a one-tailed test). The moderate group consistently fell in an intermediate position but did not, in most instances, differ significantly from the other two groups.

Further evidence of the affective reactions induced by the threat appeals was obtained from responses to the following two questions, each of which was followed by a check list of five answer categories ranging from "very worried" to "not at all worried:"

1. "When you think about the possibility that you might develop *diseased gums*, how concerned or worried do you feel about it?"
2. "When you think about the possibility that you might develop *decayed teeth*, how concerned or worried do you feel about it?"

Since these questions made no reference to the illustrated talk, it was feasible to include them in the pre- and postcommunication questionnaires given to all four groups.

TABLE 8. *Effect of Threat Appeals: Percentage Who Reported Feeling Worried about Decayed Teeth and Diseased Gums*

Group:	Strong (N = 50)	Moderate (N = 50)	Minimal (N = 50)	Control (N = 50)
One week before the communication	34%	24%	22%	30%
Immediately after the communication	76%	50%	46%	38%
Change	+42%	+26%	+24%	+8%

Reliability of Differences	Critical Ratio	Probability-Value
Strong vs. control	3.06	.01
Strong vs. minimal	1.59	.06
Strong vs. moderate	1.37	.09
Moderate vs. control	1.54	.06
Moderate vs. minimal	0.17	.43
Minimal vs. control	1.43	.08

From Janis and Feshbach [18]

The results, presented in Table 8, show the percentage in each group who reported feeling "somewhat" or "very" worried. These findings indicate that there was a marked increase in signs of disturbance among each of the three experimental groups, as compared with the control group. Paralleling the results in Table 7, the greatest increase was found in the strong group.

In general, the foregoing evidence consistently indicates that after exposure to the communications the group exposed to the strong appeal felt more worried about the condition of their teeth than did the other two groups; the moderate group, in turn, tended to feel more worried than the minimal group. The results, therefore, provide illustrative evidence in support of the assumption that content factors which augment the meaningfulness of the threat—by elaborating on its consequences and by emphasizing its applicability to the audience—tend to increase the level of emotional arousal. Whether the same factors apply to other "emotional" appeals designed to arouse guilt, aggression, disgust, and so on remains a problem for further investigation.

It seems probable that intense emotional reactions are especially likely to be elicited by symbol stimuli which evoke anticipatory responses (perceptual images and symbolic responses) that closely resemble those evoked by real life situations of actual threat. The available findings provide an initial basis for the general hypothesis that the more vividly a communication describes the unpleasant aspects of a potential threat and emphasizes its seriousness, the higher the level of emotional tension evoked.

It seems unlikely that the hypothesis just stated will prove to be true under all conditions. It has often been observed that when people are already in a state of high emotional tension—e.g., because of inescapable signs of imminent danger—elaborations of the concrete details of the threat will serve to reduce rather than to augment anxiety. As Kris [23] points out, a vague, unknown threat can sometimes result in more anxiety than a concrete, known one. Vague threats sometimes stimulate people to project their own exaggerated fantasies onto the environment, using their imagination to fill in with horrible details. Moreover, when the threat is specific and well defined, people are often able to control their anxieties by taking protective action which reduces the sense of helplessness. Hence one of the important problems requiring further investigation is to determine under what conditions vague allusions to a threat make for less emotional tension than detailed elaborations of the threat, and under what conditions the reverse is true. Some of the important conditions that appear to reduce the emotional impact of well-elaborated threats will be discussed in the sections that follow.

Source Factors

Whenever a communication contains predictions about potential threats, the emotional impact will depend to a considerable extent upon appraisals of the communicator. For instance, if the communicator is regarded as completely uninformed, his predictions may be immediately discounted and therefore fail to arouse the sort of anticipations which cue off emotional reactions (cf. pp. 21 ff.). Similarly, if the communicator is perceived as having an obvious intent to manipulate the emotions of the audience, disbelief would be the expected reaction. Moreover, a person's responsiveness to a threat appeal is probably a function not only of his initial (precommunication) appraisals of the communicator but also of the cues which the communicator gives during his communication. Members of the audience may react to an extremely exaggerated presentation of a threat by concluding that the communicator is deliberately attempting to "scare" them and hence be inclined to disregard what he says.

An exploratory study by Janis [*17*] provides some indications of the type of inferences concerning the communicator that an audience is likely to draw from the presentation of a threat appeal. Two printed selections which described the dangers of excessive cigarette smoking were used. Both contained exactly the same recommendations and the same information concerning the threats of reduced life span, of developing cancer of the lungs, of damaging one's circulatory system, of suffering from Buerger's disease, etc. In one version, however, the unpleasant aspects of these threats were described in detail whereas in the other the threats were less elaborated. Forty subjects of varying educational levels were interviewed after they had read one or the other of the selections. (Both were presented as excerpts from a popu-

lar magazine article written by a physician.) It was noted that spontaneous comments concerning manipulative intent and doubts about
the author's sincerity were more frequently elicited by the elaborated
version than by the less elaborated one. Some typical comments were
the following:

> "I was mostly amused by this propaganda effort. I felt this guy is
> an alarmist and I wondered what his real purpose is. Why is he so
> aroused about it?"

> "I think it was written to scare people—to scare them out of the
> habit of smoking—because it is so extreme . . . I think he is
> probably a smoker himself."

> "It is overdone. I realized that it might be unpleasant to other
> people but my reaction was humor. . . . I think he is a crusader,
> someone who ballyhoos an idea and he may not really believe in
> it himself; he may not have humanitarian motives."

This exploratory study suggests that a high degree of descriptive
elaboration of relatively *familiar* threats is likely to be a cue to manipulative intent and may therefore reduce the effectiveness of the communication. Especially among people who are relatively sophisticated
about propaganda techniques, as was the case with many of the subjects who made comments like those just quoted, this type of reaction
is likely to interfere with acceptance. With such audiences, the chances
that the threat statements will be disregarded can probably be reduced
by making the threat appeal as objective and as impersonal as possible.
It should be mentioned, however, that a number of the more sophisticated subjects who expressed "discounting" ideas after reading about
the dangers of smoking nevertheless indicated elsewhere in the interview that they felt extremely disturbed by what they had read. This
additional observation suggests that a strong fear appeal may sometimes succeed in arousing emotional tension but nevertheless interfere with acceptance of the message by stimulating defensive aggression toward the communicator. (See pp. 86–88 for further discussion
of this type of reaction in the light of the evidence from the experiment on threat appeals.)

Antecedent Communication Factors

Another type of factor that may influence emotional arousal is suggested by one of the incidental findings obtained by Janis, Lumsdaine, and Gladstone [20] when the opportunity unexpectedly arose to investigate the effects of a prior communication on reactions to an anxiety-arousing event (cf. pp. 261–264 for a detailed description of this experiment). Some of their evidence suggests that the level of emotional tension evoked by President Truman's announcement of Russia's first atomic explosion may have been diminished by prior exposure to communications which happened to have discussed and predicted this very event three months earlier. One of the experimental groups had received two preliminary communications, one of which presented a "pessimistic" point of view, i.e., it argued in favor of the position that Russia already had developed the A-bomb and gave details about the location of Russia's A-bomb factories. Three months later, immediately after the official announcement was made, it was found that this group expressed less worry about the A-bomb threat than the other groups, which had not received the "pessimistic" communication. For example, feelings of "worry" about the possibility that their own city might be destroyed by an A-bomb were reported by only 40 per cent in the group which had received the "pessimistic" communication as compared with 58 per cent of the control group, which had received no preliminary communications ($p < .05$, one-tail test).

This result suggests that some degree of "emotional innoculation" may have been produced by the earlier communication exposure. Although this isolated finding could be interpreted in a number of different ways, it is worth noting that it is consistent with the following hypothesis: The emotional reaction evoked by communications which announce a threatening or pessimistic event will tend to be reduced by prior exposure to preparatory communications which discuss and predict the event in advance. The hypothesis seems plausible on the assumption that the element of surprise is a major factor which determines the degree of emotional arousal evoked by bad news; i.e., less fear is aroused by *gradual* than by *sudden* awareness of a potential threat. This assumption has been discussed by Janis [*15*] in an analysis of emotional reactions to wartime threats. Taking account of the emotional adaptation that was widely observed among British, German, and Japanese civilians who were exposed to repeated threats of air raid dangers, he concluded that extreme reactions of anticipatory anxiety are most likely to occur when sharp awareness of a potential threat is elicited unexpectedly, without opportunity for prior psychological preparation.

In order to avoid extreme reactions of anticipatory anxiety, it is probably essential to bring about a stepwise increase in awareness of the reality and proximity of the . . . threat, before the danger appears to be actually at hand. In each person's private image of his own future, the threat must come gradually into focus at a time when the menace is not perceived as being overwhelmingly great.

A stepwise increase in awareness of impending danger, with a corresponding increase in feelings of insecurity, has two advantages from the standpoint of personal adjustment. First, it stimulates each individual to rehearse the future danger situation in his own imagination and this, in turn, often leads to the spontaneous development of a variety of personal techniques for handling one's own anxiety. This process of internal preparation probably leaves the person in a less vulnerable psychological position when he is confronted with subsequent anxiety-arousing events. Secondly, a slight dose of insecurity often serves as a powerful motivation for participating in group activities which are designed to ward off the danger; such participation with others can become an important source of reassurance, and, with subsequent increases in insecurity, the person is likely to turn more and more of his energies into this form of activity. ([*15*] p. 250.)

The above discussion highlights the potential importance of sequence factors as a determinant of the emotional impact of a threat appeal. In other words, the power of a threat appeal to evoke intense emotional reactions depends partly upon whether the audience has been exposed to prior communications dealing with the same threat and whether these communications provided the necessary conditions for emotional adaptation. As was implied by our earlier discussion of the meaningfulness of the threat, there is also some reason to expect that prior communications can sometimes augment the impact of an emotional appeal. For instance, when the threat is one which could not be comprehended without prior information about its consequences, an antecedent communication could sensitize an audience to its implications.

EMOTIONAL TENSION AND ACCEPTANCE

Hypotheses on Sources of Interference

Even when a threat appeal succeeds in arousing emotional tension, it may fail to produce the intended opinion changes because the communicator's reassurances fail to be reinforced. Moreover, if the reassuring recommendations are not presented at the time when emotional tension is strongly aroused, little gain could be expected from the use of a threat appeal. An obvious implication of our theoretical assumptions is that the arousal of emotional tension should immediately *precede* the presentation of the reassurances. When the need for reassurance is maximal, not only would the motivation to rehearse the reassuring recommendation be greater but the amount of reinforcement from tension reduction would also be increased. The chances of adequate rehearsal at the right time are probably augmented by repeated presentations of the threat, always followed by the reassuring recommendations.

We turn now to another major set of factors that can influence the effectiveness of an emotional appeal. Under certain conditions, the communicator's reassuring recommendations may fail to reduce emotional tension because they do not evoke anticipations of averting the threat. For instance, this would be likely to occur if the communicator's reassurances were regarded as *a*) irrelevant to the threat, *b*) impossible to carry out, or *c*) a partially successful means of averting the threat but with many "loopholes."

In line with the general theory of emotional tension as a drive, it would be predicted that if emotional tension persists at a high level after the communicator's reassurances have been rehearsed, spontaneous responses will be tried out until one is hit upon that succeeds in reducing emotional tension. Consequently, beliefs and opinions other than the ones advocated in the communication may be reinforced and the communicator may fail to produce the desired effect. A strong threat appeal which is intended to motivate the audience to take account of a realistic possibility of danger could have the unintended effect of motivating the audience to adopt "magical," "wishful," or other types of reassuring beliefs that are antithetical to the communicator's purposes. Thus, the perception of inadequacies or "loopholes" in the communicator's recommendations may prevent the reduction of emotional tension and thereby greatly diminish the effectiveness of a fear-arousing communication.

There is another, closely related class of phenomena which should be taken into account in connection with potential failures of reinforcement. When emotional tension is strongly aroused, habitual defensive reactions are likely to become prepotent responses. Thus, the tendency to rehearse the communicator's reassurances about ways and means of counteracting the threat may not be the dominant reaction to a powerful emotional appeal. For instance, when a communication produces a high degree of emotional tension, the audience may distort the meaning of what is being said or engage in overt escape activities which interfere with acceptance of the communicator's recommendations. Unintended effects of this kind can be regarded as spontaneous defensive reactions which are motivated by unreduced emotional tension.

Various sources of interference that may operate when emotional tension is highly aroused are suggested by clinical observations of patients' reactions to psychotherapeutic treatment [*1, 4, 5*]. Such observations suggest three main types of defensive behavior that can prevent a person from being influenced by verbal communications which evoke strong anxiety reactions:

1. When a communication touches off intense feelings of anxiety, communicatees will sometimes *fail to pay attention to what is being said.* Inattentiveness may be a motivated effort to avoid thoughts which evoke anxiety. This avoidance tendency may be manifested through overt attempts to change the subject of conversation to a less disturbing topic. When such attempts fail and anxiety mounts to a very high

level, attention disturbances may become much more severe: e.g., inability to concentrate, distractibility, or other symptoms of the cognitive disorganization temporarily produced by high emotional tension.

2. When exposed to an anxiety-arousing communication, communicatees will occasionally react to the unpleasant ("punishing") experience by becoming *aggressive toward the communicator.* If the communicator is perceived as being responsible for producing painful feelings, aggression is likely to take the form of *rejecting* his statements.

3. If a communication succeeds in arousing intense anxiety which is not sufficiently reduced either by the reassurances contained in the communication or by self-delivered reassurances, the emotional tension which remains after the communication is over may motivate *the development of a new habit of defensive avoidance,* i.e., the individual may learn to ward off *subsequent* exposures to the anxiety-arousing content. The experience of being temporarily unable to terminate the disturbing affective state elicited by a discussion of a potential threat can give rise to a powerful incentive to avoid thinking or hearing about it again; this may ultimately result in failing to recall what the communicator said, losing interest in the topic, denying or minimizing the importance of the threat.[5]

Experimental Evidence on Acceptance of Fear-arousing Communications

The experiment by Janis and Feshbach [*18*], the results of which were partly described earlier, was designed primarily with the above theoretical considerations in mind. One of its main purposes was to explore the potentially adverse effects of strong fear arousal.

Five questions concerning dental hygiene practices were presented to all subjects one week before the communication and again one week after. The questions, which asked the students to describe the way they were currently brushing their teeth, covered practices about which all three forms of the illustrated talk contained specific recommendations.

TABLE 9. *Effect of the Illustrated Talk on Conformity to Dental Hygiene Recommendations*

Type of Change Group:	Strong (N = 50)	Moderate (N = 50)	Minimal (N = 50)	Control (N = 50)
Increased conformity	28%	44%	50%	22%
Decreased conformity	20	22	14	22
No change	52	34	36	56
Total	100	100	100	100
Net change in conformity	+8%	+22%	+36%	0%

Reliability of Differences	Critical Ratio	Probability Value
Control vs. minimal	2.54	<.01
Control vs. moderate	1.50	.07
Control vs. strong	0.59	.28
Strong vs. moderate	0.95	.17
Strong vs. minimal	1.96	.03
Moderate vs. minimal	0.93	.18

From Janis and Feshbach [18]

The results, shown in Table 9, reveal that the greatest amount of conformity was produced by the communication which contained the *minimal* amount of fear-arousing material. The strong group showed reliably less change than the minimal; in fact, the strong group failed to differ significantly from the controls, whereas the minimal group showed a highly reliable increase in conformity as compared with the controls. The data in Table 9 show a fairly consistent trend which suggests that as the amount of fear-arousing material is increased (above some minimal level) conformity to the communicator's recommendations tends to decrease. Similar findings are also reported with respect to conformity to another of the communicator's recommendations, namely, that one should go to a dentist for a dental hygiene checkup.

The authors point out that the findings may not necessarily represent changes in overt *behavioral* conformity, since the observations are based on the subjects' own verbal reports which might reflect only lip service to the recommendations. They conclude that the results nevertheless demonstrate that the strong appeal was markedly less effective than the minimal appeal at least in eliciting verbal conformity.

In addition to describing the four essential characteristics of the "proper" toothbrush, the illustrated talk contained numerous comments and illustrations to explain the need for avoiding the "wrong" kind of toothbrush. The importance of using the proper kind of toothbrush was the theme that was most heavily emphasized throughout the entire communication. As would be expected, this proved to be one of the main opinions on which significant changes were produced by the dental hygiene communication, as measured by the shifts from one week before to one week after the communication exposure. Just before their postcommunication attitudes were tested, all of the groups were exposed to a brief counterpropaganda statement which contradicted the main theme of the original communication. The new communication was found to have a greater effect on the control group than on the three experimental groups. But the minimal appeal proved to be the most effective form of the communication with respect to producing *resistance* to the counterpropaganda. The results are shown in Table 10.

TABLE 10. *Effect of the Illustrated Talk on Reactions to Subsequent Counterpropaganda: Net Percentage of Each Group Who Changed in the Direction of Agreeing with the Statement That "It Does Not Matter What Kind of Toothbrush a Person Uses"*

Type of Change Group:	Strong (N = 50)	Moderate (N = 50)	Minimal (N = 50)	Control (N = 50)
More agreement	30%	28%	14%	44%
Less agreement	38	42	54	24
No change	32	30	32	32
Total	100	100	100	100
Net change	−8%	−14%	−40%	+20%
Net effect [experimental minus control]	−28%	−34%	−60%	

Reliability of the Differences in Net Change	Critical Ratio	Probability Value
Control vs. minimal	3.66	<.001
Control vs. moderate	2.05	.02
Control vs. strong	1.71	.05
Strong vs. moderate	0.36	.36
Strong vs. minimal	2.03	.02
Moderate vs. minimal	1.66	.05

From Janis and Feshbach [18]

The authors point out that after a communication has successfully induced attitude changes the audience's ability to resist the influence of subsequent exposures to counteracting propaganda is, in effect, an indicator of the strength or stability of the attitude built up by the original communication. The experimental results in Table 10 suggest that under conditions where people will be exposed to competing communications dealing with the same issues, the use of a strong threat appeal will tend to be less effective than a minimal appeal in producing stable and persistent attitude changes.

The results just described indicate that the minimal appeal was the most effective form of the communication in that it elicited *a*) more resistance to subsequent counterpropaganda and *b*) a higher incidence of reported adherence to a set of recommended practices. No significant differences were found on other indicators of preferences and beliefs. Thus, the moderate and strong appeals were found to have no unique positive effects that would compensate for the observed detrimental effects. The findings consistently indicate that inclusion of the additional fear-arousing material not only failed to increase the effectiveness of the communication but actually decreased its over-all success.

The outcome of this experiment does not preclude the possibility that under certain conditions very strong threat appeals may prove to be highly successful. For instance, in situations where the communicator has the power to administer severe punishment and the audience has already learned not to ignore his threats, strong fear appeals are likely to induce a high degree of conformity. That the threat of extreme punishment under such circumstances can motivate acceptance of opinions and attitudes is suggested by numerous observations, such as those reported by Bettelheim [2] in his account of the behavior of political prisoners in German concentration camps. Although strongly opposed to Nazism, many political prisoners apparently began to accept some of the attitudes and values of their Gestapo guards and manifested various signs of "identification with the aggressor," presumably as a consequence of repeated threats of severe deprivation and torture.

Another factor to be taken into account is the type of audience response which the persuasive communication is designed to produce.

Some of the experimental findings indicate that a strong threat appeal may be maximally effective in arousing interest and in eliciting a high degree of emotional tension (cf. Tables 7 and 8 and pp. 68–73). When the communicator's goal is to instigate prompt audience action (e.g., to recruit volunteers to perform a group task) such reactions might contribute to the effectiveness of the communication.

The main findings of the fear appeal experiment indicate, however, that when the goal of a persuasive communication is to create sustained preferences or attitudes, a relatively low degree of fear arousal will sometimes be the optimal level—that too strong a fear appeal can evoke some form of interference which reduces the effectiveness of the communication. The results definitely contradict the assumption that as the dosage of fear-arousing stimuli in a mass communication is increased the audience will necessarily become more highly motivated to accept the reassuring recommendations contained in the communication. For communications of the sort used in the experiment, the *optimal dosage* appears to be far below the level of the strongest fear appeals that a communicator could use if he chose to do so.

Further confirmatory evidence was obtained from two supplementary studies made in connection with the same experiment.

1. A follow-up questionnaire was administered to the same subjects one year after they had been exposed to the dental hygiene communication. The superiority of the minimal appeal over the strong appeal was still apparent: conformity to the recommended practices was shown by a somewhat higher percentage of students in the minimal appeal group than in the strong appeal group (Janis [16]).

2. From a separate analysis of the opinion changes of subjects who manifested predispositional differences in level of anxiety, it was found that the unfavorable effects of the strong appeal occurred predominantly among persons who were chronically most anxious—as manifested by overt excitability and psychoneurotic complaints [19].[6]

In general, the available evidence indicates that as the degree of emotional tension in the audience is increased there is *not* a corresponding increase in acceptance of the communicator's reassuring recommendations. It seems likely that for many types of persuasive communications the relationship will prove to be a curvilinear one, such that as emotional tension increases from zero to some moderate level acceptance tends to increase, but as emotional tension mounts to higher levels acceptance tends to decrease. Descending acceptance in the latter part of the curve is clearly indicated by the experimental data in Tables 9 and 10; ascending acceptance in the lower end of the curve might account for some of the findings on the superiority of "emotional" appeals cited at the beginning of this chapter [*13, 26*].

Mediating Processes

We turn now to a central question posed by the experimental findings: What are the major sources of interference that can reduce acceptance of the communicator's recommendations when a strong threat appeal is used? Earlier we have described three main types of spontaneous defensive reactions, observed in psychotherapy, that might give rise to failures of reinforcement when a persuasive communication evokes a high degree of emotional tension. We shall briefly assess the importance of each of the three types of interfering reactions with respect to the effectiveness of threat appeals in persuasive communications.

Inattentiveness to the communication. Observations of reactions to intense anxiety stimuli suggest that when emotional tension is strongly aroused distractibility tendencies are increased and cognitive functions tend to be temporarily impaired [*12*]. If this were to occur when a strong threat appeal is presented in a persuasive communication, there would be less attention and less learning of the content, which would result in lowered effectiveness.

In the experiment on the effects of threat appeals in a dental hygiene communication [*18*], the possibility that this type of interference might have contributed to the reduced effectiveness of the strong appeal was investigated. The three forms of the communication were found to be equally effective in teaching the factual material on dental hygiene, as measured by a comprehensive information test given immediately after exposure to the communication. Thus, the evidence concerning the amount of information acquired from the communication did not indicate that the strong appeal produced inattentiveness or any form of distraction that would interfere with learning efficiency during the communication session.[7] The absence of any observable

reduction of learning efficiency is consistent with clinical observations which imply that normal personalities can ordinarily tolerate
unpleasant information concerning potential threats to the self without manifesting any marked impairment of "ego" functions ([*15*] pp.
101–116). The findings suggest that the use of fear-arousing material
of the sort presented in the illustrated talks would rarely give rise to
any interference with the audience's ability to learn the content of the
communication.

An investigation of immediate recall by Janis and Milholland [*21*]
also provides evidence pertinent to attention and learning factors that
may be influenced by threat appeals. This experiment compared the
verbatim recall of two equated groups of subjects, one of which read
a short communication containing a strong threat appeal while the
other read an equivalent communication containing a minimal appeal. The selections were based on the material used in the illustrated
talk in the earlier experiment [*18*] and were presented as excerpts from
an article in an authoritative dental journal. The threats that were
described pertained mainly to tooth decay.

Immediately after reading the excerpt, each subject was asked to
write out as much as he could recall of the communication. The verbatim recall responses were analyzed according to a coding scheme
which represented each item of information contained in the passage.
No difference was found in the mean number of items of information
acquired by the two groups, as measured by the verbatim recall test.
This finding shows the same outcome as the information test results
of the earlier experiment. But there were some additional findings in
the later experiment which indicate that the strong fear appeal had
a selective effect upon *what* was learned.

The investigators broke down their results according to two main
categories of information items common to both forms of the communication: *a*) *causes* of the threat (e.g., food adheres to the teeth,
acids are formed, and the enamel coat dissolves) and *b*) *unfavorable
consequences* of the threat (e.g., necessity to go to the dentist for treatment, painful mouth conditions, inflamed gums). The first type of
information was better recalled by the minimal appeal group, whereas
the second was better recalled by the strong appeal group. These findings suggest that under conditions where relatively minor threats are

depicted, elaborations of the potential dangers have the effect of focusing attention on the threatening consequences, making them more vivid and therefore better learned; but the heightened learning of the consequences detracts from attention to and learning of other material contained in the communication—in this case, material on the causes of the threat. In this experiment, however, both groups recalled equally well the main recommendations made by the communication. Nevertheless, the selective recall tendency noted in this experiment suggests that threat appeals can exert an important effect on what is learned and retained from a communication. Under certain circumstances (notably where subsequent preferential actions are contingent upon understanding the causes of a threat) this tendency could conceivably reduce the ultimate effectiveness of a communication. This lead warrants further investigation.

Aggression toward the communicator. In our earlier discussion of cues to manipulative intent, we have considered the possibility that attitudes of distrust toward the communicator can interfere with the effectiveness of emotional appeals. It was mentioned that in an exploratory study [*17*] of reactions to a communication on the dangers of cigarette smoking some of the subjects felt extremely disturbed by the threat appeal even though they inferred that the communicator was deliberately trying to "scare" his audience. Cues to manipulative intent may result in failure to rehearse the communicator's recommendations (e.g., because competing thoughts about the communicator are being rehearsed instead) or in deliberate rejection of the recommended conclusion motivated by aggression directed toward the communicator. Hence the various factors mentioned above in the discussion of the effect of cues to manipulative intent on the arousal of emotional tension might also apply to the learning and acceptance of the communicator's recommendations.

Even when manipulative intent is not attributed to the communicator, he may nevertheless be regarded as a frustrator, i.e., as the cause of distressing, painful feelings. This, too, could arouse aggression in the recipients and incline them to reject the communicator's conclusions.

Some evidence pertinent to attitudes toward the communicator's presentation was obtained in the experiment on the effects of strong, moderate, and minimal appeals in a dental hygiene communication [*18*]. It was found that the strong appeal evoked a more mixed or ambivalent attitude toward the communication than did the moderate or minimal appeal. On the one hand, the students exposed to the strong appeal were more likely than the others to give favorable appraisals of the interest-value and quality of the communicator's presentation. On the other hand, they expressed the greatest amount of subjective dislike of the communication and made more complaints about the content.

Some of the comments, particularly about the slides, highlight the differentiation between the students' favorable appraisals of the quality of the strong appeal communication and their unfavorable personal reactions to it:

"I did not care for the 'gory' illustrations of decayed teeth and diseased mouths but I really think that it did make me feel sure' that I did not want this to happen to me."

"Some of the pictures went to the extremes but they probably had an effect on most of the people who wouldn't want their teeth to look like that."

"I think it is good because it scares people when they see the awful things that can happen."

Such comments suggest that the ambivalence may have been resolved by adopting the attitude: "This is disagreeable medicine but it's good for us."

In general, the evidence does not suggest that the use of the strong appeal evoked marked hostility of the sort that would motivate rejection of the conclusions.[8] The low level of aggression, however, may have been due to the absence of cues which would arouse the audience's suspicions of the communicator's intentions. A fear-arousing communication presented by a communicator who is initially regarded with suspicion—or by one who makes statements containing obvious signs of manipulative intent—might evoke a considerable amount of hostility in the audience, with a correspondingly strong motivation to resist his influence. This possibility highlights the need for further investigations on the conditions under which interfering aggressive reactions are elicited by the use of strong threat appeals.

Defensive avoidance. From the findings of the threat appeal experiment, it can be inferred that the audience exposed to the strong appeal was left in a state of emotional tension that was not relieved by rehearsing the reassuring recommendations contained in the communication. The data are consistent with the "defensive avoidance" hypothesis: When fear is strongly aroused but is not adequately relieved by the reassurances contained in a persuasive communication, the audience will become motivated to ignore or to minimize the importance of the threat. This hypothesis can be regarded as a special case of the following general proposition which pertains to the effects of exposure to any fear-producing stimulus: Other things being equal, the more persistent the fear reaction, the greater will be the acquired motivation to avoid subsequent exposures to internal and external cues which were present at the time the fear reaction was aroused.

If the defensive avoidance hypothesis is correct, it would be predicted that the group displaying the greatest degree of residual fear would be most strongly motivated to ward off those internal symbolic cues—such as anticipations of the threatening consequences of improper dental hygiene—which were salient during and immediately after the communication. The main findings, particularly those showing that the greatest degree of resistance to the subsequent counterpropaganda occurred in the group exposed to the minimal appeal, seem to be consistent with this prediction.[9] The most direct evidence cited in support of the defensive avoidance hypothesis came from the spontaneous write-in answers given by the subjects when they were asked to explain their evaluation of the counterpropaganda. Among those subjects who disagreed with the counterpropaganda, those who had been exposed to the minimal amount of fear-arousing material were found to be the ones who were most likely to refer to the illustrated talk as an authoritative source and to make use of its arguments (cf. Janis and Feshbach [*18*] p. 87). The relative absence of such references in the spontaneous answers given by those who had been exposed to the moderate and strong appeals implies that there was some tendency among these subjects to avoid recalling the content of the fear-arousing communication.

Further investigations are obviously needed in order to specify the conditions under which defensive avoidance reactions interfere with acceptance of a communicator's recommendations. One would expect that defensive avoidance with respect to a given threat would be most likely to occur under the following set of conditions: *a*) when emotional tension is strongly aroused by a communication which deals with the threat; *b*) when the reassurances offered by the communicator and those spontaneously tried out by the communicatee fail to reduce emotional tension to a tolerable level; and *c*) when signs of the threat are ambiguous or can be easily ignored.

OTHER IMPLICATIONS

Earlier in this chapter we have given a schematic account of the way in which threat appeals can lead to increased acceptance of the communicator's conclusions. The successful use of threat material in persuasive communication was described in terms of the acquisition of an habitual chain of responses $(C \rightarrow E \rightarrow R)$ such that when the topic or subject matter is subsequently brought to the person's focus of attention it again elicits the emotional reaction, which in turn is followed by mental rehearsal of the reassuring verbal statements presented by the communicator.

The discussion concerning the implications of the theoretical assumptions has focused mainly on only one major type of communication effect, namely, sustained changes in beliefs or opinions. But the theoretical assumptions also suggest a number of hypotheses about the effectiveness of communications that are designed to achieve other effects. Without going into specific deductions, the applicability of the assumptions to three other communications goals will be briefly indicated. The main purpose of this final discussion is to suggest additional lines of research that might increase our understanding of emotional factors in persuasive communication.

1. Mass communications are sometimes used to instigate immediate audience action, such as donating money or volunteering to devote time and energy to a task. In such instances, the communication may be directed to people who already share the communicator's attitude, and the purpose is primarily to elicit an overt action that is compatible with that attitude. For example, Kate Smith's radio mara-

thon during the War Bond drive made extensive use of "guilt" appeals for the purpose of stimulating resolutions to the effect that "the proper thing for me to do right now is to phone in my pledge to buy a War Bond" [27]. Here the sustained effects with respect to building up an habitual chain of responses would be of comparatively little importance. In eliciting a single action immediately after exposure to the communication, the use of a very strong "emotional" appeal would probably be much more successful than in creating sustained attitudes. Insofar as defensive avoidance reactions are unlikely to develop until after the audience leaves the communication situation, the degree of emotional tension could probably be increased to a much higher level before there would be any diminishing returns with respect to eliciting the recommended action. (The above considerations would not apply, of course, in the case of recommendations that concern actions to be carried out long after the communication has been presented. When the goal of the communication is to induce a delayed action, the same sources of interference would be expected to affect the outcome as when the goal is to create sustained opinion changes.)

2. Public statements of a reassuring character are often made by political and social leaders in periods of crisis to prevent excited, disorganized behavior. For example, in order to counteract a potential outburst of community violence at a time when hatred toward a minority group has been touched off by incidents of rape or murder, local authorities sometimes attempt to give reassurances to the effect that the offending criminals will be severely punished. In such instances the threat appeal comes from a different communication source than the reassurances. But although the threat anticipation has already been evoked (e.g., via newspaper stories) and the level of emotional tension may already be extremely high before the communication is presented, the effectiveness of the communicator's reassurances would be governed by the same principles as in the case where a single communication contains both a threat appeal and the corresponding reassurances. Hence the factors discussed in connection with changing beliefs and opinions would apply equally to situations where reassuring communications are used to prevent excited behavior.

3. Mental hygiene and character training material often has the goal of teaching people to respond in an adjustive way whenever they

feel shame, anger, insecurity, or other disturbing emotions. In this case the communicator may deliberately evoke emotional tension in order to give the audience some guided practice in responding appropriately when strong feelings are aroused. The goal is to create a verbally mediated habit such that the recommended form of behavior will regularly occur instead of impulsive behavior (e.g., teaching a child how to control his anger so he will not "start fights"). Taking account of the need for "transfer" and "generalization," one could expect that the acquisition of habits of emotional control might be facilitated by using emotional appeals which depict many different instances of the threat, so as to increase the chances that the tension-reducing response will generalize to a wide variety of situations.

Another aspect of training in emotional control consists of preparing people to face future danger by performing specific defensive action (e.g., military training to take cover in the event of a bombing attack). For delayed contingent actions of this sort, it is probably essential to give the individual guided practice under conditions where the same cues are present that will occur later on, in the critical situation. In order to accomplish this, the emotional appeals contained in preparatory communications would be used to evoke emotional reactions so that the internal cues will closely resemble those that will be elicited when the real threat is subsequently encountered. This poses an important set of problems for further research on emotional training techniques: What types of emotional appeals can be used to produce the same kind of emotional reactions as those that are likely to occur in actual danger situations? In what ways can communications be used to prevent emotional reactions from gradually dropping out during a series of training trials? Systematic research on problems of this sort could not only have the practical value of increasing the effectiveness of various types of educational devices but also contribute to psychological theory by testing specific implications derived from theoretical assumptions concerning the reinforcing effects of tension reduction.

Notes

1. It is assumed that relationships between alterations in the motivational state of the audience and acceptance of the communicator's conclusions can be directly tested by controlled experiments which investigate the opinion changes produced by incentive stimuli or by drive-producing stimuli. There are, of course, other less dependable methods by which the same dynamic relationships can be indirectly tested. Cf. pp. 199–202 for a discussion of the way in which predispositional differences among different audiences can be taken into account so as to provide data pertinent to the effects of motivating appeals.

2. Attention, comprehension, and acceptance probably determine, to a very large extent, the degree of persistence of the opinion changes induced by a communication. But in addition other factors might be involved as determinants of the recipient's resistance to subsequent pressures which interfere with continued acceptance. For example, an "emotional" appeal may sometimes elicit sustained emotional tension which could have the effect of increasing the recipients' need to communicate their opinion changes to others, and thereby commit themselves more strongly to the new position. Hence the three aspects of communication responsiveness are not intended to be exhaustive but rather to highlight the need for differentiating alternative *modi operandi* that require systematic exploration.

3. So little is known about the motivating effects of arousing *pleasant* emotional reactions that we shall make no attempt to formulate any specific propositions about the conditions under which the use of a "positive" emotional appeal in persuasive communication operates as an incentive for accepting the communicator's conclusions. This omission calls attention to one of the major gaps in current research—not only in the field of persuasive communication and attitude change but also in the more general field of the psychology of human learning. In contrast to their intense interest in investigating the causes and consequences of anxiety and other unpleasant emotions, specialists in the human sciences have devoted extraordinarily little attention to the motivational aspects of pleasant, ego-syntonic emotions. Up to the present time this shortcoming has also characterized our research program.

4. Subsequent evocations of the habit chain $(C \longrightarrow E \longrightarrow R)$ would be expected to result in additional reinforcement, so long as the emotional reaction does not extinguish and the terminal response continues to be followed by tension reduction. When repeatedly evoked, however, the habit chain may gradually become "short-circuited," so that ultimately the content cues (C) are immediately followed by the reassurance response (R). In other words, after many subsequent exposures to the content cues, the intervening link in the chain (E) may tend

to become attenuated and drop out of the sequence. Observations of "emotional adaptation" phenomena [*11, 15*] suggest that habits which are mediated by emotional responses may tend to undergo a subsequent attenuation process of this kind. Experimental evidence on "anticipatory goal reactions" also point up the short-circuiting tendency that occurs when a complex habit chain is repeatedly elicited [*14*]. Further research on the retention of opinion changes produced by fear-arousing communications is needed to determine the conditions under which this type of short-circuiting does and does not lead to extinction of the reassuring response.

5. The three reaction tendencies, while formulated in general terms, take account of three specific types of behavior observed during psychoanalytic and psychotherapeutic sessions. The first two refer to *immediate* reactions that often occur when a therapist gives an interpretation which brings anxiety-laden thoughts or motives into the patient's focus of awareness: 1) attention disturbances, blocking of associations, mishearing, evasiveness, and similar forms of "resistance"; and 2) argumentativeness, defiance, contempt, and other manifestations of reactive hostility directed toward the therapist. The third refers to certain types of *subsequent* "resistance," displayed during the later course of treatment, as a carry-over effect of the therapist's disturbing comments or interpretations.

Although the three types of defensive behavior have been observed primarily in clinical studies of psychoneurotic patients (whose anxiety reactions are generally linked with unconscious conflicts), it seems probable that similar reactions may occur among normal persons during or after exposure to communications which make them acutely aware of severe threats of external danger. Nevertheless, independent evidence is needed to determine whether such sources of emotional interference play any significant role in influencing the net effectiveness of fear-arousing material in mass communications—especially when the communications are presented in an impersonal social setting where emotional responses of the audience are likely to be greatly attenuated.

6. At the end of the school year the emotional status of every student was rated according to the following categories by the four or five teachers with whom he or she had taken courses: "Hyperemotional; excitable; usually well balanced; well balanced; exceptionally stable; apathetic; unresponsive." As an independent source of data a personality inventory, administered at the time of the precommunication opinion test, was used. It contained items concerning neurotic anxiety symptoms.

The teachers' ratings, together with the set of items from the personality inventory provided separate indices of individual level of anxiety. On each of these indices, the experimental and control groups were dichotomized into a relatively high anxiety and a relatively low anxiety subgroup. These predispositional indices were then studied in relation to the effects of the dental hygiene communication. Two main measures of attitude change were used: 1) changes in dental hy-

giene practices in conformity with the communicator's recommendations and
2) resistance to the counterpropaganda on the importance of using the proper
type of toothbrush.

A fairly consistent trend was found with respect to both indices of attitude
change. Among those exposed to the strong fear appeal, the subjects with a relatively high level of anxiety generally showed little or no positive change, whereas
those with a relatively low level of anxiety tended to be more influenced. Among
those exposed to the communication containing little fear-arousing material, differences between the highs and lows were much less. The findings appear to be in
line with the generalization that a high degree of emotional tension tends to reduce
the over-all effectiveness of a persuasive communication. That is to say, if one
assumes that personalities who chronically manifest a high level of anxiety have
a lower threshold of fear arousal than others, the findings bear out the following
prediction: persons who are predisposed to experience the highest level of emotional tension in response to a strong fear appeal tend to be least influenced by
the communicator's recommendations.

7. Beliefs concerning the desirable characteristics of the "proper" type of
toothbrush were also acquired equally well. One might even surmise that the
strong appeal may have had a beneficial effect on attention, because in response
to questions asked immediately after exposure to the communication a significantly
higher percentage of the strong group reported that a) it was very easy to pay
attention to what the speaker was saying and b) they experienced very little
"mind-wandering" (cf. Janis and Feshbach [18], pp. 82–83).

It is necessary to bear in mind, however, that in this experiment the communication was given to a captive classroom audience. When people are at home
listening to the radio (or in any situation where they feel free to choose whether
or not to continue attending to the communication) the use of strong threat appeals might sometimes have the drastic effect of stimulating the audience to "turn
it off." In general, the amount of inattentiveness resulting from the use of a strong
threat appeal might prove to be a major source of ineffectiveness in the case of
communications given under conditions where there are no obvious social norms
or situational constraints which prevent the audience from directing attention
elsewhere. Even with a captive audience, it is quite possible that under certain
extreme conditions a strong threat appeal might interfere with learning efficiency.
For instance, the same sort of temporary cognitive impairment that is sometimes
observed when verbal stimuli happen to touch off unconscious personal conflicts
or emotional "complexes" might also occur when a fear-arousing communication
elicits sharp awareness of unexpected danger—particularly if the audience perceives the threat to be imminent and inescapable.

8. The fact that the strong appeal group expressed the greatest amount of subjective dislike of the communication and made the most complaints about the

content might be interpreted as a sign of *potentially* aggressive attitudes toward the communicator. But if the aggressive reactions of the strong appeal group were intense enough to motivate rejection of the conclusions, one would not expect to find this group giving the most favorable appraisals of the communicator's presentation and of the interest value of his illustrated talk. Consequently, it seems improbable that the reduced attitude effects of the strong appeal could be explained as being due primarily to oppositional tendencies arising from aggression toward the communicator. In drawing this tentative conclusion, Janis and Feshbach [*18*] point out that in their experiment the communication was administered as an official part of the school's hygiene program and contained recommendations that were obviously intended to be beneficial to the audience. Even under these comparatively favorable conditions the strong appeal evoked subjective criticisms which seem to reflect aggressive feelings. Under markedly different conditions, where the auspices and intent of the communication are perceived to be less benign, the audience would probably be less disposed to suppress or control aggressive reactions.

9. The results in Table 10 show that the use of the strong appeal, as against the minimal one, resulted in less rejection of a subsequent communication which discounted and contradicted what was said in the original communication. In effect, the second communication asserted that one could ignore the alleged consequences of using the wrong type of toothbrush, and in that sense it minimized the danger which previously had been heavily emphasized by the fear-arousing communication.

The results obtained from the students' reports on their dental hygiene practices (Table 9) could be interpreted along the same lines. It would be expected that those students who changed their practices, after having heard and seen one of the three forms of the illustrated talk, were motivated to do so because they recalled some of the verbal material which had been given in support of the recommendations, most of which referred to the unfavorable consequences of continuing to do the "wrong" thing. In theoretical terms, one might say that their conformity to the recommendations was mediated by symbolic responses which had been learned during the communication. The mediating responses (anticipations, thoughts, or images) acquired from any one of the three forms of the illustrated talk would frequently have, as their content, some reference to *unpleasant consequences* for the self, and consequently would cue off a resolution or an overt action that would be accompanied by anticipated success in warding off the threat.

Returning now to the hypothesis concerning the effects of experiencing residual emotional tension, the prediction would be that defensive avoidance of the mediating responses would reduce the amount of conformity to whatever protective action is recommended by the fear-arousing communication. If rehearsal of the statements concerning potential danger is accompanied by strong emotional tension during and after the communication, the audience will become motivated to avoid recalling those statements on later occasions when appropriate action could ordinarily be carried out. An avoidance motivation of this kind acquired from the illustrated talk would tend to prevent the students from adopting the recommended changes in their toothbrushing habits because they would fail to think about the unpleasant consequences of improper dental hygiene at times when they subsequently perform the act of brushing their teeth.

References

1. Alexander, F., and French, T. M. *Psychoanalytic therapy*. New York, Ronald Press, 1946.
2. Bettelheim, B. Individual and mass behavior in extreme situations. *J. Abnorm. Soc. Psychol.*, 1943, *38*, 417–452.
3. Brown, J. S., and Farber, I. E. Emotions conceptualized as intervening variables—with suggestions toward a theory of frustration. *Psychol. Bull.*, 1951, *48*, 465–495.
4. Dollard, J., and Miller, N. E. *Personality and psychotherapy*. New York, McGraw-Hill, 1950.
5. Fenichel, O. *Problems of psychoanalytic technique*. Albany (N.Y.) Psychoanal. Quart. Inc. 1941.
6. Feshbach, S. The drive reducing function of fantasy behavior. Unpublished Ph.D. dissertation. Yale Univ., 1951.
7. Freud, S. *The future of an illusion*. London, Hogarth Press, 1928.
8. Freud, S. *Civilization and its discontents*. New York, J. Cape & H. Smith, 1930.
9. Glover, E. Notes on the psychological effects of war conditions on the civilian population: III, The Blitz. *Int. J. Psychoanal.*, 1942, *23*, 17–37.
10. Grinker, R. R., and Spiegel, J. P. *Men under stress*. Philadelphia, Blakiston, 1945.
11. Guthrie, E. R. *The psychology of human conflict*. New York, Harper, 1938.
12. Hanfmann, Eugenia. Psychological approaches to the study of anxiety. In P. H. Hoch and J. Zubin, eds., *Anxiety*. New York, Grune & Stratton, 1950. Pp. 51–69.
13. Hartmann, G. W. A field experiment on the comparative effectiveness of "emotional" and "rational" political leaflets in determining election results. *J. Abnorm. Soc. Psychol.*, 1936, *31*, 99–114.
14. Hull, C. L. *A behavior system*. Yale Univ. Press, 1952.
15. Janis, I. L. *Air war and emotional stress*. New York, McGraw-Hill, 1951.
16. Janis, I. L. A follow up study on sustained effects of fear arousing communications. 1953. (In preparation.)
17. Janis, I. L. Intensive interviews on reactions to fear-arousing propaganda. (Unpublished study.)
18. Janis, I. L., and Feshbach, S. Effects of fear-arousing communications. *J. Abnorm. Soc. Psychol.*, 1953, *48*, 78–92.
19. Janis, I. L., and Feshbach, S. Personality differences associated with responsiveness to fear-arousing communications. 1953. (In preparation.)
20. Janis, I. L., Lumsdaine, A. A., and Gladstone, A. I. Effects of preparatory communications on reactions to a subsequent news event. *Publ. Opin. Quart.*, 1951, *15*, 487–518.
21. Janis, I. L., and Milholland, W. The influence of threat appeals on selective learning of the content of a persuasive communication. *J. Psychol.*, 1954, *37*, 75–80.

22. Knower, F. H. Experimental studies of changes in attitudes: I. A study of the effect of oral argument on changes of attitude. *J. Soc. Psychol.*, 1935, *6*, 315–347.
23. Kris, E. Danger and morale. *Am. J. Orthopsychiat.*, 1944, *14*, 147–155.
24. Lasswell, H. D., Leites, N., and associates. *Language of politics: studies in quantitative semantics.* New York, Geo. W. Stewart, 1949.
25. MacCurdy, J. T. *The structure of morale.* New York, Macmillan, 1943.
26. Menefee, S. C., and Granneberg, Audrey G. Propaganda and opinions on foreign policy. *J. Soc. Psychol.*, 1940, *11*, 393–404.
27. Merton, R. K. *Mass persuasion.* New York, Harper, 1946.
28. Miller, N. E. Learnable drives and rewards. In Stevens, S. S., ed., *Handbook of experimental psychology.* New York, John Wiley, 1951. Pp. 435–472.
29. Mowrer, O. H. *Learning theory and personality dynamics.* New York, Ronald Press, 1950.

CHAPTER 4: *Organization of Persuasive Arguments*

THE effectiveness of persuasive communications depends not only on the choice of motivating appeals but also upon the organization of the arguments used in support of the position advocated. Thus, writers on methods of persuasion discuss the number of repetitions, amount of emphasis, methods of refutation, and similar factors (Brembeck and Howell [4]). Typical problems raised are: Should one start with his strongest arguments or save them until the end? Which types of content are most effective when stated explicitly and which types are best left implicit? Answering questions of this sort at present is much more of an art than a science, but the underlying factors upon which the effects of alternative ways of organizing a message depend are ones which are of considerable concern to the scientist interested in communication.

The theoretical factors underlying the choice of alternative organizations do not constitute a closely integrated system, but require reference to a large number of principles of attention, perception, motivation, and learning. For example, in deciding whether to use one's major arguments at the outset or to save them for the climax, one must often take into account the initial position of the audience. The most relevant considerations here are those derived from the analysis of *motivational factors,* particularly when the communication involves refutation of arguments strongly held by the audience. Similarly, the decision may depend upon the initial interest of the audience in the material presented. But the problem also involves theoretical issues concerned with *learning factors,* such as the degree of compatibility or interference between the arguments involved. Thus the problems of the organization of a communication are theoretically complex and only a small beginning has been made in unraveling the numerous factors involved. Accordingly it is not possible to present in this chapter a systematic treatment of the many questions which can be raised with respect to the organization of persuasive arguments. Instead only sample problems in this area will be considered. The specific ones

99

selected are those which are believed to involve significant theoretical issues and upon which experimental evidence is available from our research program and from the work of other investigators.

The first problem to be discussed is the effectiveness of explicitly stating in the communication the conclusion that is to be drawn from the arguments, as compared with leaving it entirely to the audience to draw the conclusion. A second problem is the relative effectiveness in persuasion of concentrating all the arguments upon the side of the issue the communicator favors, as compared with including the arguments on the "opposite side." The last question concerns the optimal order of arguments. Two subproblems are considered: 1) When all the arguments concern a *single* side of an issue, what is the effectiveness of a climax order (in which the strongest arguments are used at the end) as compared with an anticlimax order (in which the strongest arguments are used at the outset)? 2) When *both* sides of an issue are advocated successively does the side presented first or the side presented second have an advantage?

PROBLEM 1: *What are the effects of a) explicitly drawing the conclusion, and b) leaving the conclusion implicit?*

Greater effectiveness of letting the audience draw its own conclusions might be predicted from the assertion sometimes made that indirect suggestion is more effective than direct (Dunlap [9]), as well as from the frequently cited tenet of the nondirective school of psychotherapy that decisions are more effective when reached independently by the client than when suggested by the therapist (Rogers [22]). On the other hand, the opposite prediction can be made on the grounds that for many members of the audience the conclusion must be explicitly stated to be clearly perceived.

Some incidental observations on this problem were obtained by Cooper and Dinerman [6] in a study of reactions to an antiprejudice film. One of the important messages to be transmitted was "never explicitly stated in the film . . . and it was hoped that the lesson would be inferred by the audience . . ." (p. 249). They report that the implicit message influenced the more intelligent members but not the less intelligent members of the audience. They conclude: "By virtue of their implicit form, such messages may well have been actually inaccessible to this less intelligent group" (p. 263).

RESEARCH EVIDENCE

An experiment by Hovland and Mandell [*14*] was designed to study systematically the relative effectiveness of the explicit and implicit procedures. Experimental comparison was made of two types of communication which were identical in every way except that in one the communicator drew the conclusion at the end while in the other it was left to the audience.

A communication was developed in which the general *principles* of the topic were presented together with a statement of the *conditions* existing, so that conclusion drawing consisted essentially in fitting the particulars and the generalizations together to determine the appropriate implications.

The topic was "Devaluation of Currency." A highly simplified account of general economic principles was given, with a statement of the conditions which make devaluation desirable or undesirable. From these principles and a statement of the conditions prevailing in the United States, the logical conclusion which would follow was the desirability of devaluating American currency.

The communication was tape-recorded and presented as a transcription from a radio program called "Education for Americans." All subjects heard the identical communication, but for half of them the part containing the explicit conclusion drawing was omitted. Other aspects of the study are discussed in an earlier chapter (cf. pp. 33–35).

The communications were presented to groups of college students ostensibly as a pretest by a commercial organization of a new type of current events program on which the opinion of the audience was sought. The "audience reaction" questionnaire contained not only items dealing with the subjects' evaluation of the program but also several key opinion questions concerning monetary devaluation which had been used in an earlier questionnaire and a series of fact quiz items to test the extent to which the "principles" and "conditions" presented in the communication had been learned.

The over-all results on opinion change are given in Table 11. The data are derived from the responses to two key questions concerning the subjects' opinions about the desirability of devaluating the dollar. Comparison of the version in which the speaker drew the conclusion with the one in which he did not, reveals a very large difference in favor of conclusion drawing by the communicator. Over twice as many subjects changed their opinions in the direction advocated by the communicator when the conclusion was explicitly drawn as did when it was left to the audience.

TABLE 11. *Per Cent of Subjects Changing Opinion on "Devaluation" from before to after Communication*

Direction of Change *	Conclusion Not Drawn by Communicator (N = 114)		Conclusion Drawn by Communicator (N = 121)
Positive	30.7		51.2
No change	57.9		45.5
Negative	11.4		3.3
Net per cent changing	19.3		47.9
Mean difference		28.6	
p		.001	

* "Positive" is here defined as changing in direction of position advocated by communicator, "negative" as changing in direction opposite that advocated by communicator. Net per cent changing = per cent changing in positive direction minus per cent changing in negative direction.

From Hovland and Mandell [14]

No significant relationship was obtained between the influence of the conclusion-drawing variable and responses on a personality test designed to measure "resistance to suggestion" and "independence." Nor was any obtained between intelligence test score and the efficacy of conclusion drawing. This may have been due to the fact that a metropolitan university population with ability considerably above average was employed (two-thirds of the subjects were above the national average for college students).

IMPLICATIONS

It is not to be expected that there will be an invariable superiority of conclusion drawing by the communicator. What are the factors upon which the relative effectiveness of the two procedures may depend?

1. Kind of communicator. An hypothesis tested in one portion of the Hovland-Mandell study was that a communicator who arouses suspicion is apt to have less effect when he draws the conclusion. In one version the communicator was described as an importer, who would have something to gain by having his conclusion followed, while in the other an impartial economist was the speaker. Although the two communicators were perceived to differ in their trustworthiness, conclusion drawing was equally effective with both. But with other types of issues this factor may be of greater significance (cf. below, and also Chapter 2, pp. 45 ff.).

2. Kind of audience. The degree of sophistication of members of the audience concerning the issue presented is likely to be an important factor. This may be the result of specific knowledge about the problem, or a function of the general ability level of the audience. Thus, with an audience composed of highly intelligent individuals, there may be less need to have the implications of the premises spelled out and less benefit from conclusion drawing by the communicator. On the other hand, with less intelligent individuals, there is the likelihood that they will be unable to arrive by themselves at the correct conclusion from the premises alone. The observations of Cooper and Dinerman [6] suggest such an effect. While no support for this was found in the Hovland and Mandell research, it is likely that this was because of insufficient difference between "high" and "low" intelligence subjects in the population studied. The issue was sufficiently complex so that it may have been difficult for all members of the audience. It would be extremely interesting to study this problem with a wide range of intellectual ability, like that represented in an Army population.

Personality differences may also play a role, although they did not appear in the present study. It is likely that, if individuals at the extremes are selected, those who are highly suggestible will make up their minds on the basis of conclusions presented by others. At the opposite end there may be persons who are resistant to suggestions of others and like to make up their own minds. What may then be needed will be parametric studies to determine the frequencies of each type of individual in various audiences. But the results of Hovland and Mandell raise some question as to how critical this factor is for normal types of population. Their results seem to indicate that other factors play a much more significant role.

Here is an interesting field which will need extensive research to delineate the basic factors and to determine their interactions.

3. Kind of issue. One important factor might be expected to be the degree to which the issue is of primary concern to the individual. It would be hypothesized that on certain issues it is more convenient to "borrow" the opinions of others. This type of borrowing is likely to occur not only when the individual himself is less informed on the topic than the communicator but also when he has little involvement in the issue. But where strong "ego-involving" issues are concerned his independence may be more vigorously asserted, and he may be more motivated to examine the arguments and implications closely. In many cases these are issues on which the individual has found that others will try to influence his decision for motives of their own. Under the latter conditions drawing the conclusion for oneself may be more effective.

The complexity of the issue is a second factor. If it is easy to see the implications, it is not to be expected that the communicator's drawing the conclusion will make much difference. If, on the other hand, the issue is quite involved and the steps in drawing the conclusion from the premises are difficult, the advantage of having the conclusion drawn explicitly may be quite pronounced. As suggested above, it is likely that the issue used by Hovland and Mandell was above average in complexity, and this may account for the superiority of explicit drawing of the conclusion in their research.

A nondirective approach, in which no conclusion is drawn, may be more effective when the communication deals with highly personal matters of the sort involved in psychotherapy, where direct suggestions are especially likely to meet with strong resistance. But for relatively impersonal issues, there may be little or no gain from indirect suggestion. We have seen that in the Hovland-Mandell study, which dealt with an impersonal topic and presented arguments requiring several steps and assumptions in order to reach the conclusion, the superiority of conclusion drawing was clearly evident, even in the case where the communicator was regarded as biased. Thus, the available evidence suggests the following general hypothesis: In persuasive com-munications which present a complicated series of arguments on im-personal topics, it is generally more effective to state the conclusion *explicitly* than to allow the audience to draw its own conclusions.

PROBLEM 2: *What are the relative effects upon opin-ion change of a) presenting only those arguments favoring the recommended conclusion and b) discussing also argu-ments opposed to the position advocated?*

Two patterns are usually available to the communicator: concen-tration on the points supporting the position he advocates, or presenta-tion of these *plus* discussion of the opposed arguments. Which is more effective? This problem is to be distinguished from a related one on the effects of successive exposure to opposite sides of an issue, where the two communications reach opposite conclusions. Here a number of experiments with debates and with mass communications (e.g., Schanck and Goodman [23]) have indicated that the two communica-tions usually tend to produce cancellation of effects ([18] pp. 55–57). In the experiments to be considered in the present section, a conclu-sion favoring only one side of the issue is advocated, and the research problem concerns the effects of including or omitting discussion of the arguments on the opposite side.

RESEARCH EVIDENCE

Experimental data on the problem are provided by Hovland, Lums-daine, and Sheffield [13]. To two experimental groups of 214 soldiers each and to a control group of 197 soldiers they presented communica-tions on the question of an early end of the war with Japan follow-ing Germany's surrender. Beliefs about the issue were tested before the communication and immediately after. One experimental group was given a 15-minute talk including only the arguments for thinking that the war with Japan would be a long one. The material contained much factual information stressing Japan's advantages and resources. The second experimental group was given a communication which contained the same arguments plus some consideration and refutation of arguments on the other side, e.g., concerning Japan's weaknesses.

The major hypothesis governing the preparation of the communication giving both sides was that "those who were opposed would be stimulated by a one-sided argument to rehearse their own position and seek new ways of supporting it" (p. 203). They might also distrust a one-sided presentation as coming from a biased source that had failed to mention the opposed arguments. In line with this formulation, a number of principles were utilized concerning the optimal order of presentation. These included the following: 1) the main arguments against the position advocated, especially those that cannot be easily refuted, should be mentioned at the very outset; 2) appeals to the motives of those members of the audience opposed to the communicator's point of view should be presented early; 3) an attempt to refute arguments on the other side should be made only when an obviously compelling and strictly factual refutation is available; 4) any refutations, and those positive arguments which are potentially most antagonizing, should come late in the presentation; 5) members of the opposition should not be given a chance to identify themselves as such.

In order to evaluate the effectiveness of the two programs, subjects were asked to estimate the probable length of the war with Japan. Both programs were found to be extremely effective, with marked changes shown for both experimental groups (with practically no change for the control group). No advantage of one program over the other for the audience *as a whole* was revealed. As suggested earlier, however, a critical feature in the theory underlying the experiment was the expectation of greater effectiveness of the two-sided program on men initially opposed to the commentator's view that the war would take at least two years after V-E Day. The data obtained support this hypothesis.

Figure 4 shows that the net effects were different for the two ways of presenting the material, *depending on the initial stand of the listener*. The program giving both sides was more effective for men initially opposed, that is for men who, contrary to the programs, expected a short war (less than two years). On the other hand, the program giving the one-sided picture was more effective for men initially favoring the stand taken, those who agreed that the war would take at least two years.

Another hypothesis of the authors was that the better educated men would be less affected by a conspicuously one-sided presentation and, conversely, would be more likely to accept the arguments of a presenta-

NET PER CENT OF INDIVIDUALS CHANGING OPINION
IN DIRECTION OF POSITION ADVOCATED
BY COMMUNICATOR

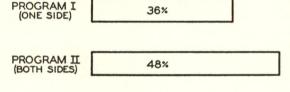

A. AMONG MEN INITIALLY OPPOSED
TO COMMUNICATOR'S POSITION

PROGRAM I
(ONE SIDE)   36%

PROGRAM II
(BOTH SIDES)   48%

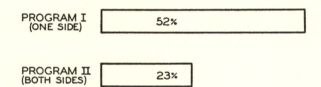

B. AMONG MEN INITIALLY FAVORABLE
TO COMMUNICATOR'S POSITION

PROGRAM I
(ONE SIDE)   52%

PROGRAM II
(BOTH SIDES)   23%

FIGURE 4. Effects of a One-sided vs. a Two-sided Presentation on Beliefs. *From Hovland, Lumsdaine, and Sheffield [13].*

tion that appears to take all factors into account in arriving at a conclusion. On the other hand, the consideration of both sides of an issue could weaken the immediate force of the argument for the less well educated insofar as they are less skilled in critical thinking and more likely to be impressed by the strength of the one-sided argument without thinking of objections.

When the results were broken down according to educational level, it was found that the program which presented both sides was more effective with better educated men, while that which presented one side was more effective with less educated men.

When both education and initial position were considered, the communication giving both sides proved to be more effective among the better educated regardless of initial position, whereas the one-sided presentation was primarily effective with those who were already convinced among the less well-educated group. From the results obtained it would be expected that the total effect of either kind of program on the group as a whole would depend both on the group's educational composition and on the initial division of opinion in the group. Thus, obtaining information about the educational level and initial position of an audience might be of considerable value in choosing the most effective type of presentation.

In the Hovland, Lumsdaine, and Sheffield experiment, effects of the communication were measured only in terms of *immediate* changes in opinion; it was not possible to compare the effects of one-sided versus two-sided communications in terms of resistance to the effect of subsequently presented counterarguments or "counterpropaganda." A more recent study by Lumsdaine and Janis [20] was designed to extend the evidence on the one-sided versus two-sided question by comparing the effectiveness of the two forms of presentation after part of the audience had been exposed to a second, or counterpropaganda, communication.

The Lumsdaine and Janis experiment was conducted several months before the announcement by President Truman that Russia had produced an atomic explosion. It compared the effects of two forms of a persuasive communication. Both forms consisted of a transcribed "radio program" in which the same communicator took the position that Russia would be unable to produce large numbers of atomic bombs for at least the next five years.

Program I, the one-sided presentation, contained only the arguments that supported this conclusion (for example: Russian scientists have not yet discovered all the crucial secrets, they cannot learn all of them through espionage; even after acquiring all the know-how Russia does not have sufficient industrial potential to produce the bombs in quantity).

Program II, a two-sided presentation, contained the same arguments presented in identical fashion, but also presented and discussed arguments for the other side of the picture (for example: Russia has many first-rate atomic scientists; Russian industries have made a phenomenal recovery since the war; Russia has uranium mines in Siberia). As in the previous study, the content of opposing arguments was selected partly on the basis of spontaneous arguments given in pretest interviews with representatives of the intended kind of audience. The opposing arguments were interwoven into the communication and in some instances no attempt was made to refute them. The total content of both programs was designed to lead unambiguously to the conclusion that Russia would be unable to produce A-bombs in quantity for at least five years. Except for the presence of the opposing arguments, the two communications were identical: Program II was recorded first, and Program I was constructed by simply deleting the opposing arguments from the tape recording.

One experimental group received the one-sided program (I) and another the two-sided program (II). A week later half of each group was exposed to a countercommunication and the other half was not. The counterpropaganda consisted of a second communication in which the same issue was discussed by a different commentator who took a position opposite to the first. He argued that Russia had probably already developed the A-bomb and within two years would be producing it in large quantities. Most of this communication consisted of playing up and elaborating the opposing arguments that had been mentioned earlier in Program II, but some new material was also introduced, including a description of four plants in Russia alleged to be already producing A-bombs. A control group received neither the original communication nor the countercommunication. All groups were given an initial questionnaire, several weeks before the experimental communications were presented, to determine initial level of opinion, and a final questionnaire at the end of the experiment.

The main question designed to measure the effects of the communications was: "About how long from now do you think it will be before the Russians are really producing *large numbers* of atomic bombs?" This "key" question was asked in both the initial and the final questionnaires.

As in the earlier experiment, there was little over-all difference in the effectiveness of the two programs for those groups that were not exposed to counterpropaganda. In the later experiment the main interest of course attaches to the results for the groups that were exposed to counterpropaganda, and to the comparison between these results and those for the group that received no counterpropaganda.

The pattern of results is quite clear-cut: in spite of the lack of over-all difference for the groups who did *not* receive counterpropaganda, the results for the groups that were exposed to counterpropaganda show that Program II was decidedly superior to Program I. These data are presented in Figure 5 below.

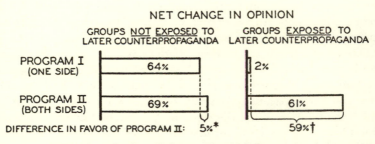

NET CHANGE IN OPINION

FIGURE 5. Comparison of a One-sided vs. a Two-sided Presentation for Groups Exposed and Not Exposed to Subsequent Counterpropaganda. *From Lumsdaine and Janis* [20].

* p-value >.30
† p-value <.01

The findings of the two experiments can be summarized briefly as follows:

1. A two-sided presentation is *more* effective in the long run than a one-sided one *a*) when, regardless of initial opinion, the audience is *exposed* to subsequent counterpropaganda, or *b*) when, regardless of subsequent exposure to counterpropaganda, the audience initially *disagrees* with the commentator's position.

2. A two-sided presentation is *less* effective than a one-sided if the audience initially *agrees* with the commentator's position and *is not exposed* to later counterpropaganda.

IMPLICATIONS

One rationale for the results on counterpropaganda would run as follows: Regardless of initial position, a convincing one-sided communication presenting only positive arguments will tend to sway many members of the audience farther in the direction advocated by the communicator. Subsequently, however, these persons hear the opposite point of view, also supported by cogent-sounding arguments. Their opinions now tend to be swayed back in the negative direction, especially if the new arguments appear to offset the previous positive arguments. However, if the initial communication is, instead, a two-sided one it will already have taken into account both the positive and negative arguments and still have reached the positive conclusion. When the listener is then subsequently exposed to the presentation of negative arguments in the counterpropaganda he is less likely to be influenced in the negative direction. He is already familiar with the opposing point of view and has been led to the positive conclusion in a context where the negative arguments were in evidence. In effect, he has thus been given an advance basis for ignoring or discounting the negative arguments, and thus "innoculated" will tend to retain the positive conclusion.

In both of the studies discussed the opposing arguments were introduced in a manner which the investigators considered most likely to achieve clear-cut effects, and no attempt was made to vary experimentally the way in which the opposing arguments were presented. This, however, is an extremely important research problem. Further work could profitably be directed at investigating the manner in which opposing arguments are introduced into two-sided communications, the character of the arguments, the extent to which they are explicitly refuted, and a host of related problems. Such studies would provide not only information on the conditions for maximum effectiveness of two-sided communications but better understanding of the general problem of refutation as well.

PROBLEM 3: *What are the effects of different orders of presentation of arguments in persuasive communications?*

Discussion of this problem is typically subsumed under the topics of *primacy* and *recency*, with consideration of the relative effectiveness of the first portion of a communication as compared with the last. But two somewhat different situations, often discussed together, must be distinguished. In the first, only a single communication is to be presented which advocates a particular point of view, and the communicator must decide whether to present his major arguments at the beginning or save them for a strong ending. In the other, two different sides of an issue are to be presented and the question is whether the side presented first or that presented second will have greater influence on opinion. These two problems have much in common, but there are also some important differences between them, so that the ensuing discussion is separated into two subdivisions:

A. *When only a single side of an issue is to be presented, is it more effective to utilize the strongest arguments at the outset or at the end?*

A communication in which the strongest and most important arguments are reserved until the end is frequently referred to as having a "climax" order. Conversely, presentation of the major arguments at the beginning and the weaker points at the end is called "anticlimax" order.

RESEARCH EVIDENCE AND ANALYSIS

There have been two extensive studies of the relative effectiveness of these two alternative arrangements. The first was conducted by Sponberg [24], using communications dealing with the desirability of wartime marriages. Each communication was divided into three parts: "large" (eight minutes long and containing the argument previously rated by judges as being most important); "medium" (five minutes of an argument of intermediate importance), and "small" (three minutes of the least important argument). These were presented to one group of 92 college students in climax order (with least important arguments first) and to another group of 93 in the reverse (anticlimax) order. Opinion questionnaires dealing with the over-all issue and with each of the three supporting arguments were administered immediately before the communication and immediately after, and again 10 to 13 days later. Sponberg concludes: "The study revealed the operation of the law of primacy in the presentation of oral material, and, in general, favors the anticlimax order of speech composition" (p. 44).

The other major study, by Cromwell [7], reaches an opposite conclusion. He presented recorded speeches to four groups of college students, making a total of 441 subjects. The topic was the desirability of federal medical aid. Each communication consisted of two speeches, one containing the strongest arguments for the position advocated and the other a speech of the same length but weaker in argumentative content and organization. His a priori characterization of the speeches as "strong" or "weak" was confirmed by the ratings of effectiveness assigned to them by judges. One group of subjects listened to a strong affirmative speech followed by a weak one. A second group listened to the same speeches in reverse order. The other two groups heard in similar manner "strong" and "weak" speeches on the negative side of the question. Tests of attitude, using a modified form of a Thurstone scale, were given before and after each speech.

The results show that the shift in audience attitude was significantly greater for speeches in the weak-strong order (climax order) than in the opposite or anticlimax order. Only 27 per cent of the auditors who heard the speeches presented in anticlimax order made a shift greater than one standard error in the direction of the proposition advocated, whereas 42 per cent of the listeners who heard the speeches in climax order made a shift of this magnitude ($p < .01$).

Thus Sponberg's results support an anticlimax order while those of Cromwell indicate the superiority of a climax sequence. There seem to be two major variations in the procedures of the two experiments which may have affected the outcomes. In Sponberg's study the differences in emphasis were confined to a single speech, while in the Cromwell study the difference was in the strength of two speeches on the same topic. The other variation was that in the Sponberg study the difference in strength of argument was defined partly on the basis of the amount of time devoted to it in the talk, while in the Cromwell research the speeches were of equal length but were designed to differ in convincingness.

In view of the contradictory conclusions it is unlikely that one or the other order will turn out to be universally superior. Our interest is then in an analysis of the factors which will make either the climax or the anticlimax order more effective under a particular set of conditions. The factors and hypotheses discussed will be for the most part only suggestive, since the researches in this area do not yield direct information on theoretical variables. They have been done primarily by students of speech whose orientation was toward practical problems of presentation. Thus characterization of speeches as "weak" or "strong" does little to indicate the theoretical factors involved. In one sense, therefore, the ensuing discussion is an attempt to give "psychological" explanations of the possible factors and mechanisms involved in procedures designed by communication practitioners.

"LEARNING" FACTORS

The extent to which a communication is effective in changing opinions depends in part on the extent to which the content of the communication is attended to, understood, and remembered. When none of the supporting arguments are grasped and retained, beliefs and expectations based on them will generally be unaffected. Consequently, we must examine the possibility that the differential effectiveness of climax and anticlimax order may depend on the extent to which one or the other order facilitates learning the material presented. Both "motivational" and "associative" factors must be considered.

1. Motivation to Learn

One possible difference between "weak" and "strong" portions of a communication is in their effectiveness in arousing interest and attention. In mass communication situations it is very common for the individual who lacks interest in the material presented to "turn off" the communication, either physically (by switching off the radio or television set) or psychologically (by no longer paying attention).

Hence it is possible that the effectiveness of climax or anticlimax order may depend on the contribution of one or the other order to the arousal or maintenance of attention. At the one extreme where the audience has little interest in what is being said one would expect that placing the strongest and most interesting material at the beginning would be more effective since it would arouse the listeners' interest and motivate them to learn what was being said. This consideration would favor an anticlimax order, and may have been involved in an experiment of Adams [1]. Subjects thumbed through a prepared magazine having several advertisements for each advertiser arranged in either climax or anticlimax order. In the former the small ads were placed at the beginning, while for the latter (anticlimax) the largest ads came first and the smaller ones toward the end. It was found that subjects remembered the name of the product better with the anticlimax order (where the large ads came first, followed by the small) than when the reverse order was employed. An explanation of the results may be given in terms of attention and interest. The large ads may gain attention. With the anticlimax order the subjects may become set to notice other smaller ads for the same product. When the small ads come first there may be a tendency not to notice them and to see only the larger ones at the end.

Under other conditions the opposite type of outcome might be expected, where the communicatees have enough initial curiosity about a topic to cause them to pay attention to the opening portions but where their interest and attention will fall off rapidly unless sustained by interesting and impressive arguments. Thus attention-getting devices which attract initial attention are useful only if there is other material to sustain attention once it has been aroused. Research would be most helpful on the conditions under which various orders of arguments affect the arousal and maintenance of interest and hence influence the effectiveness of climax or anticlimax order.

One possible hypothesis suggested by the preceding considerations is that *the presentation of the major arguments at the outset* (anticlimax order) *will be most effective where the audience is initially little interested in the communication.* Where high attention is guaranteed by the interest of the audience, other factors would be of greater significance in determining the outcome.

Other determinants may play a part under special circumstances. With anxiety-arousing communications, for example, strong arguments which arouse anxiety may be disruptive if placed at the beginning. Weak arguments at the beginning (climax order) may prepare the audience better for the later arguments (through "negative adaptation"). Some aspects of this problem have been discussed in Chapter 3. The data presented there appear to indicate that the intensities of anxiety arousal involved in ordinary communications are not sufficient to interfere with learning the content of the communication, although they can interfere with modifications in opinion and behavior.

2. "Associative" Factors

The effectiveness of the order of presentation depends in part upon whether the major arguments are placed in the position where they can be learned most rapidly.

The problem of whether material placed at the beginning or the end of a communication is better learned when exposure is controlled and motivation likely to be constant has been investigated by a number of researchers. The pioneer study in this area is that of Jersild [17]. He had his subjects read a series of narrative biographical statements and subsequently tested how well each was retained. The "memory value" of the individual statements was controlled by having each of ten different groups, totaling 253 subjects, read the same statements arranged in different orders. He found that the statements read at the beginning were better remembered than those read at the end. The subjects remembered 64.3 per cent of the first three statements compared with 50.9 per cent of the last three. Although Jersild did not test for statistical significance, a test put to his data shows that the probability of obtaining this difference through chance is less than .01.

Ehrensberger [10] conducted an experiment which essentially repeated Jersild's. He used ten different experimenters, to remove the communicator as a source of bias. The subjects were told that they were to read a series of statements and would be tested for memory immediately afterward. They were then tested for recognition of the items read. This experiment indicated a statistically significant superiority for the material presented toward the end of the communication, the opposite of Jersild's finding.

Here again there are contradictory results. The lack of generality is further illustrated in a study by Doob [*8*]. He explored the effects of a communication presented under conditions where the audience did not expect to have retention tests. His experiment consisted of two parts: 1) Three hundred and fifty-seven subjects read each of five short passages relating to controversial issues and indicated their attitude toward each. From a subsequent test for recall, he found that "Items coming first in [this] situation tend to be recalled in greater numbers and to be recalled sooner, but they are not recalled more accurately or with a greater number of words" (p. 204). Whatever difference existed, then, favored primacy. 2) One hundred and thirty-seven subjects from the same class saw a featured film at a local theater under the impression they were to study communication technique. They were quizzed afterward about the newsreel shown with the film. Under these conditions, recall clearly and significantly favored those items appearing at the end of the newsreel (recency).

Here again it is clear that there is no universal rule that either the first or the last item in a series will have superior retention. This outcome parallels that for learning simple materials. Experimental psychology for a long period of time postulated a Law of Primacy and Law of Recency (Carr [*5*]). Research with simple learning materials clearly demonstrated that there is no universal phenomenon of greater difficulty at the beginning or the end of a series of items. If there is any common phenomenon it is the greater difficulty of the middle portions of the material. Results from an experiment of one of the authors (Hovland [*11*]) with learning lists of three-letter syllables in serial order are shown in Figure 6a. It will be observed that the beginning and the end are of about equal difficulty but the middle of the list is of greater difficulty.

In the case of simple serial learning the greater difficulty of the central items is usually attributed to interference effects which are maximal near the middle of the list. The question arises as to whether there are similar serial position phenomena with the material and conditions that are typical of persuasive communications, where the content is meaningful and where the subject has no special set to learn the items in serial order. Data approximating the required conditions for ordinary communications are provided by Jersild [*17*]. He presented a long series of statements and subsequently tested the extent to which

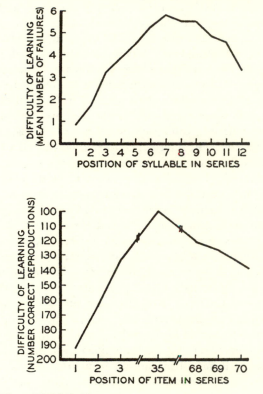

FIGURE 6.   Effect of Serial Position.

    a. Number of failures in each syllable position during learning. *From Hovland* [*11*].

    b. Recall scores as a function of serial position of narrative items. Arbitrary value of 100 assigned to serial position 35. *Data from Jersild* [*17*].

they were retained. When his results are plotted for the middle items of the list and for the beginning and end items, a serial position curve is obtained which closely approximates that obtained with simpler materials (Figure 6b). Compared with the greater difficulty of the middle items the differences between the first and last items in the list are not of great significance. Thus while serial position effects do play a significant role they do not explain the relative importance of climax and anticlimax effects.

"ACCEPTANCE" FACTORS

Another set of factors affecting the relative effectiveness of climax and anticlimax order concerns the degree to which one or the other order brings about acceptance of the communicator's message. One hypothesis which might be advanced to explain the advantage of a climax versus an anticlimax order is suggested by a learning-theory analysis of changes in size of incentives. From Hull's postulates ([16] pp. 140–148) it would be expected that a greater reaction potential will be produced if a small incentive is given at first, followed by a large, than if a large one is given first and then followed by a small, even though the total incentive is the same. If we assume that "strong" and "weak" arguments imply that the former possess higher incentive value than the latter, the possibility is suggested that, other things being equal, we should expect strong arguments followed by weak to be less effective than weak arguments followed by strong. There are at present insufficient data available to check this deduction from theory, but it is interesting to note that the data from Cromwell [7] indicate that "the effect of the weak speech seems to be made weaker by following a strong one" (p. 119). It is easy to imagine that the presentation of strong arguments at the outset leads to expectations which are frustrated by the subsequent presentation of weak arguments which "let you down," while with the climax order one would be impressed by the later arguments which exceeded the expectations created by those presented initially.

IMPLICATIONS

In the preceding analyses several assumptions have been considered as to ways in which climax and anticlimax orders may differ. From the available evidence it does not appear likely that the major explanation of differences in outcome is to be found in differences in ease of remembering the points made at the end as compared with those at the beginning. A more likely factor may be the attention-evoking potentiality of the "strong" as compared to the "weak" positions of the message. Consideration of this factor suggests that under conditions where the audience has low interest and low motivation to learn it may be particularly important to place one's most interesting and important arguments at the beginning. Under conditions of low interest one would then expect the anticlimax order to be superior. But analysis of the incentive value of various arrangements suggests that other factors must be considered. Under conditions where at least minimal attention is guaranteed, placement of the weak arguments after the strong would be expected to reduce the incentive value of the total set of arguments, thus favoring the climax order.

The foregoing discussion suggests that one should not expect either climax or anticlimax order of presentation to be invariably effective. The advantages of one over the other order will depend upon the particular conditions under which the communication is presented, including the predispositions of the audience and the type of material being communicated. The most useful generalizations will accordingly be concerned with "interaction" effects. Two tentative propositions of this type are advanced: that climax order will be favored on issues with which the audience is familiar and where deep concern is felt, but that anticlimax order will be favored on unfamiliar topics and with uninterested audiences.

B. When both sides of an issue are to be presented successively, does the side presented first or the side presented last have an advantage?

In the preceding section we discussed the effectiveness of different sequences of arguments when only a single side of an issue is presented. We shall now consider the order of arguments when one set of arguments advocates one point of view and the other presents the opposite side of an issue. These are the considerations which would apply if one were to ask whether the side of a debate presented *first* is more effective than the side presented *last*, other things being equal.

RESEARCH EVIDENCE

The most widely known study of this problem is that of Lund [21] who labeled his findings the Law of Primacy in Persuasion. Lund prepared six communications, consisting of an affirmative and negative position on each of three topics. The issues were "Should all men have equal political rights?" "Is the protective tariff a wise policy for the United States?" and "Will monogamous marriage continue to be the only socially accepted relation between the sexes?" Three groups, consisting of about 40 subjects each, were presented with first one side of the issue and then the other. Counterbalanced order was employed by giving the communications to half the group in the affirmative-negative order and to the other half in the negative-affirmative order. This controlled for possible differences in the persuasiveness of the communications.

The attitudes of the subjects toward the issues were measured two days before the communications, and again immediately after each communication. Thus there were three measures of the subject's attitude toward each issue. Lund found that the first communication caused a shift in attitude in the direction advocated, and the second caused a shift back toward the original attitude, but not all the way back; so the final attitude remained changed in the direction advocated by the first communication, indicating a "primacy" effect. These results were consistent for five of the six groups of subjects.

The results of Knower [19] are often quoted in support of primacy. Knower used 107 subjects tested on attitudes toward prohibition. Speeches on opposite sides of the question were given to the subjects to read. He concludes from his study that "When two speeches on opposite sides of the question were read, primacy in the order of reading influenced the amount and possibly the direction of change in attitude which occurred in the group" (p. 532). But the evidence he presents indicates that only one of his four groups shows sizable effect.

In another portion of the study by Cromwell [7] discussed earlier in this chapter (pp. 113 f.), data are presented on the relative effectiveness of primacy and recency with opposing arguments. Affirmative and negative speeches were prepared concerning socialized medicine and federal arbitration of labor disputes. In one version of each side "strong" arguments were used and in another "weak" arguments. Separate groups, ranging in size from 100 to 123 students, were given: 1) the weak affirmative first and then the weak negative, 2) the weak negative first and then the weak affirmative, 3) the strong affirmative followed by strong negative, and 4) the strong negative followed by strong affirmative. The subjects' attitudes were measured before the communications and again after both speeches had been presented. While no clear-cut differences were obtained with the weak speeches, Cromwell found that with the strong speeches the preponderance of the changes were in the direction of the speech presented *last*. This result was significant beyond the .01 level of significance on both topics. Thus, whatever differences were obtained favored *recency*, in contradiction to Lund's findings.

A study by Hovland and Mandell [*15*] on the effects of "commitment" on questionnaires also provides data on the role of primacy in persuasion. In one part of the study Lund's experimental conditions were reproduced as closely as possible. Two of his topics were used: "Should all men have equal political rights?" and "Is the protective tariff a wise policy for the United States?" Half the experimental groups received the affirmative version first and half the negative. Three hundred and thirty-one college students served as subjects. They were given opinion questionnaires before and after each communication.

The results were strikingly different from those of Lund. No significant primacy effects were obtained. The trend was, in fact, slightly in favor of recency. The experiment was repeated, with 191 subjects, using issues of more current interest: "Antihistamines should be sold without a prescription" and "An atomic submarine is feasible at the present time." The results again failed to confirm Lund's results.

Here, as in the section on climax and anticlimax order, there appears to be considerable variability in outcome. Many of the factors discussed in the previous section are relevant here. The principal additional consideration is the effect on acceptance of having the same communicator advocate both sides of an issue. A review of relevant learning factors and a discussion of the factors affecting acceptance follows.

"Learning" Factors

We assume here, as earlier, that the degree to which a communication produces opinion change depends in part on learning the content of the communication. However, few relevant data are available.

1. Motivation to Learn

As in the case of a single communication, the motivation of the audience is one important factor affecting the extent to which the two sides of an issue are learned. Under some conditions there may be a high motivation to learn the communication presented first.[1] As additional communications are presented, interest may either be satiated or aroused, depending upon a variety of factors. Declining interest would produce a primacy effect; increasing interest a recency effect. Motivation to learn would drop off in simple verbal material if the subject rapidly became bored, or in complex material where, for instance, the subject found the communication to be of little interest to him. Motivation to learn would increase as a result of the first exposure whenever new drives are aroused or there is an increase in the original drive. A person may, for example, initially attend a debate out of a sense of duty. But the skill of the debaters may arouse interest and curiosity and thereby increase the motivation necessary for learning.

To determine the motives involved and the strength of these motives in an experimental setting the conditions of the situation must be analyzed. In the experiment of Lund the experimenter was the subjects' regular classroom instructor. How would this fact influence the effect of his procedure of presenting first one side and then the other? Since there were no instructions given, the class at first may have assumed that the views in the first communication were those of the instructor, and have been motivated to learn the material. However, when the instructor proceeded to present a diametrically opposed position, it is entirely possible that the student subjects became confused by the sudden reversal in arguments, realized they were being subjected to an experiment, and in this way lost their ordinary classroom learning motivation. This may have contributed to the observed primacy effects. (Cf. also p. 127 for discussion of the possible influence of this procedure on acceptance.)

To a considerable extent the motivational factors affecting attention and learning of a single communication would also be involved with two opposed communications. Thus it is likely, other things being equal, that primacy would be favored where the side presented first arouses interest in the topic and then satiates interest before the second side is presented.

2. "Associative" Factors

If the motivation of the subjects can be kept constant through the experimental session and the communications are of equal interest, the interactions between the learning of the first and second communications must be considered. In the experiments of Lund, Cromwell, and Hovland and Mandell the subjects in effect first learn one response and then learn an incompatible contrary response. The situation may be diagramed as follows:

First communication: Learn: $A \to B$

Second communication: Learn: $A \to C$

Retention test: Measure: $A \lessgtr \begin{matrix} B \\ C \end{matrix}$

A may be regarded as the set of considerations to which the individual learns a response, B. A may raise a general issue, like "How long will it be before we have true racial equality?" and B may be the conclusion drawn by the communication, e.g., "At least 100 years" in the example given. But then, to the same issue or set of considerations, A, the second communication provides a contradictory conclusion, C. The questionnaire after the communication then raises the issue A and measures the extent to which the two opposed conclusions (B and C) are retained.

This poses two sets of problems from the standpoint of a learning analysis.

a. Will the second side be *learned* as effectively as the first? If more effectively learned, the term *associative facilitation* is used, but if less effectively one speaks of *associative interference* [*12*]. The general principle derived from an extensive series of studies under laboratory conditions over the last 30 or 40 years is that when *B* and *C* are incompatible responses to the same stimulus there will be interference effects in learning the second response, so that from the standpoint of learning it may be said that it will be harder to learn the second set of materials than the first. The effectiveness of the second set of materials is particularly likely to be reduced when interest in the communication is low. Under these conditions there will be considerable difficulty in learning a new incompatible response. If the communications are both very interesting and the subjects are highly motivated to learn, then we may find that they will overcome the extra difficulty by dint of greater concentration.

    b. After the two sides are learned, which will be better *retained?* If the two are equally well learned, the problem comes under the rubric of *reproductive interference* or *reproductive facilitation.*²

    But one cannot, of course, assume that both the first and second sets of materials are equally well learned in a naturalistic situation, as one can in laboratory studies where two sets of materials are learned to the same criterion before differences in retention are evaluated. Classical experimental work involving verbal learning finds that when both sets of associations are equally well learned $A \rightarrow C$ associations are better retained than $A \rightarrow B$ associations. With communications, this would be equivalent to saying that the *recency* effect would predominate if equal learning was insured. In predicting the relative superiority of the second learned response over the first, however, temporal factors would be important. The general finding is that the greater the time interval between the two learning situations, the greater the operation of recency. This certainly would be expected, since a long time interval elapsing after the first communication is learned would mean that much of the content would be forgotten by the time of the second communication. There would, therefore, be little interference with the learning of the second communication and only the latter would tend to be remembered.

    Yet another important factor to consider is the time interval between the learning of the second communication and the occasion when remembering is required. In experimental results on simple verbal material one would predict recency effects when the time interval is short. But the passage of time would tend to decrease this recency effect and permit the other factors making for primacy to become relatively stronger.[3] Underwood [25] has shown that for verbal learning the relative superiority of the second list with respect to retention decreases as the time between learning and testing becomes greater. If the same factors operate in social communication one would expect to find that when the issue is raised quite a while after the communication, recency would be less likely to be operative. Striking data are offered on this point in an experiment by Bateman and Remmers [3]. Seventy senior high school students were subjected to propaganda unfavorable to labor unions. The next day they were given propaganda favorable to unions. The students' attitudes were tested before and after the communications, as well as two months later. The results show that immediately after the two communications the attitudes changed in the direction of the second communication. This is the predicted recency effect. Two months later, however, the attitudes had changed in the direction of the first communication. Thus primacy effects occurred with time. While the data are consistent with the analysis suggested here, the experiment cannot be considered as presenting conclusive evidence because it did not include a control group and the order of presentation was not rotated. A better controlled study of the same type would be valuable.

"ACCEPTANCE" FACTORS

If conditions are controlled so as to yield comparable learning of two successive communications, then the degree to which primacy or recency effects occur is dependent upon the extent to which the audience *accepts* the different communications. Differences in degree of acceptance which are attributable to the particular content of one or the other communication are meant to be counterbalanced in studies of primacy-recency. Our present concern is therefore only with factors which can cause an interaction between acceptance and sequence effects. Let us then turn to acceptance factors which may affect the operation of primacy or recency.

1. Attitude toward the Communicator

There are strong reasons to suspect that the attitude toward the communicator may have played a significant role in Lund's results. In naturalistic situations, conflicting communications are usually presented by different communicators. This occurs in debates, forums, courtrooms, and similar settings. But in Lund's experiment it will be recalled that the experimenter (the class instructor) presented first one side and then the other. Thus the side of the issue presented first may have been readily accepted and its effect reflected in the questionnaire administered after the first communication. But when the instructor presented the opposite conclusion in the same fashion, there is a strong possibility that the subjects were suspicious and not only did not learn the material (as suggested earlier) but did not accept it. This lack of acceptance would then be reflected in the opinions expressed in the questionnaire after the second communication. Thus the primacy effect obtained could have been due in part to the artificial conditions which prevailed in the experiment. In subsequent studies it will be important to present the materials under more naturalistic conditions, where opposed arguments are presented by different communicators.

2. Commitment and Self-consistency

A second acceptance factor which can produce primacy effects is any tendency for individuals to maintain a position to which they have committed themselves publicly or privately; commitment then acts to produce a certain irreversibility of opinion change. This is the factor that Lund believed to be most important. He postulates a "striving for consistency." There is doubtless a motive of this type operative in our culture, but it is not clear what conditions elicit it.

The consistency motive is particularly likely to operate if the individual has expressed his beliefs publicly and thus committed himself. Just how strong this tendency to consistency is when the belief is kept private is uncertain. Hovland and Mandell [15] found no differential results between groups of subjects who answered an attitude questionnaire both after the first and again after the second communication and those who expressed their opinion only after the second. "Committing themselves" on the first questionnaire did not change their responsiveness to the second. Thus, self-consistency and commitment to a position do not seem to be effective causes of primacy effects where the commitment involves only stating one's position on an attitude questionnaire.

Although the sort of commitments discussed above are at best not very strong causes of primacy effects, it is quite possible that an interpersonal, social type of public commitment would have a considerably greater effect in maintaining a position once it is adopted. An individual who has reached a conclusion and discussed his conclusion with others may be highly resistant to further communications. One would expect this type of phenomenon to vary greatly among different individuals; it may be linked with personality characteristics such as "rigidity" and "strong superego."

3. Initial Position of Audience

Primacy is only relative. Sometimes the particular issue being presented is new; more frequently it has been thought about before. Thus what is presented first in a communication may not be first at all in the larger context of all communications received by the individual on the issue (cf. Lund, p. 183). The relative effectiveness of the first and second communications will accordingly be dependent upon prior familiarity with the topic and sophistication about the issues involved. For example, an individual who has thought little about a topic may be much more susceptible to "scare" appeals and emotionally loaded messages than someone who has greater prior familiarity with the issues (cf. pp. 75–77).

Lack of prior knowledge by the subjects about the topic may explain the primacy effect found in the experiments of Asch [2]. Subjects were asked to characterize an unknown individual on the basis of a series of descriptive terms read to them by the experimenter. Two groups of subjects heard identical lists but in two different orders. One group was given the list in the order "intelligent, industrious, impulsive, critical, stubborn, envious" while the other group was given "envious, stubborn, critical, impulsive, industrious, intelligent." The adjectives read first had a greater effect in "structuring" the subsequent descriptions by the subjects than those that followed.

In the case of issues which are clearly structured at the outset, the likelihood of obtaining primacy may depend on the initial opinion of the members of the audience. This is particularly likely to be true when the same communicator presents both sides of the issue. As was mentioned earlier, if the side with which the listeners predominantly disagree is presented first, they may tend to ignore or refute the communicator's arguments while rehearsing to themselves their own points. Thus the side presented first may have little effectiveness. On the other hand, if the arguments with which they agree are presented first, they may pay closer attention to them and then subsequently be more affected by the second side, since they are thus assured at the outset that the communicator is taking their own arguments into account. This factor has already been discussed above (pp. 105–111).

As with learning factors, so also with acceptance factors, either primacy or recency may be predicted, depending upon the conditions of the communication situation. Under one set of circumstances one would obtain decreased acceptance of the second communication, as in situations where the first communication "innoculates" the hearer against subsequent arguments or emotional appeals (Lumsdaine and Janis [20]). Under other conditions the effect of the second may be heightened through increased awareness of the issues or through overcompensation in responding to the opposite position.

IMPLICATIONS

The foregoing considerations suggest that it is doubtful it will ever be meaningful to postulate a Law of Primacy in social psychology which states that the material presented first will be more effective than that presented second. It may turn out empirically that "primacy" is obtained more frequently than "recency," but if so it is due to special combinations of events which can individually produce either primacy or recency, or equal effectiveness of both. It would seem, therefore, that further work might profitably go in one or the other of two divergent directions. It might be directed toward analyzing the conditions obtaining under various naturalistic situations and determining the empirical outcomes. Thus studies of debates or political campaigns could be examined to determine which of the factors discussed above predominate and affect the outcome. Or theoretical analysis might be made of various factors responsible for the greater effectiveness of the first or second communication. Such studies might, for example, endeavor to keep all other factors constant and assess only the influence upon belief of the time interval between the first and second presentations. This information would then provide the data needed for predicting the outcome when this combination was known to be involved in a specified situation of interest to the communicator.

Notes

1. In all the experiments cited, the audience's exposure to the communication is assured. In many naturalistic types of communication, where there is no "captive audience," an important problem is self-selection of the audience (Klapper [18]). In these situations the investigator must determine what the effect of presenting a communication first or second will be upon the attentional or motivational factors within the subject which determine whether or not he exposes himself to the latter communication at all. Situations can be conceived where presentation of the first communication increases the likelihood of the subject's exposing himself to the second. On the other hand, there can be situations where boredom and fatigue reduce interest and decrease the individual's motivation to expose himself to the second communication. Factors such as the novelty of the communication, the type of setting (classroom, radio, newspapers, etc.), and the initial position of the subject on the issue are all of importance.

2. It should be emphasized that the paradigm presented can produce reproductive *facilitation* as well as reproductive *interference*. The interference effects will occur where the two learned responses are incompatible, and these are the usual conditions for the Lund phenomenon. For a general theory, however, responses bearing other than an incompatible relationship to each other must be analyzed. In the verbal learning situation, it is generally found that the interference effects become less as the responses become more similar to each other. At the point where the responses are identical, the intervening learning material can be regarded as additional learning trials of the original material, and thus more of the original learning occurs (producing facilitation). Under complex learning conditions, where meaningful but not identical material is involved, the first communication sometimes makes the second more meaningful; greater comprehension resulting from the first would benefit the second. This outcome would be an instance of "positive transfer" in learning, and *recency* would be the phenomenon obtained. Either facilitation or interference can thus be obtained as a result of successive communications, depending upon the relationship which the communications bear to each other and the level of meaningfulness of the communications for the subjects.

3. This learning factor, like other factors mentioned earlier, operates in complicated ways in communication situations, where the time between learning and testing is not a learning vacuum. The intervening social experiences of the individual have an effect on the retention of a complex, socially significant communication. Social approval or disapproval of the learned communication can either facilitate or interfere with one of the originally learned communications. A similar effect would occur when there is a long time interval between the learning of two communications (cf. Chapter 8).

References

1. Adams, H. F. The effect of climax and anti-climax order of presentation on memory. *J. Appl. Psychol.*, 1920, *4*, 330–338.
2. Asch, S. E. Forming impressions of personality. *J. Abnorm. Soc. Psychol.*, 1946, *41*, 258–290.
3. Bateman, R. M., and Remmers, H. H. A study of the shifting attitude of high school students when subjected to favorable and unfavorable propaganda. *J. Soc. Psychol.*, 1941, *13*, 395–406.
4. Brembeck, W. L., and Howell, W. S. *Persuasion: A means of social control.* New York, Prentice-Hall, 1952.
5. Carr, H. A. The laws of association. *Psychol. Rev.*, 1931, *38*, 212–228.
6. Cooper, Eunice, and Dinerman, Helen. Analysis of the film "Don't Be A Sucker": a study in communication. *Publ. Opin. Quart.*, 1951, *15*, 243–264.
7. Cromwell, H. The relative effect on audience attitude of the first versus the second argumentative speech of a series. *Speech Monogr.*, 1950, *17*, 105–122.
8. Doob, L. W. Effects of initial serial position and attitude upon recall under conditions of low motivation. *J. Abnorm. Soc. Psychol.*, 1953, *48*, 199–205.
9. Dunlap, K. *Civilized life.* Baltimore, Williams & Wilkins, 1934.
10. Ehrensberger, R. An experimental study of the relative effectiveness of certain forms of emphasis in public speaking. *Speech Monogr.*, 1945, *12*, 94–111.
11. Hovland, C. I. Experimental studies in rote-learning theory. II. Reminiscence with varying speeds of syllable presentation, *J. Exp. Psychol.*, 1938, *22*, 338–353.
12. Hovland, C. I. Human learning and retention. In S. S. Stevens, ed., *Handbook of experimental psychology.* New York, John Wiley, 1951. Pp. 613–689.
13. Hovland, C. I., Lumsdaine, A. A., and Sheffield, F. D. *Experiments on mass communication.* Princeton Univ. Press, 1949.
14. Hovland, C. I., and Mandell, W. An experimental comparison of conclusion-drawing by the communicator and by the audience. *J. Abnorm. Soc. Psychol.*, 1952, *47*, 581–588.
15. Hovland, C. I., and Mandell, W. Is there a "law of primacy" in persuasion? Paper presented before the Eastern Psychological Association, April 1952.
16. Hull, C. L. *A behavior system.* New Haven, Yale Univ. Press, 1952.
17. Jersild, A. Primacy, recency, frequency and vividness. *J. Exp. Psychol.*, 1929, *12*, 58–70.
18. Klapper, J. T. *The effects of mass media.* New York, Columbia Univ. Bureau of Applied Social Research, 1949 (Mimeo.)
19. Knower, F. H. Experimental studies of changes in attitude. II. A study of the effect of printed argument on changes in attitude. *J. Abnorm. Soc. Psychol.*, 1936, *30*, 522–532.
20. Lumsdaine, A. A., and Janis, I. L. Resistance to counterpropaganda produced by a one-sided versus a two-sided propaganda presentation. *Publ. Opin. Quart.* (in press).

21. Lund, F. H. The psychology of belief: IV. The law of primacy in persuasion. *J. Abnorm. Soc. Psychol.,* 1925, *20,* 183–191.
22. Rogers, C. R. Some observations on the organization of personality. *Am. Psychologist,* 1947, *2,* 358–368.
23. Schanck, R. L., and Goodman, C. Reactions to propaganda on both sides of a controversial issue. *Publ. Opin. Quart.,* 1939, *3,* 107–112.
24. Sponberg, H. A study of the relative effectiveness of climax and anti-climax order in an argumentative speech. *Speech Monogr.,* 1946, *13,* 35–44.
25. Underwood, B. J. Retroactive and proactive inhibition after five and forty-eight hours. *J. Exp. Psychol.,* 1948, *38,* 29–38.

CHAPTER 5: *Group Membership and Resistance to Influence*

THE effects of a communication are determined not only by the characteristics of the communicator, the types of appeals he uses, and the manner in which he organizes his arguments but also by the motives and abilities of the individuals in his audience. In this and the next chapter our major concern will be with audience predispositions which are relevant to the effectiveness of communication. Some of the most important of these predispositions have to do with the conformity tendencies which stem from membership in groups. These tendencies are based on knowledge of what behavior is expected by the other members and on motives to live up to the expectations. The present chapter will be concerned primarily with the motives underlying conformity and the social cues which elicit them.

An analysis of the influence of groups upon the attitudes of their members is of obvious importance to the general problem of changing opinions through communications. Communicators often use these social incentives to facilitate acceptance of the opinion they advocate. For instance, community leaders frequently assert that group approval will follow upon the adoption of their recommendation or that disapproval will be the consequence of failure to accept it. On the other hand, a specific recommendation may encounter resistance because a group provides strong incentives for holding the original opinions. Certain methods of persuasion entail lowering the importance of the incentives delivered by the group (e.g., making the person less resistant to change by decreasing his dependence upon the group) or increasing the incentive value of competing groups.

The present discussion of group factors as they affect persuasive communications will be limited in its scope in two major respects. First, these factors will be examined mainly as they relate to *resistance to change*. The focus will be upon the special class of communications (referred to as "counternorm communications") which propose a point of view that is at odds with the opinions approved by the groups in which the recipients hold membership. We shall attempt to analyze some of the factors which underlie the resistance encountered by communications of this sort. The factors and principles governing the effects of counternorm communications are expected to be useful, with appropriate adaptations, for predicting the effects of communications which are favorable to group-sanctioned opinions. To some extent, the same factors and principles probably also govern the effectiveness of the intragroup influence processes by which conformity to group standards is elicited and maintained. The present focus upon counternorm communications has a further consequence: it leaves out of consideration the methods which attempt to change the individual's perceptions or knowledge of group norms, for example, by communicating information about the majority opinion on a given issue [*1, 3, 7*] or by group discussion and decision [*11, 30*]. Our interest here is in communications which argue in direct opposition to group norms rather than in communications that attempt to reinterpret them.

Second, we shall consider only instances where a person's attitudes depend upon the opinions or characteristics of groups in which he holds *membership*. There is considerable evidence in social science literature for the existence of relative homogeneity with respect to certain attitudes among persons who are members of a given group, i.e., those who frequently interact with one another, take part in common activities, and are generally considered as "belonging together." Studies of the changes in opinions which accompany joining or leaving groups (for example, cf. Newcomb [*36*]) indicate that this homogeneity is not due entirely to selective formation of groups but is at least in part a reflection of intragroup influence processes. In addition to the evidence on membership groups, there are indications that opinions are sometimes related to groups to which the individual does not belong (e.g. [*2, 6, 8, 23*]). In order to take account of the importance of both membership and nonmembership groups, the term "reference group," introduced by Hyman [*23*], has come into use to denote *any* group which has an effect on a person's opinions. The writings of Sherif [*41*], Newcomb ([*37*] pp. 225 ff.), Merton and Kitt [*33*], and others present an emerging theory of reference groups consisting of a series of statements about the influence upon attitudes of groups in general. While we have restricted the present discussion to membership groups, we expect that the basic generalizations reported can be incorporated into the reference group framework and will be descriptive of the manner in which opinions are affected by nonmembership groups as well.[1]

Given the above limitations, our interest is in the factors underlying the resistance to change of opinions which are held in conformity with the behavioral standards of a group to which the individual belongs. These standards, shared among the members of a group and representing the behavior and attitudes they expect of one another, will be referred to as "norms." Viewed from the standpoint of a group, conformity of its members results from a complex social process which includes teaching them about the norms, motivating them to conform, and, in various situations, providing reminders of the norms and the associated sanctions. The adequacy with which these various aspects of the process are performed within a group will determine the degree of conformity exhibited by its members. It will also determine the degree to which the members resist persuasive communications which propose nonconformity, especially those from outside the group.

Viewed in terms of the individual member, conformity will ensue if, as a result of these social communication processes, he attains some conception of the expected behavior (or opinion) and at any given point in time is motivated to bring his own behavior (or opinion) into line with it. If the individual knows the norms to which conformity is expected, he will exhibit conforming behavior in any given situation to the extent that:

First, he is dependent upon the group for the satisfaction of various motives, and this forms the basis for *motivation* to conform.

Second, there are social stimuli or *situational cues* which operate to arouse the motives related to conformity.

These sets of factors will be discussed in the two major parts of this chapter.

PART I: *Valuation of Membership*

BACKGROUND

A variety of motives are involved in attitudinal and behavioral conformity to group norms. Some of them have to do with maintaining social approval and avoiding disapproval, the importance of which the individual learns during the early stages of his socialization. Others have to do with the person's desire to understand his fellows, to be understood by them, and to share their solutions to recurrent problems. Confidence in the accuracy of communication depends upon sharing with one's associates certain common ways of viewing things and common meanings for words and other symbols. In brief, to the extent that a person is motivated to establish effective two-way communication relationships with other persons, he tends to adopt their standards of evaluation. A related basis of conformity motives is suggested by the feelings of security, the sense of "rightness," which seem to come from holding opinions similar to those of other persons. Part of this security is undoubtedly due to the desire to gain social acceptance, but there also seem to be instances where social acceptance is not at stake. These are the cases where the person has of necessity to make a judgment on an issue, has no expert opinion or direct reality check as a basis for validating that judgment and, as a consequence, seeks to validate it through agreement with others.

An important question is why an individual becomes motivated to conform to one group rather than to another. The answer to this requires an understanding of his motives for seeking and maintaining membership in a particular group. It is clear that different persons may have quite different reasons for joining and remaining in a group. Common knowledge and some research data [*44*] indicate that a person's membership in a group can involve any one or combination of the following three factors:

1. Positive attractions within the group based on friendship for the other members and the desirability of the status and activities which membership makes possible. In determining the net positive attractions of a group, account must be taken of undesirable aspects of the group which must be endured and desirable activities outside

the group which must be foregone if membership is to be maintained.

2. Outside threats or deprivations which are avoided by maintaining membership in the group.

3. Restraints which act to keep the person within the group without regard to his desires in the matter.

Whichever of these factors are involved, they render the individual susceptible to the influence of the group and form the basis for conformity to its norms. Such conformity may be motivated by a need to resemble highly esteemed persons, to maintain social approval, or to avoid unpleasant circumstances (e.g., loss of the privileges of membership).

The degree of conformity exhibited by any given member depends in part upon the importance to him of the membership factors mentioned above.[2] The more highly esteemed the other members, the greater are the satisfactions derived from adopting their opinions and values. The more important is the group as a refuge from external dangers, the more powerful become any threats of exclusion and, other things being equal, the closer the conformity. Thus, the more strongly the person is motivated to maintain membership in a group, the greater will be his behavioral conformity to its norms, and, at least under some circumstances, the more conforming will be his *opinions*.

Existing evidence on this general point comes mainly from studies of groups in which membership is voluntary and where escape from external threats probably contributes little to the maintenance of membership. These studies are not primarily concerned with the motives involved in taking refuge in a group or with the consequences of restricted contact, but bear largely on the importance of the positive attractions within the group or the total quantity of positive values perceived to be mediated by membership. This we shall refer to as "valuation" of membership. Taking cognizance of individual differences in this respect, we shall distinguish "high valuation" members (i.e., those for whom the group provides much gratification of needs) from "low valuation" members.

A correlational study by Festinger, Schachter, and Back [15] provides the clearest demonstration of the importance of this factor for opinion conformity. They examined differences among small social groups within a housing project in degree of "group cohesiveness," which they defined in terms of the average attractiveness of a group for its members. They measured cohesiveness in terms of the number of friendships formed within each group, and found this to be related to the degree of uniformity among the members of each unit in regard to a controversial issue. The authors defined the concept "power of the group" as the ability of the group to produce attitudinal changes among its members, and interpreted the correlation between cohesiveness and attitudinal uniformity as indicating that the "power" of a group is a direct function of its cohesiveness. The circumstances in which this investigation was carried out make it unlikely that spurious factors could account for this correlation and therefore this interpretation seems justified. A subsequent laboratory study by Back [4], in which the attractiveness of membership was experimentally varied, produced confirming evidence indicating that greater interpersonal influence tends to occur in the more attractive groups.

A correlation between group attractiveness and attitude changes in conformity with its norms was also found in Mussen's [35] investigation of changes in ethnic attitudes resulting from a four-week stay in an interracial camp for boys. His results show that the boys who changed in accordance with the approved unprejudiced attitudes of the camp tended also to be the ones who were generally satisfied with the camp and their fellow campers.

In summary, the available evidence seems to indicate that the more highly a person values his membership in a group the more closely will his opinions and attitudes conform to the consensus within the group. The implication of this phenomenon is that the person who places high value on the group is highly influenced by communications from other members, particularly with respect to issues about which he believes the group to have norms.

RESEARCH EVIDENCE

VALUATION OF MEMBERSHIP

If the member who values the group highly is greatly influenced by intragroup communications relevant to the norms, he might also be expected to be highly resistant to influence which is contrary to the norms, particularly when such influence comes from outside the group. If the attractiveness of the group is related to its ability to produce opinion changes, attractiveness should also be a factor in its ability to maintain these attitudes against counterpressures. This involves the assumption that the processes involved in the maintenance of norms are generally the same as those involved in their formation.

The following hypothesis on this point was investigated by Kelley and Volkart [26]: High valuation members (i.e., those who place high value upon the group) will be less influenced by a communication contrary to its norms than will low valuation members. According to this hypothesis, the amount of opinion change produced by such a communication will be inversely related to degree of valuation of membership.

To test this hypothesis, Kelley and Volkart gave communications and questionnaires to the members of 12 Boy Scout troops. The pertinent norm consisted of the positive attitudes which Scouts have in common concerning woodcraft skills, forest lore, and camping activities. (General knowledge of the Scouting program, together with a preliminary comparison of Scouts' and non-Scouts' opinions, indicated that it was reasonable to assume Scouts do have group norms on these topics.) At a regular weekly meeting of each troop the Scouts answered two questionnaires, one to determine how highly they valued their membership in the troop and the other to measure their precommunication attitudes toward woodcraft activities as compared with activities characteristic of city life.

A week later an outside adult appeared before the troop and delivered a standardized communication, criticizing woodcraft activities and suggesting that in the modern world boys would profit more from learning about their cities and from various activities possible in town. Immediately after the speech the scale measuring attitudes toward woodcraft as opposed to city activities was readministered in order to determine the postcommunication attitudes. The same person who had given the questionnaire earlier asked the Scouts to answer the questions again and to indicate how they felt about the various activities after having heard the speaker. At this point however, the troop was divided into random halves. To one half the attitude scale was administered under "private" conditions, i.e., the usual assurances of anonymity and secrecy were given. To the other half it was administered under "public" conditions, i.e., the Scouts were led to expect that their responses to the questionnaire would soon be made known to other members of the troop. For the purpose of testing the present hypothesis about the relation between valuation and opinion change, we shall consider only the "private" subjects within each troop and assume that their questionnaire responses reflect their true opinions. (The private and public conditions will be compared in the next section.)

The results of this procedure were analyzed by determining the following indices for the "private" samples within each troop: 1) the average amount of change in the direction of the communication and 2) the average degree of valuation of membership. The inverse relationship specified by the hypothesis was supported by the data. For the 12 troops (private samples only), the rank order correlation between amount of change and valuation of membership was —.71, significant at the 1 per cent level of confidence, using a one-tailed test.

The net changes produced by the counternorm communication, with the different troops combined and the Scouts grouped according to their valuation of membership, are shown in Figure 7. The expected inverse relationship between valuation and change is again apparent. The low valuation members tended to change in the direction advocated by the communication (as shown by the positive net change) while the high valuation members actually changed in the opposite direction. In brief, it appears that persons who place most value upon their group membership are least influenced in the direction advocated by a counternorm communication.[3]

The results in Figure 7 suggest that the communication had a negative or boomerang effect among the high valuation Scouts. In the absence of a special control group which did not receive any communication, one cannot rule out the possibility of attributing the negative effect to the intervention of irrelevant factors during the period between the before- and after-tests. For example, the before-test may have stimulated thought and discussion about the norms and hence may have produced an increase in conformity even before the speaker appeared. While these considerations do not change the over-all conclusion about the relationship between valuation and resistance to counternorm communications, they raise some question as to whether the negative values represent a true boomerang effect. If we interpret the minus values as a boomerang effect, an important problem arises with respect to the use of counternorm communications: In

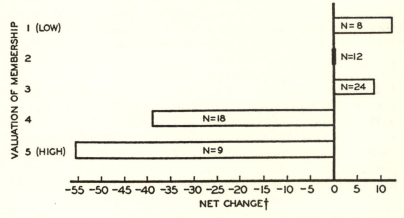

FIGURE 7. Opinion Change in Response to Counternorm Communication for Scouts with Various Degrees of Valuation of Membership.* ("Private" Samples Only.) *Data from Kelley and Volkart* [26].

 * Combining categories 1, 2, and 3 and comparing them (in terms of net change) with 4 and 5 combined, p <.02 using one-tailed test.

 † Net change equals the per cent changing in direction advocated by the communication minus the per cent changing in the opposite direction.

describing the norms in order to argue against them, the communicator may add to the recipients' knowledge of the norms and thereby heighten their conformity. The communication in the present study mentioned the general emphasis in Scouting upon outdoor activities and implied that Scout leaders do not agree with the criticism of these activities contained in the speech. This may have increased the Scouts' understanding of this norm and suggested it to be of greater importance to the organization than the boys had previously assumed. An effect of this nature would increase the tendency of the more loyal Scouts to express opinions extremely favorable to outdoor activities. The general problem posed here resembles that of presenting one side versus both sides when advocating a given point of view: Should a counternorm communication mention the norms explicitly or should it give only the counterarguments and leave the norm implied? Research has not been done on this specific aspect of the one-side versus two-side problem discussed in the preceding chapter.

Additional evidence for the correlation between valuation and change under private conditions was obtained incidentally in an investigation of salience of group membership, described later in this chapter. College students of the Catholic faith answered anonymously a questionnaire containing items related to Catholic norms. At the same time, some were exposed to a communication consisting of information about the alleged responses of other students to the questionnaire. These responses diverged from the end of the opinion continuum most acceptable to Catholics. A rough index of valuation of membership was provided by the responses to the question, "How frequently do you attend religious services?" The students indicating high valuation of membership (i.e., frequent attendance) were compared with the others, referred to here as low valuation members. Figure 8 presents separately for the high and low valuation members a comparison of those who received the communication with those

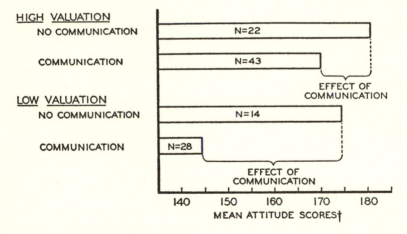

FIGURE 8. Effect of Counternorm Communication on High and Low Valuation Members.* *Data from Kelley* [25].

    * Effect of communication is larger for the low than for the high valuation members; p $<$.06 using a one-tailed test.

    † High score indicates high degree of conformity to group norms.

who did not. It can be seen that this difference is greater for the low valuation members. It appears that they were more influenced by the communication than were high valuation members.

Thus, both studies indicate that persons who most highly value their membership in a group are least influenced in their opinions by a counternorm communication. In both instances opinions were measured by responses given to questionnaires under conditions where secret and anonymous treatment of the results was assured.

Public versus Private Conditions

The public and private variations in the investigation by Kelley and Volkart were introduced to test an hypothesis about the conditions under which group norms become "internalized" (i.e., genuinely accepted and adhered to even in the absence of external social pressures). Specifically, the hypothesis is that a person internalizes the norms of a group to the degree that he finds positive attractions in holding membership in it.

From the evidence in the preceding section, it appears that resistance to counternorm communications is directly related to valuation of membership. This can be interpreted as a special case of the relation between strength of motives to conform to group norms and valuation of membership. If it can be assumed that under private conditions individuals express their true opinions, then the foregoing result suggests that the degree of acceptance (or internalization) of the norms is a function of valuation. The tenability of this crucial assumption is increased if one can demonstrate that a contrasting condition of opinion expression, such as that represented by the public variation, yields a different pattern of results.

The specific rationale for comparing public and private conditions is as follows: Consider two group members, one having internalized the group's norms and the other not. The first member expresses opinions in conformity with the norms because he has an inner conviction regarding their propriety and desirability. The second expresses conforming opinions *only* because of rewards or punishments which are delivered by others and which depend upon the degree of overt conformity he exhibits. When these two members are exposed to a counternorm communication, the resistance to change displayed in their opinion responses will be based on different factors: that of the first will depend on internal factors and that of the second, if any, will be based on external pressures. If the assumptions made above are correct and if those persons who value highly their membership in a group internalize its norms to a greater degree than those who value it little, then the resistance to change shown (in their expressed opinions) by high valuation members should depend upon internalized factors to a greater extent than the resistance displayed by low valuation members.

It might further be assumed that the private condition of attitude expression, by and large, involves only internal controls, while the public condition involves both internal and external controls.[4] If the resistance to change of high valuation members is based upon internalized controls to a greater degree than that of low valuation members, then the difference between the "highs" and "lows" in their resistance to change (as measured by responses to the questionnaire) should be greater under the private condition. In other words, the negative correlation between amount of change and valuation of membership should be greater under private than under public conditions.

Evidence pertaining to this hypothesis was obtained from the study of Boy Scouts' attitudes. As noted in the preceding section, for the private samples of the 12 troops, the rank order correlation between amount of change and valuation of membership was −.71. For the public samples the corresponding correlation was +.35 (not significantly different from zero). These two coefficients are significantly different from each other. Table 12 presents separately for the public and private conditions the amount of net change for the various degrees of valuation. An inverse relation between valuation and change appears with fair consistency under the private condition but is not apparent under the public one.

The evidence appears to support the hypothesis concerning a stronger inverse relation between valuation and change under private conditions than under public. However, in Table 12 it can be seen that there was greater over-all change under the public condition than under the private. This is inconsistent with the earlier assumption

TABLE 12. *Opinion Change under Public and Private Conditions, for Various Degrees of Valuation of Membership*

Degree of Valuation of Membership *	N	Public Net Change †	N	Private Net Change †
1 (low)	9	−11.1%	8	+12.5%
2	12	+41.7	12	0.0
3	18	+33.3	24	+ 8.4
4	17	+29.4	18	−38.9
5 (high)	18	− 5.6	9	−55.5
Total	74	+19.0%	71	−12.7%

* Combining categories 1, 2, and 3 and comparing them (in terms of net change) with 4 and 5 combined: for private sample, $p < .02$ using a one-tailed test; for public sample, $p = .24$ using a one-tailed test.
† Net change equals the per cent changing in direction advocated by the communication minus the per cent changing in the opposite direction.

From Kelley and Volkart [26]

that the private condition arouses only internal sources of resistance to change whereas the public condition arouses *both* internal and external sources. If this assumption is violated, is it reasonable to interpret the differential correlation between valuation and change for the two experimental conditions as indicative of greater internalization on the part of the high valuation members? A close examination of the public instructions suggests that they may have heightened the resistance to change, as planned, but at the same time produced an increased pressure to change. The latter could readily have resulted from perceptions that some of the powerful adults present who favored the speech (the speaker's assistants and possibly some of the Scout officials) would know the extent to which each boy conformed to it. Thus, whereas the theoretical analysis above assumes that the public condition merely heightened the external pressures on the low valuation members to resist the communication, this condition may also have heightened the external pressure on all members to conform to the communication. This would account for the tendency for high valuation members to exhibit increased change under public conditions. The low valuation members, influenced by both kinds of pressure, would show less increase from public to private conditions. If this interpretation of the inconsistency is correct, the evidence can be regarded as supporting the hypothesis that internalization of group norms is greater for persons who place high value on their membership than for low valuation members.

IMPLICATIONS

INTERNALIZATION

The various findings presented in the preceding section, considered together, tend to be consistent with the hypothesis that there is a direct relationship between positive attachment to a group and internalization of its norms. Some such relationship seems generally acknowledged in theoretical discussions of internalization and of the related concept of "identification" [*18, 38, 43, 47*]. However, relatively little is known about the processes which underlie this relationship as it occurs in adolescent or adult groups. In this connection, suggestive leads may be provided by psychoanalytic discussions of identification and related mechanisms involved in the child's internalization of the values of loved persons ([*17*]; [*34*] pp. 573–616).

Earlier in this chapter we have distinguished three main conditions underlying motivation for maintaining membership: 1) positive attractions of the group due to opportunities to satisfy personal goals through membership, 2) opportunities to avoid external dangers and unpleasantness by maintaining membership, and 3) presence of restraints acting to keep the person within the group and under its power. The evidence on valuation of membership in the preceding section suggests that the first of these factors facilitates internalization; we may next inquire as to whether the other two factors play any part in this phenomenon. On this point there are few findings and several conflicting views which we shall review briefly.

While subscribing to the view that positive attachment to the group produces internalization (or what is termed "private acceptance"), Festinger [*13*] contends that this is the *only* relation to the group which brings about this effect. He believes that the other two conditions, both of which involve danger or punishment, bring about public compliance but not private acceptance. The latter is thought to occur only by virtue of a positive desire on the part of the person to maintain the existing relationship with those attempting to influence him.

A contradictory view with regard to the role of physical restraints and punishment in producing internalization is provided by the psychoanalytic conception of "identification with the aggressor" (cf. Anna Freud [*17*]). This mechanism seems to be a defensive reaction which depends upon threat and anxiety rather than upon affection alone. Taking the example of a child being disciplined by a powerful, punishing parent, Mowrer ([*34*] pp. 588 ff.) asserts that if the child "sides" with or pretends to be the parent, he has much less reason to fear the parent. The conflict between the child's infantile desires and the social prohibitions disappears and his anxiety abates. With the development of this "defensive identification," the child takes on the necessary restraints, attitudes, or values which enable him to keep his unacceptable impulses under control.[5]

While avoiding conflict in this manner could conceivably account for internalization in the absence of any affection or positive regard for the source, its effects would certainly be heightened by such attitudes. The severity of punishment meted out by the members of a group is greatly increased if it involves the threat of loss of love and support. One of the crucial questions, as we have seen, is whether such positive regard, often one component of an ambivalent attitude, is a necessary condition for internalization.

A complicating factor in answering this question by examining everyday life situations is that if a person's interactions are restricted to the members of a given group he is likely to develop affection for them and come to depend upon their opinions. Most persons need social support for certain of their opinions and particularly for their opinions of themselves. At the same time, most people probably find it difficult to continue to obtain such support from groups which are absent for long periods of time. When a person is removed from the groups he loves and is forcibly placed among strangers, he gradually loses his feelings of being supported by his former associates and comes to depend upon the opinions of the immediately present persons for his feelings of dignity and self-esteem.

An extremely important problem for future research and theoretical development is the investigation of these and other processes which may underlie internalization and an analysis of the conditions favoring each. A thorough specification of the pertinent factors may eliminate some of the apparent disagreements among present views of internalization. For example, we have seen that Festinger stresses the value of positive attachment to the group whereas the "defensive identification" theory seems to indicate the importance of restraints and punishment. These views may be compatible if we take account of different levels of drive strength and different degrees of severity of the inhibiting measures. Festinger is primarily concerned with influence occurring in peer groups. In such groups there rarely exist the strong impulses and the severely restrictive social influences which characterize the childhood training situation and which seem to be necessary for defensive identification. In other types of adult or adolescent groups, however, this mechanism may, under extreme circumstances, play an important role in attitude change. The report by Bettelheim [5], mentioned earlier (p. 82), describes how the prisoners in a German concentration camp identified with the extremely aggressive and punitive guards to the extent of trying to simulate their appearance, enforcing rules long forgotten by the guards, and accepting some of their views which were strongly resisted previously. Similar effects might be found to occur in more "normal" circumstances if the person is extremely powerless in relation to a group or if he is limited physically or socially to contact with its members. The implications of this mechanism for opinion change remain to be explored.

Social Status and Resistance to Influence

We have seen some evidence that a person's conformity to group norms is directly related to how highly he values his membership. This relationship may be considerably altered by other factors related to conformity, particularly those which affect the amount of social pressure exerted upon the individual and the degree of freedom he feels with respect to nonconformity. One of the most important of these factors is likely to be the individual's status within the group. We shall now consider the possibility that, however much he may value the group, a person of high status will, under certain conditions, deviate from its norms and accept a communication which advocates an unorthodox point of view.

A possible assumption here would be that conformity depends not only upon the importance of the group for the individual but also upon his expectations about the rewards or punishments that will follow any given degree of deviation from the standards. It seems likely that the sanctions for nonconformity are applied with differential force to the various members of a group. Not all members contribute equally to the well-being of a group—some bring to it much more than their share of the abilities, knowledge, and possessions which promote its success and welfare. These persons, whose presence and participation are highly valued by the other members (and who, in that sense, have high status), may be permitted greater nonconformity before receiving rebukes or rejection. Presumably, the person becomes aware of how highly other members value his membership, and this affects the amount of security he feels in his relations with them or the amount of power over the group he perceives himself to possess.[6] It would seem reasonable, on these grounds, to propose the hypothesis that the more highly a person is valued by the other members the more tolerance will be shown his deviations from the group norms and therefore the greater freedom he will feel in accepting communications contrary to them. In other words, the higher the person's social rank in the group, the less will be his anxiety concerning nonconformity.

This hypothesis would be difficult to test. Note that it has to do with the person's awareness of his freedom to deviate and not his willingness. Several considerations indicate that the more valued person may actually have stronger conformity motives than the less valued one. For example, the more valued member should have greater influence upon the activities and norms of the group and, consequently, shape them more closely in line with his own interests and attitudes. Furthermore, the position of high value in a group may be especially satisfying because it permits a broad range of activities and yields various satisfactions not available to persons in less valued positions. To the extent that this is true, persons who are highly regarded will place greater value upon their membership and, therefore will display greater conformity to group norms.

A related hypothesis would apply in instances where the person believes that he can retain his high rank only as long as he continues to conform to the existing norms. Persons in positions of high conferred status may tend to conform to the group norms to a higher degree than the rank-and-file members, because the role expectations for these positions are stronger and more exacting than the expectations impinging upon ordinary members. We would expect this to be particularly true in groups where these persons of high rank are used as the comparison points or models to exemplify the norms of the group.

These considerations indicate that correlations between how highly the group values a person and his conformity will generally be positive. The suggested hypothesis would merely be that, as compared with others, the person of high value to the group will be freer to deviate from the group norms *if he wishes to.* This freedom will only be apparent on certain occasions such as, for example, when a communication from outside the group makes him dissatisfied with internal conditions and convinces him of the need for innovations. In those situations it would be expected that, as compared with other members, he will feel able to govern his behavior more in accord with his personal reactions to the arguments and conclusion of the communication and less in accord with the demands of the group.

Relatively little research data bear directly upon this problem. Hughes [22] gives an anecdotal report of an industrial work group in which the degree of conformity required of a member appeared to be inversely related to the extent to which he was accepted by the others. A clique of long-tenure employees had established a production norm to which new employees were required to conform. Hughes observed that as a newcomer gained acceptance, conformity pressures were relaxed; the "well-established" worker could consistently "break" the rate to some degree without receiving the severe punishment given for similar deviations to workers who were as yet unaccepted.

Relevant correlational evidence is provided by Newcomb [36] in his study of the degree to which various members of a small college community accepted the norm of liberalism in political and economic attitudes. Newcomb used as a measure of community prestige the frequency with which each person was nominated to represent the college at an intercollegiate gathering. This measure was found to be highly correlated with popularity (which can be regarded as one type of social rank) and with number and importance of college positions held. In terms of conformity to the community norm, greater prestige was associated with greater liberalism and also with greater increase in liberalism. In other words, persons who attained the highest prestige in the community changed their opinions most in the direction of its norms.

Evidence on popularity as it correlates with resistance to change was obtained by Kelley and Volkart in their investigation of Boy Scouts' attitudes. Popularity, measured in terms of frequency of choice as a friend by one's associates, was inversely related to the amount of change produced by the communication. In other words, the more popular boys offered more resistance to the attempt to change their group-anchored attitudes than did the less popular ones ($p = .04$ under private conditions and .08 under public). Thus, popularity had much the same relation to resistance to change of the group-anchored attitudes as did valuation of membership. The measures of popularity and valuation did not, however, turn out to be correlated significantly in the present study.

In brief, correlational analysis indicates that persons of high prestige and popularity hold attitudes in conformity with the prevailing norms and are highly resistant to external influence contrary to those norms. This apparently contradicts the suggested hypothesis that the higher the person's social rank the more freedom he will feel to accept counternorm communications. However, this result may indicate either *a*) that the effects of the felt freedom that accompanies high social rank are not evident in static correlations (as mentioned earlier) or *b*) that the person with high rank feels that his status is highly dependent upon his conformity with group norms rather than upon his contribution to the group.

The latter possibility is specifically raised by Newcomb who suggests that persons who desired prestige in the college community found it necessary to conform to the norms. Additional evidence in line with this explanation is provided by Schachter's experimental study of the relation between popularity and conformity [*39*]. He investigated the effect upon sociometric status of deviation from group consensus.

Trained confederates were introduced into discussion groups and they proceeded to deviate from the consensus of opinion in standard ways. Analysis of the subsequent pattern of communication and sociometric choice indicated that with consistent nonconformity a confederate's popularity declined markedly. This suggests that sociometric status is awarded, at least in part, on the basis of social conformity. To the extent that this is true, the continuation of popularity depends upon visibly conforming to group norms. We should not expect this kind of status to be related positively to feelings of freedom to deviate.

Viewing popularity as a status contingent upon conformity gives meaning to the correlations obtained by Kelley and Volkart among popularity, valuation of membership, and resistance to change. Popularity is probably valued by most group members and, as indicated by Schachter's study, probably depends upon their conformity to social norms. In order to maintain the social approval and satisfactions associated with high popularity, we would expect the popular person to adhere more closely to social norms than the less popular one. In such cases, popularity will be positively correlated with resistance to change. The lack of relation between popularity and valuation suggests that the satisfactions associated with high popularity—being in the limelight, being well known, and having many speaking acquaintances—are different from the satisfactions derived from membership in general which include intimate friendships, participation in a program of activities, being in a successful and prestigeful group. Thus, a member enjoying the satisfactions of popularity need not be among those members who are most satisfied with the other aspects of membership.

In summary, one particular aspect of social rank, popularity, has been found to be positively correlated with conformity and resistance to counternorm communications. Some additional evidence suggests that conformity is required of popular members if they are to retain their rank. However, there is little experimental evidence one way or the other on the hypothesis that the higher a member's power position (or the more valued he is) the greater his freedom to accept ideas contrary to the norms of the group. As indicated above, correlational analysis of the relation between rank and conformity is likely to be confounded by natural relations between rank and 1) valuation of membership and 2) control over norm setting. A controlled experiment may provide the only means of disentangling these variables.

A suggestion as to how this might be done is provided by Sherif's investigation of hostility between experimentally formed groups [*42*]. A number of boys without prior acquaintance were brought together in a summer camp and divided into two competitive groups. By observation and sociometric techniques it was possible to determine the social rankings which developed within each group with respect to popularity and power. Note was also taken of the development of norms within each group and conformity of the various members. While the data were not collected specifically to test the hypothesis being considered here, several suggestive results emerged. For one thing, it was evident that the popularity rankings did not correspond perfectly with the power hierarchies within the groups; several boys exerted greater influence over group affairs than would have been expected from their popularity ranks. Secondly, on several occasions it was observed that low status members were especially zealous in their conformity to group norms, apparently attempting to gain recognition in this manner. This is consistent with the inverse relationship between status and conformity which was hypothesized earlier.

In general, this is an important area for future research particularly as it bears upon the problem of producing opinion change through communications. If our analysis is correct, we would expect the person most highly valued by the group generally to be as resistant to change as the less valued person. However, we would also expect the person of high rank to be more easily changed *independently of changes occurring among other members of the group*. Thus, he may prove to be a strategic person to approach in initiating opinion change among the members of a large group. (For a related discussion, cf. Merton [*32*].) The hypothesis also has interesting implications for the freedom of group members to initiate innovations and internal change. One of the problems here is to determine the conditions under which such innovations come primarily from the least satisfied members at the periphery of the group and the conditions under which changes originate with persons in central positions who are thoroughly familiar with the operations and needs of the total organization.

PART II: *Situational Cues and Salience of Membership*

BACKGROUND

An individual's potential conformity is determined by his knowledge of group norms and by the types of predispositional factors discussed in the foregoing section—valuation of membership and social status. But in any specific situation the actual conformity will depend somewhat upon situational cues which evoke the relevant motives and knowledge. Understanding of the operation of these situational factors is particularly important in investigations of communication effectiveness, because communications are largely dependent upon the proper manipulation of cues. The phenomenon we have singled out for consideration has to do with situational variations in the degree to which symbols or "reminders" of the group are present, and the effects of these variations upon the person's resistance to counternorm communications. Underlying this phenomenon is the fact that a person typically belongs to a number of different groups, all of which exert some sort of influence over his attitudes. In addition, other groups, individuals, and impersonal factors influence his opinions. These various social and nonsocial influences rarely act in concert but usually affect different opinions or act upon the same opinions in different ways. In any given situation, conformity is likely to depend upon the extent to which the cues associated with a given membership successfully compete with other cues in the person's environment, capture his attention, and consequently arouse his conformity motives.

We shall refer to the degree to which, in a given situation, a specific group is present and prominent in a person's "awareness" as the *salience* of that group. In some instances high salience will correspond to presence in the center of the person's attention, but we do not wish to restrict the notion to instances where there is a fully conscious or reportable awareness of the group. We shall also disregard possible differences in the salience of the various aspects of the group or its norms and speak simply of salience of the group as a whole, on the tentative assumption that salience of any aspect of the group heightens the tendency to conform to its norms at that particular time.

Several theoretical discussions deal with this phenomenon, but only recently has it been investigated experimentally.[7] Charters and Newcomb [9] studied the effects of the immediate situation on expressed opinions under conditions where no communications were presented. They administered an attitude questionnaire to three comparable groups of Roman Catholics under the following conditions: 1) in a large class with many other students, 2) in a small group by themselves but with no mention of their church membership or of the reason for their being together, and 3) in a small group by themselves where, before answering the questionnaire, they were told that they had been called together as Catholics in order to obtain their help in constructing a questionnaire on religious beliefs and were asked to discuss some of the "basic assumptions" behind the opinions of all Catholics. In the last variation, the common religious affiliation of all subjects in the room was repeatedly emphasized.

In all three variations the subjects anonymously answered an opinion questionnaire. This questionnaire contained a number of critical items related to Catholic norms but so worded that they could also be answered by the subjects in their roles as members of other groups. The results showed that subjects in the third variation answered these critical items more in the manner prescribed for Catholics than did subjects in the other two variations.

There is some ambiguity as to whether this result is, as the authors suggest, due simply to "heightening the individual's awareness of his membership in the specified group by vivid reminders of this membership" (p. 415). First is the possibility that the initial discussion in the third variation gave the subjects a clearer idea of how Catholics should feel about certain issues. Charters and Newcomb attempted to minimize this through instructions to their discussion leaders. Another possibility is that there were tendencies to answer as "good" Catholics, because of anticipations, for example, that outsiders would view the data with respect to how uniformly Catholics adhered to their church's norms. Again, the investigators attempted to eliminate this possibility through instructions to the subjects, and they conclude from their findings that "an individual's expression of attitudes is a function of the relative momentary potency of his relevant group memberships" (p. 420).

If, as this suggests, situational cues affect the opinions a person expresses, they also affect his resistance to counternorm communications. It would seem reasonable to assume that the salience of a group determines its availability as a possible source of resistance to change, the strength of the resistance being determined by other factors such as how highly membership is valued. However, if a group is not salient in a given situation, it can provide no support for attitudes no matter how highly it is valued. If a group is divided into comparable halves and group membership is highly salient for one half and not for the other, we should expect a higher frequency of resistance to counternorm communications in the highly salient half; but within both halves there might be some persons to whom the group is of so little concern that under no circumstances would they offer resistance based on group loyalty.

RESEARCH EVIDENCE

SALIENCE AND RESISTANCE TO CHANGE

An experiment by Kelley investigated the relation between salience of a group and resistance to a counternorm communication [25]. In addition, the procedure was designed so as to determine whether the phenomenon would appear under conditions where subjects are mixed together in terms of their religious affiliations and are not told that this factor is involved in the investigation. The following hypothesis was tested: When group-anchored attitudes are exposed to counterpressures, their resistance to change at the particular time will be greater with high salience of the relevant group than with low.

With the above purposes in mind, attitudes of members of the Roman Catholic Church were studied within high school and college age groups. The experiment was conducted during their regular class sessions when members of all religious faiths were present and when, because of cues which arouse competing loyalties and interests, the salience of any particular religious affiliation could be expected to be lower than when cues to that religion are present. The students were first given short readings, followed by an opinion questionnaire. The readings were different for different samples of students, some receiving material intended to heighten the salience of Catholic Church membership and others receiving unrelated "neutral" material. The salience-heightening material described the leader of the Catholic Church and some of the church's functions, but carefully avoided any reference to those church norms related to items contained in the subsequent opinion questionnaire. The neutral material described public figures and organizations having no relation to the Catholic Church.

Following the reading, all subjects were given a questionnaire. This contained items which were related to certain Catholic norms but were carefully selected so as to involve other roles and memberships and to heighten the salience of Catholic membership as little as possible. The items had to do with such issues as censorship of books and movies, parental control over children with regard to choice of beliefs, and traditionalism in religious practices. In addition, two out of every three of the subjects received, as part of the questionnaire, a communication intended to modify their opinion responses. This was done by including for each item in their questionnaires information purporting to give the opinion of the typical student at the same level in school. The "typical opinions" were indicated at positions fairly divergent from those most acceptable to Catholics and thus constituted a counternorm communication for them.

Through appropriate combinations of these materials, two main experimental conditions were created: 1) communication, high salience; and 2) communication, low salience. In addition, an experimental condition with no communication and high salience was created in order to check on the effectiveness of the communication. A random procedure was used for assigning subjects to each experimental variation, so the subjects within the three samples can be assumed to be comparable initially, within the limits of sampling error. The basic data consisted of a comparison of the attitudes expressed by members of various religious groups under these conditions, the questionnaire providing an immediate after-test of the experimental treatments. The results for the high school students are presented in Figure 9, where higher scores represent closer conformity to what are prejudged to be Catholic norms. The validity of this prejudgment is apparent in Figure 9 from the fact that for the no communication, high salience variation the Catholic subjects showed significantly higher scores than the non-Catholic subjects. While there are clear differences between the two religious classifications, the communication represented such extreme positions on the issues raised in the questionnaire that it operated to shift the responses of non-Catholics as well as Catholics. The evidence reveals that the communication produced statistically significant effects for both religious classifications.

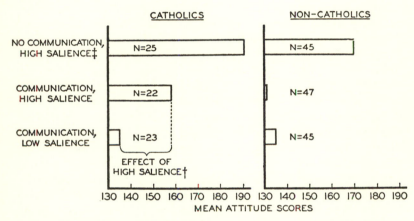

FIGURE 9. The Effects on Mean Attitude Scores * of Variations in Salience of Catholic Membership for High School Students. *From Kelley* [25].
* A high score indicates high conformity to Catholic norms.
† For the difference between the communication, high salience sample and the communication, low salience sample, p <.05 using a one-tailed test.
‡ Catholics vs. non-Catholics, p <.01.

The expectation of greater resistance to change for the Catholic subjects with high salience of their church than for those with low is borne out by the data in Figure 9. Of the Catholics receiving the communication, those for whom the church was highly salient showed higher attitude scores than those for whom it was not. Subjects of other religious affiliations who received the communication expressed much the same attitudes whether receiving the salience-arousing materials or not, which is to be expected because the salience of the Catholic Church is not relevant to their attitude anchorage.

The results from the college subjects do not support the hypothesis even though identical procedures were carried out with the two age groups. There were differences between the Catholics and non-Catholics in opinions expressed, and the communication was effective for both groups. However, the experimental variation intended to produce differences in salience of Catholic membership failed to produce any differences in the Catholics' resistance to the communication.

Several factors might account for the apparent ineffectiveness of the experimental procedures intended to produce variations in salience of church membership for the college students. One possibility is that the Catholics sampled in a metropolitan college include large numbers who have drifted away from their church and feel little attachment to it. If so, heightening the salience of church membership may have little or no effect on their expressed opinions or resistance to counternorm ideas. Another possibility is that Catholic college students are more sophisticated about how various controversial issues relate to the norms of their church, so that the questions on the opinion scale may have heightened the salience for all subjects and thus eliminated the differences created by the reading materials. As compared with a sample of high school students, a sample of college-age Catholics would probably include more persons in both of these categories—those who have lost their earlier attachment to the church and those who have gained in awareness of the various implications of the church's norms. If these factors operated in the present case to attenuate the effects of the experimental salience-arousing cues, the phenomenon obtained with the high school students may appear only for persons of high valuation of membership and relatively low sophistication about relevant opinion issues.

In summary, this study provides partial confirmation of the hypothesis that, other factors operating at an appropriate level, the resistance to change of group-anchored attitudes is directly related to the degree of salience of the group. The results from the experimental procedure indicate that for high school students, while in their classes, salience of membership in the Catholic Church can be heightened by brief reading materials which described the church's leader, symbols, and functions. However, the same procedure did not appear to have a similar effect for Catholics in college classes.

RETENTION OF CHANGES PRODUCED UNDER HIGH AND LOW SALIENCE

The data presented above suggest that a communication will produce more immediate change when the opposing group norms are at a low level of salience than when they are highly salient. In terms of the strategy of mass communication, this might indicate that when group anchorage must be overcome the communicator would be wise to approach his listeners at a time when the pertinent group is in the background and they are preoccupied with other loyalties and interests.

However, the problem immediately arises as to the fate, with the passage of time, of changes produced under these conditions. When the group becomes salient in subsequent situations, we would expect the resistance to the communication to be restored and to produce a reversion to the old attitudes. This would eliminate the difference in final attitudes between persons initially with low salience and those initially with high. Later on we shall see that there are also reasons for expecting changes produced under conditions fostering low salience to be maintained *less well* than those produced under conditions fostering high salience.

The expectations discussed above would be contrary to the usual finding that the greater the immediate effect of a communication the greater its long-run effects. This last consideration would imply that if low salience makes for greater opinion change at the time of the communication, it would also yield greater delayed effects.

Evidence pertaining to the retention of initial changes was obtained from the high school students in the study of salience described above. The opinion questionnaire (given initially under the three conditions of 1) no communication, high salience; 2) communication, high salience; and 3) communication, low salience) was readministered three days later under uniform conditions of no communication, high salience. For the Catholic students initially receiving the communication, a comparison of the high and low salience samples is shown in Figure 10. It can be seen that both samples made large shifts on the delayed after-test in the direction of greater conformity with Catholic norms.

The size of this shift over the three-day interval was virtually identical for those given the communication initially under low salience and those exposed under high. In addition, it is apparent that the highs had returned to the level of the control (no communication) sample while the low salience sample still showed a sizable effect of the original communication.

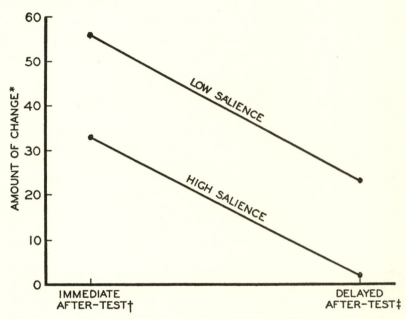

FIGURE 10. Retention over Three-day Interval of Opinion Changes Produced under Conditions of High and Low Salience. *Data from Kelley* [25].
* Amount of change equals the difference between the sample initially receiving the communication (either high or low salience) and the sample receiving none.
† For difference between high and low salience samples, p <.05 using one-tailed test.
‡ For difference between high and low salience samples, p = .06 using two-tailed test.

Thus the results bear out the common observation that the greater the initial change the greater the opinion change shown on subsequent occasions. There is no evidence that when changes are induced under conditions of low salience the subjects completely revert to the initial position. While this may possibly occur for certain classes of attitudes and situations, it is not important under the conditions represented here. It is possible, of course, that with such a short time interval between the immediate and delayed tests the subjects did not encounter pro-norm opinions or become aware of their nonconformity. A more rigorous test of the persistence of opinion changes induced under high and low salience conditions will require procedures to insure that subjects become aware of their nonconformity and are exposed to pro-norm communications following the original influence situation.

IMPLICATIONS

The effects of the situational cues discussed in the foregoing section undoubtedly depend upon the predispositional factors which have been the central concern of this chapter. For example, whether or not cues elicit conformity depends upon whether or not the individual values his membership enough to find satisfaction in being like the other members and maintaining their approval. Situational cues will be relatively ineffective in producing conformity if, because of his group status, the individual feels considerable freedom to deviate from the norms and finds that other considerations compel him to hold a deviant point of view. The specific kind of conformity behavior elicited by "reminders" of membership will be a function of the person's knowledge or beliefs about the kind of behavior that is expected and approved. In brief, the analysis of a group member's resistance to counternorm communications must take account of *both* the predispositions related to conformity and the situational cues which serve to elicit them.

One of the ways that situational cues can operate is to heighten the individual's awareness (salience) of his membership in a given group. The postulation of some such process appears necessary to account for the evidence that under certain conditions cues of a group seem to increase the individual's resistance to persuasive communications contrary to the group's norms. When such cues are absent, counternorm communications have greater immediate effects upon opinions and, at least under the conditions of the present research, appear to produce more lasting changes. Of particular interest for further investigation is the problem of determining the conditions which affect the persistence of opinion changes produced under high and low salience. The results reported above indicate that under certain circumstances the greater immediate change made possible by low salience also appears at a later time. Under other circumstances, particularly where persons become sharply aware of their nonconformity after being influenced by the communication, a complete loss of the change might be expected.

Several other theories would suggest not merely that the greater change produced under low salience will be completely lost but that the end result will be a kind of boomerang effect with the low salience condition giving rise to less persistent change than the high salience condition. One possibility of this sort is that subsequent situations of high salience may produce guilt and anxiety among those persons initially low if they become aware of having been caught off guard and seduced into deviating markedly from the group norms. One way of alleviating this guilt and of warding off possible social punishment for the nonconformity is to conform more closely to the group norms than ever before. As a result, persons exposed to low salience conditions (and hence most influenced initially by the counternorm communication) would finally be more in conformity with the norms (and less in agreement with the communication) than those exposed to high salience conditions.

A second mechanism would have almost the same end effect. If during the communication situation the resistance stemming from the group can be aroused and dealt with, then the likelihood is increased that the change will endure through later situations where the group happens to be salient (cf. discussion of one-sided versus two-sided presentations, pp. 105 to 111). The problem becomes one of providing the person with a method either for resolving the conflict between the appeals of the communication and the counterpressures of the group or for becoming adapted to it. This may involve revaluation of the group, redefining the issue, resigning oneself to a special role or position in the group, and so on. It may also be useful to prepare him for the social criticism that his new views will eventually evoke. He may be shown how to justify his nonconformity by relating it to other norms or by citing precedents, or he may be taught certain acts and sentences which will aid other people in making the discrimination between his nonconformity on a specific issue and his general conformity with respect to other group norms. The assumption here is simply that when a person changes an attitude in full awareness of the norm that has supported the old position, the reorganization produced will tend to have a better chance of enduring than one produced without such awareness. Accordingly, changes produced under high salience would endure more than those produced under low. This and other hypotheses related to the persistence of changes brought about under various conditions of salience require further experimental analysis.

Notes

1. Taking account of the different phenomena to which the term "reference group" has been applied, a distinction has been made elsewhere [24] between the two major sets of functions that reference groups serve in producing conforming behavior: 1) the "normative" functions of "pointing to" norms and of providing the incentives for conformity to them; and 2) the "comparison" function of exemplifying the norms or providing a comparison point against which the individual can evaluate his own or others' behavior. Conformity behavior on the part of a group member is usually a consequence of the fact that the group has performed both sets of functions for him: the other members have communicated to him that certain behavior is "expected," have given him approval or disapproval according to how well he has met the expectations, and have exemplified the expected pattern by means of their own behavior. In some cases one or more of these functions are performed by groups of which the individual is not a member.

The notion of "reference group" has been developed to cover *all* instances where groups, either membership or nonmembership, serve these functions of *enforcing* standards or *being* standards. The central assumption is that the same basic dynamic factors underlie a group's ability to evoke conformity motives, whether from its members or from other persons. Similarly, the general factors involved in the use of one's associates as comparison points are the same as those related to using members of other groups.

For example, reference group concepts are intended to apply to cases where the membership group enforces conformity to a standard which is exemplified by the behavior of members of a different group. It is not uncommon, especially in upwardly mobile social classes, for parents to set as standards for their children the behavior and circumstances of persons outside the family, with whom contact is minimal. In other cases a child may be informed by his parents that conformity to the norms of an outside group will lead to rejection or loss of approval from the family. The outside group, referred to as a negative reference group, may then serve as a negative comparison point for the child; when he learns that an attitude or behavior is distinctively characteristic of the negative reference group, he will tend to reject the attitude or behavior and even exhibit the opposite.

Occasionally, a group in which a person does not hold membership serves both the normative and comparison functions. One important case where this appears to be true is that of low status persons who desire membership in a high status group. Research on these persons strongly suggests that they are motivated to share the attitudes of the high status group even without having attained mem-

166

bership in it [*14*]. A businessman who desires membership in an elite social club may regard the behavior of its members as providing an example for him to follow, evaluate his own behavior in terms of how similar it is to that of the members, and anticipate reward or punishment (invitation or rejection) on the basis of the degree of this similarity.

Although much interest has been focused on reference *groups*, it is clear that not only groups but individuals can serve the same functions, i.e., act as communicators of standards, conformity enforcers, and comparison points. Persons who are important to an individual for any reason can specify the behavior they desire of him and promise rewards or threaten penalties to insure fulfillment of that behavior. There are other important instances where, independently of others' opinions, the individual sets goals for himself and proceeds to discipline himself according to the adequacy with which those goals are reached.

In the future, the theory gradually developing around the idea of "reference group" should be broadened so as to take account of different types of judgmental standards and their various sources. The normative aspects of reference groups will, it is hoped, be related eventually to more general theories of goal setting and motivation, including the processes whereby the individual sets his own standards and enforces them upon himself. The comparison functions of reference groups will be related to general theories of perception and judgment such as the current conceptions of "frames of reference" and judgmental scales (cf. Helson [*21*], and Volkmann [*46*]). Given these more general developments, "reference group" theory promises to occupy an important position in the social sciences, relating sociological theories of social control, group roles, and communication, on the one hand, to psychological theories of motivation, symbolic processes, and frames of reference in perception and judgment, on the other.

2. The degree of conformity shown by a member will depend, of course, upon his expectations of being rewarded for conformity and of being punished for nonconformity. Thus, conformity motives depend in part upon the pattern of formal and informal sanctions applied within the group. The more severe the formal punishments and the stronger other members' reactions to deviancy, the stronger will be the individual member's tendencies to conform and resist counterinfluence. These social reactions or pressures toward conformity depend, in turn, upon various circumstances within and around the group. For example, they have been shown to depend upon the cohesiveness of the group [*39*], the external demands upon the group for uniformity of opinion [*16*], and the importance or relevance of any given norm to the life and success of the group [*39*]. Apparently the sanctions for conformity are also applied differentially to the various members of a group, depending upon such considerations as their tenure [*22*], their position in the communication network of the group, and their social status. The last factor is discussed more fully on pp. 149 to 154.

Concerning the factor of importance: when a given norm is important to the group great pressure will be exerted on a member to conform and he will come to perceive its importance. The perceived importance of any given norm will depend upon the extent to which it is emphasized and discussed within the group, the degree to which surveillance is maintained over the relevant behavior, and the quantity and quality of direct incentives used to produce conformity. As regards surveillance, conformity should be greatest in those areas where surveillance is most complete and where the delivery of sanctions is most immediate. One of the most usual cues as to the importance of conformity on a given issue is the degree of unanimity among the members. The greater the unanimity, the more likely it is that deviant behavior will be noticed and conforming behavior rewarded. Consequently the greater the unanimity perceived by any given member, the stronger will be his motives to conform.

3. As an alternative interpretation, this negative relationship might be explained by assuming that the questions on "valuation of troop" measure the same attitudes as those measured by the attitude scale. If this were true, members receiving high valuation scores would also have the most favorable initial attitudes toward woodcraft activities and hence might be expected to be least influenced by the antiwoodcraft communication; thus the apparent relationship between valuation and resistance to change would be an artifact of differences in initial opinion. However, the data reveal an absence of correlation between valuation scores and precommunication attitudes, and this fact reduces the likelihood that this alternative interpretation is correct.

4. This distinction between public and private conditions of attitude expression parallels certain usages in the literature. In a classic study of attitudes among various religious groups, Schanck [40] found considerable divergence between public and private views on the proper form of baptism. In a study of conflicting social norms, Stouffer [45] compared one situation where the subject's resolution of the conflict was unknown to the people supporting one of the norms with another situation where there was some likelihood that they would discover it. Doob ([12] pp. 39–40) has distinguished between internal public opinion (the attitudes people "really" possess) and external public opinion (the actual expression of these attitudes). Most recently Gorden [19] has shown how acutely aware a person is of the presence of other group members when he is asked to express his own opinion publicly. He finds that "The typical pattern is for the individual to compromise between his private opinion and his conception of the group opinion when expressing his public opinion" (p. 58). The central idea in these distinctions is that openly expressed opinions are subjected to different pressures than are unexpressed opinions or those expressed under conditions of anonymity (cf. discussion of opinion measures, pp. 8–9). These pressures are social in character and serve to facilitate socially acceptable expressions and to inhibit socially unacceptable ones.

5. Necessary conditions for this type of internalization appear to be: 1) the recipient of the influence must have a sustained and strong impulse to behave in

a manner opposite that specified by the influencer, and 2) the source of the influence must have sustained power and repeatedly arouse strong anticipations that failure to conform in the specified manner will lead to punishment. These conditions imply that the recipient is in a conflict which he cannot resolve by escape or compromise, or by adequately satisfying his own impulses. The possibility of a solution through alternation between impulse gratification (when the punishing agent is absent) and conformity (when the agent is present) is not psychologically available because the consequences of "being caught" are extreme and anticipations of punishment are omnipresent. Hence the person exists in a continuing state of conflict and anxiety. This he finally avoids by taking sides with the influencer and by denying or suppressing his own impulses.

6. Evidence bearing on these assumptions is provided by Lippitt, Polansky, and Rosen [*31*]. Summarizing a series of investigations in boys' camps, they report that there is considerable agreement among the boys in their judgments of "who is able to get others to do what he wants them to." Boys who are frequently judged in this manner (the authors describe them as having "attributed power") are found to have certain physical, intellectual, and social abilities which seem to account for this evaluation. They find that most group members correctly perceive the degree to which they have such power within the group and that they tend to use this power in successfully influencing the behavior of other members. Most relevant to our present consideration is that they are also *less receptive to direct influence coming from others within the group.* Unfortunately for our purposes, this excellent series of studies has little evidence on conformity to the patterned social influences that constitute group norms and no evidence relevant to resistance to counternorm communications.

7. Discussions relevant to salience are to be found in a symposium on inconsistencies in attitudes and behavior [*10*]. It is well-known that expressed attitudes vary from situation to situation and often exhibit apparent inconsistencies. In analyzing the contributing factors several theorists suggest that inconsistencies may stem from situational fluctuations in the relative contributions of overlapping social roles and memberships.

In their recent textbook on social psychology, Eugene and Ruth Hartley discuss the problem of "evoking specific reference groups" ([*20*] pp. 478–480). They describe several investigations, such as, for example, the studies of "interviewer effect" in public opinion polling, which can be interpreted in terms of the particular group role the respondent assumes in a given situation.

As to the factors determining the level of salience, most explicit note has been taken of the situational cues which serve to remind the person of the group. Internal motivational factors should be considered as well. It seems reasonable to expect persons strongly attached to a group always to relate controversial questions to its norms, whether or not the group or its symbols are externally present. Thus, the degree to which a given group is salient in a variety of situations is likely to be positively correlated with how highly the group is valued. In this regard, Lewin ([28] p. 35) postulated that an increase in the intensity of the need related to a certain goal increases the relative potency (read "salience") of the situation containing that goal. Lewin specifically noted in discussing the psychological consequences of multiple group membership that sometimes a person's belonging to one group is dominant and sometimes his belonging to another, depending upon the character of the particular situation in which he is acting [27]. Lewin suggested that the dominant group would largely determine the person's feelings and actions and proposed that a quantitative weighting be given the various overlapping sets of factors affecting behavior at a given time ([28] pp. 34–35, 201–209).

In passing, we may note that many of the propositions about salience can be translated into the theory of tension systems, developed by Lewin and his colleagues [29] from research on the relation between task completion and such behavior as recall and resumption. The person who highly values a group develops an identification with that group, which is to say that he develops a number of tension systems (motives) the fate of which depends upon the group's successes and failures in moving toward its goals. Although it is not necessary to go into the relationship here, there is a high degree of interdependence between the goals of a group and its norms, this being most clearly seen in the case of norms which govern the individual behavior essential to group locomotion. With his set of tension systems related to the group goals and norms, the highly group-oriented person would be expected, as a special case of the "Zeigarnik effect" (memory for uncompleted tasks), to have generally high awareness of the goals and norms, and, as a special case of the resumption effect, to tend to behave according to the norms in a variety of situations.

References

1. Allard, W. A test of propaganda values in public opinion surveys. *Social Forces*, 1941, *20*, 206–213.
2. Arnett, C. E., Davidson, Helen H., and Lewis, H. N. Prestige as a factor in attitude changes. *Sociol. Soc. Res.*, 1931, *16*, 49–55.
3. Asch, S. E. Studies in the principles of judgments and attitudes: II. Determination of judgments by group and ego standards. *J. Soc. Psychol.*, 1940, *12*, 433–465.
4. Back, K. W. Influence through social communication. *J. Abnorm. Soc. Psychol.*, 1951, *46*, 9–23.
5. Bettelheim, B. Individual and mass behavior in extreme situations. *J. Abnorm. Soc. Psychol.*, 1943, *38*, 417–452.
6. Bowden, A. O., Caldwell, F. F., and West, G. A. A study in prestige. *Am. J. Sociol.*, 1934, *40*, 193–204.
7. Burtt, H. E., and Falkenberg, D. R., Jr. The influence of majority and expert opinion on religious attitudes. *J. Soc. Psychol.*, 1941, *14*, 269–278.
8. Chapman, D. W., and Volkmann, J. A social determinant of the level of aspiration. *J. Abnorm. Soc. Psychol.*, 1939, *34*, 225–238.
9. Charters, W. W., Jr., and Newcomb, T. M. Some attitudinal effects of experimentally increased salience of a membership group. In G. E. Swanson, T. M. Newcomb, and E. L. Hartley, eds., *Readings in social psychology* (rev. ed.). New York, Holt, 1952. Pp. 415–420.
10. Chein, I., Deutsch, M., Hyman, H., and Jahoda, Marie. Consistency and inconsistency in intergroup relations. *J. Soc. Issues*, 1949, *5*, No. 3.
11. Coch, L., and French, J.R.P., Jr. Overcoming resistance to change. *Hum. Rel.*, 1948, *1*, 512–532.
12. Doob, L. W. *Public opinion and propaganda*. New York, Holt, 1948.
13. Festinger, L. An analysis of compliant behavior. In M. Sherif and M. O. Wilson, eds., *Group relations at the crossroads*. New York, Harper, 1953.
14. Festinger, L., and Kelley, H. H. *Changing attitudes through social contact*. Ann Arbor, University of Michigan, Institute for Social Research, 1951.
15. Festinger, L., Schachter, S., and Back, K. *Social pressures in informal groups*. New York, Harper, 1950.
16. Festinger, L., and Thibaut, J. Interpersonal communication in small groups. *J. Abnorm. Soc. Psychol.*, 1951, *46*, 92–99.
17. Freud, Anna. *The ego and the mechanisms of defence*. New York, International Universities Press, 1946.
18. Freud, S. *Group psychology and the analysis of the ego*. New York, Liveright, 1922.
19. Gorden, R. L. Interaction between attitude and the definition of the situation in the expression of opinion. *Am. Sociol. Rev.*, 1952, *17*, 50–58.
20. Hartley, E. L., and Hartley, Ruth E. *Fundamentals of social psychology*. New York, Knopf, 1952.

21. Helson, H. Adaptation-level as a basis for a quantitative theory of frames of reference. *Psychol. Rev.*, 1948, *55*, 297–313.
22. Hughes, E. C. The knitting of racial groups in industry. *Am. Sociol. Rev.*, 1946, *11*, 512–519.
23. Hyman, H. H. The psychology of status. *Arch. Psychol.*, New York, 1942, *38*, No. 269.
24. Kelley, H. H. Two functions of reference groups. In G. E. Swanson, T. M. Newcomb, and E. L. Hartley, eds., *Readings in social psychology* (rev. ed.). New York, Holt, 1952. Pp. 410–414.
25. Kelley, H. H. Salience of membership and resistance to change of group-anchored attitudes, 1953. (In preparation.)
26. Kelley, H. H., and Volkart, E. H. The resistance to change of group-anchored attitudes. *Am. Sociol. Rev.*, 1952, *17*, 453–465.
27. Lewin, K. Psycho-sociological problems of a minority group. *Character & Pers.*, 1935, *3*, 175–187.
28. Lewin, K. The conceptual representation and the measurement of psychological forces. *Contr. to Psychological Theory*, 1938, *1*, No. 4.
29. Lewin, K. Formalization and progress in psychology. Studies in topological and vector psychology, I. *Univ. Iowa: Studies in child welfare*, 1940, *16*, No. 3, 9–42.
30. Lewin, K. Group decision and social change. In T. M. Newcomb and E. L. Hartley, eds., *Readings in social psychology*. New York, Holt, 1947. Pp. 330–344.
31. Lippitt, R., Polansky, N., and Rosen, S. The dynamics of power. *Hum. Rel.*, 1952, *5*, 37–64.
32. Merton, R. K. Patterns of influence: A study of interpersonal influence and of communications behavior in a local community. In P. F. Lazarsfeld and F. N. Stanton, eds., *Communications research, 1948–1949.* New York, Harper, 1949. Pp. 180–219.
33. Merton, R. K., and Kitt, Alice S. Contributions to the theory of reference group behavior. In R. K. Merton and P. F. Lazarsfeld, eds., *Continuities in social research*. Glencoe, Ill., Free Press, 1950. Pp. 40–105.
34. Mowrer, O. H. *Learning theory and personality dynamics.* New York, Ronald Press, 1950.
35. Mussen, P. H. Some personality and social factors related to changes in children's attitudes toward Negroes. *J. Abnorm. Soc. Psychol.*, 1950, *45*, 423–441.
36. Newcomb, T. M. *Personality and social change.* New York, Dryden Press, 1943.
37. Newcomb, T. M. *Social psychology.* New York, Dryden Press, 1950.
38. Redl, F. Group emotion and leadership. *Psychiatry*, 1942, *5*, 573–596.
39. Schachter, S. Deviation, rejection and communication. *J. Abnorm. Soc. Psychol.*, 1951, *46*, 190–207.
40. Schanck, R. L. A study of a community and its groups and institutions conceived of as behaviors of individuals. *Psychol. Monogr.*, 1932, *43*, No. 195.
41. Sherif, M. *An outline of social psychology.* New York, Harper, 1948.
42. Sherif, M. A preliminary study of inter-group relations. In J. H. Rohrer and

M. Sherif, eds., *Social psychology at the crossroads.* New York, Harper, 1951. Pp. 388–424.

43. Sherif, M., and Cantril, H. *The psychology of ego-involvements.* New York, John Wiley, 1947.

44. *Special research supplement to scouting for facts.* New York, Boy Scouts of America, 1944, No. 7.

45. Stouffer, S. A. An analysis of conflicting social norms. *Amer. Sociol. Rev.*, 1949, *14*, 707–717.

46. Volkmann, J. Scales of judgment and their implications for social psychology. In J. H. Rohrer and M. Sherif, eds., *Social psychology at the crossroads.* New York, Harper, 1951. Pp. 273–294.

47. Waelder, R. *Psychological aspects of war and peace.* Geneva, Geneva Research Centre, 1939.

CHAPTER 6: *Personality and Susceptibility to Persuasion*

THE preceding chapter has dealt with predispositional factors associated with group membership of the audience. In the present chapter we shall continue the discussion of audience predispositions, focusing on individual personality factors (abilities and persistent motives) that are related to susceptibility to persuasion.

Propositions about communication stimuli—characteristics of the communicator, the content, and the structure of the communication —provide a basis for predicting the effects for the majority of cases within a specified audience. But, as is generally recognized, the same social pressures may be experienced in different ways by different people, and consequently the effects of a communication are partly dependent upon the characteristics of individual members of the audience. By taking account of personality predispositions, as well as group affiliations, it should be possible to improve predictions concerning the way a given type of audience (or a given individual within the audience) will respond. Thus, investigations of personality factors should enable us to arrive at a more comprehensive set of general principles for predicting the degree to which a persuasive communication will succeed in changing beliefs and attitudes.

It is useful to differentiate two general classes of personality characteristics which influence a person's responsiveness to persuasion: 1) his readiness to accept or reject a given point of view on the particular topic that is being discussed, and 2) his general susceptibility to various types of persuasion and social influence.

The first set of factors has long been recognized as a major determinant of an individual's susceptibility to opinion change. A great deal of research has been devoted to studying personality factors associated with acceptance of various beliefs and attitudes within one or another topic area. In recent years much of this type of research has centered upon personality correlates of attitudes toward minority groups. Some of the results, for example, indicate that acceptance of antiminority group attitudes is associated with such characteristics as ideological adherence to conventional moral standards, compulsive submission to parents, and strong ambivalence toward authority figures.[1] Presumably such findings could be useful for predicting the way in which different individuals are likely to respond to communications concerning minority groups, but would not be relevant to communications dealing with most other topics. Thus, although personality factors of this type may prove to be determinants of the individual's readiness to accept one or another broad class of attitudes, they nevertheless can be characterized as "topic-bound," in the sense that they apply only to communications which deal with a more or less restricted range of topics.

The second class of personality predispositions, to which this chapter will be devoted, is assumed to be relatively independent of the subject matter of the communication. Consider, for example, the problem of predicting the changes in attitudes, beliefs, and expectations induced in a large group of people who, over a period of one year, are exposed to a given series of several hundred discrete communications, each dealing with a different topic or issue. Some individuals might display a tendency to be influenced by a very large proportion of the communications while others might show strong resistance to change. Predispositional factors from which predictions can be made concerning the extent of opinion change in response to a series of diverse communications, without taking the subject matter into account, can be characterized as "topic-free." General predispositions of this type are assumed to be relatively independent of such factors as initial attitude, ideological commitments, and those "personality needs" which predispose the individual to accept or reject *any particular* opinion or attitude that is fostered by a given communication.

As compared with personality predispositions that are topic-bound, those that are topic-free are likely to be much more general in scope in that they pertain to a person's responsiveness to many different types of communications, cutting across many different subject matters and covering a wide range of specific beliefs and attitudes. The term "topic-free" means only that the predispositional trait is not dependent on the content of the *conclusion*, or the content of the attitude or belief that is advocated, but does not imply complete independence of other aspects of the communication situation. In fact, some of the predispositions to be discussed later are clearly "bound" to specific characteristics of the communication. For instance, some of the hypotheses concerning topic-free predispositions deal with factors which predict a person's responsiveness only to those persuasive communications that employ certain types of argumentation. Investigations of topic-free predispositions ultimately may reveal some that are associated primarily with the nature of the communicator, others that are associated with the social setting in which the communication takes place, and perhaps still others that are so broad in scope that they are relatively independent of any specific variables in the communication situation.[2]

Thus, for any communication, we assume that there are likely to be several different types of personality predispositions, topic-bound and topic-free, whose joint effects determine individual differences in responsiveness. The essential point is that, by also taking account of topic-free factors, it should be possible to improve predictions concerning the degree to which members of the audience will be influenced by persuasive communications. Such factors have generally been neglected in analyses of audience predispositions.

In this chapter we shall examine the available evidence pertinent to topic-free predispositions. As will be seen, the data are too fragmentary and unreliable to permit more than tentative attempts to isolate, define, and classify the predispositional factors that might account for individual differences in responsiveness to persuasive influence. There are some preliminary findings, however, that suggest the lines along which future research on such factors might profitably be directed. In the section on "Research Evidence," tentative hypotheses concerning the relationship between personality factors and susceptibility to persuasive communications will be formulated and examined in the light of the available findings. In seeking to discover such relationships, the assumption is made that people can be ordered in some consistent fashion with respect to "persuasibility." The "Background" section which follows will discuss this assumption and will consider a number of methodological problems pertinent to research on topic-free predispositions.

BACKGROUND

CONSISTENCY OF INDIVIDUAL DIFFERENCES

In suggesting the existence of topic-free predispositions, we assume that there are *consistent* individual differences in susceptibility to persuasion, that some people regularly tend to accept the conclusions put forth in diverse communications, whereas others fail to do so. It is an empirical question, however, whether individual differences in responsiveness to social influence are actually sufficiently consistent to constitute a useful variable.

Although the available correlational findings on conformity, suggestibility, and related phenomena are not in complete agreement, there are some factor analysis studies, based on behavioral ratings made by trained observers (e.g., Fiske [10], Richards and Simons [32]) and on self-ratings (e.g., Layman [23], Brogden and Thomas [3]) which suggest that there are general factors of responsiveness to social influence.[3] Positive evidence of some consistent individual differences in susceptibility to persuasion is also provided by investigations in which opinions were measured before and after exposure to persuasive communications. The most pertinent evidence comes from Ferguson's study [8] which used objective indices of susceptibility to persuasion based on measures of the amount of opinion change induced by a series of informative statements. Ferguson administered three attitude scales (dealing with religionism, humanitarianism, and nationalism) to 200 college students. On a later occasion he retested the same subjects under identical conditions except that this time they were provided with information (in one group, correct; in another group, fictitious) concerning majority opinion on each item. The changes shown on each of the three scales were found to be highly intercorrelated, and centroid analysis revealed a unitary factor. The possibility that a common ideological factor might account for the intercorrelations seems precluded by the fact that no significant correlations were found between initial attitudes and susceptibility scores. Ferguson's evidence suggests that susceptibility to influence by communications of majority opinion is a general trait, not specific to the particular attitudes that were investigated.

Until data are available from more comprehensive research, one cannot be at all confident about the existence of unitary predispositional traits on which accurate predictions can be based as to how people will respond to various persuasive communications presented in diverse communication situations. Ideally, further research on this problem should secure data on actual changes induced by exposure to communications, as in the case of Ferguson's study, but employing a large series of communications which vary not only in subject matter but also with respect to media, type of appeals used, arrangement of arguments, and other stimulus characteristics. The scanty evidence already available, however, suggests that at least in some types of communication situations people show fairly consistent tendencies to be highly influenced or to remain uninfluenced by each of a series of discrete communications on different topics.

Probably there is no single general factor, in the sense that every individual can be assigned a single score which will represent his degree of susceptibility to any and all situations where changes in attitudes or opinions are elicited. On the other hand, the opposite assumption of complete specificity seems to be unwarranted. That is to say, the available evidence apparently contradicts the assumption that individuals exhibit completely unrelated degrees of susceptibility that are unique to each opinion topic or to each communication situation. Consequently, there is reason to expect that a number of more or less general factors will eventually be isolated, some of which may apply to a fairly broad range of communication situations.

In this chapter we shall use "persuasibility" as a generic term to refer to any topic-free aspects of responsiveness to persuasive communications, without prejudging the question of which components, if any, form unitary variables. For the present we must expect that whatever indices of persuasibility are used will be relatively impure measures, representing (to unknown degrees) various general and more specific predispositional tendencies. But this limitation does not necessarily preclude the possibility of finding significant relationships between personality factors and objective measures of persuasibility, as will become apparent from the evidence to be described below.

METHODOLOGICAL PROBLEMS

Throughout this chapter, our inquiry will focus on one central question: what are the personality characteristics that incline a person to be receptive or resistant to social communications which attempt to modify his beliefs or attitudes? Broadly speaking, what we seek to discover are the personality factors which are related to individual differences in the amount of opinion change induced by many different types of persuasive communications. We shall examine individual differences in persuasibility in relation to two general types of personality factors. One type has to do with a person's intellectual abilities, which are likely to determine the way he attends to, interprets, and assimilates the multitude of communications to which he is constantly exposed. For persons who possess at least a certain minimum of essential intellectual abilities, a second set of personality characteristics, which we refer to as "motive factors," may be major determinants of individual differences in persuasibility. Motive factors involve predominant personality needs, emotional disturbances, defense mechanisms, frustration tolerance, thresholds of excitability, etc., which may facilitate or interfere with a person's responsiveness to many different types of persuasive communications.

Thus, the hypotheses with which we shall be concerned specify a relationship between two classes of predispositional traits—between general personality characteristics and susceptibility to various kinds of persuasion. In investigations of such relationships, the measures of persuasibility should be treated as the dependent variable while other personality traits, based on indices of a person's tendency to perform quite different kinds of implicit and overt acts, should be treated as independent variables. Research on these problems, however, cannot be expected to provide definitive evidence on causal relationships of the sort discussed in some of the earlier chapters, where evidence could be obtained from controlled experiments. Use of the full experimental method is generally precluded when the independent variables to be investigated are traits that are fairly constant for each individual and cannot be experimentally manipulated. Nevertheless, the experimental method can be used to assess the dependent variable, persuasibility. Individual differences in responsiveness to various types of persuasions can be assessed by measuring opinion changes *when the investigator exposes his subjects to a series of communications*—a series that represents the population of communications about which the investigator wishes to generalize. Thus, in order to obtain precise data, a research design can be used in which communication exposure is experimentally controlled: measures of opinion can be obtained before and after exposure to a series of communications, and the amount of opinion change can then be compared for various subgroups that are sorted according to a personality trait. In order to check on various artifacts (regression effects, etc.) that may give rise to spurious relationships between a given trait and the amount of opinion change, it is necessary to include an *equivalent control group* that has not been exposed to the series of communications but for whom the same opinion measures and the same personality measures are obtained (cf. Hovland, Lumsdaine, and Sheffield [*17*], pp. 329–340).

The controlled exposure design—which includes opinion measures before and after a series of communications along with comparable measures for a control group—is capable of yielding results which show the extent to which people on different levels of a personality dimension are influenced by communications of the type represented by the series used in the investigation. From such results, it should be possible to arrive at general propositions which specify how different personalities respond to one or another general type of persuasive influence.

When one examines the voluminous literature pertinent to predispositional factors, one finds that the controlled exposure design has rarely been used. Most of the pertinent data consist of static correlations which come from studies designed primarily to investigate other problems. All too often the evidence reported on predispositional factors, having been only of minor or incidental interest to the investigator, is fragmentary and inconclusive. Nevertheless, at the present stage of research on this problem, the formulation of hypotheses based on the available data may prove to be beneficial in giving some direction to subsequent empirical investigations. From a careful examination of the existing evidence it is possible to extract a few tentative generalizations which seem to be fairly well supported by evidence obtained by different investigators, using a variety of methods, in diverse communication situations. Thus, despite various methodological limitations, the available empirical results throw some light on the relationships between specific personality predispositions and responsiveness to persuasive communications.

RESEARCH EVIDENCE

INTELLECTUAL FACTORS

Investigations pertinent to capacity or skill factors have relied primarily upon measures of intelligence, educational level, or similar indices which reflect general intellectual ability. From laboratory and classroom studies in the field of verbal learning, it would be expected that this general factor would be positively related to persuasibility, insofar as opinion change is dependent upon ability to comprehend and interpret verbal symbols. Persons at the lowest end of the intelligence scale, who have great difficulty in understanding any but the simplest messages, would presumably remain uninfluenced by the majority of mass communications.

When the obvious cases of mental deficiency are excluded, what relationship, if any, exists between general intellectual ability and persuasibility? In reviewing the available evidence, we shall see that the answer to this question is by no means a simple one. Murphy, Murphy, and Newcomb ([28] p. 930), in their summary of the literature of social psychology up to 1937, point out that zero or near-zero correlations have consistently been found between intelligence and susceptibility to propaganda. More recent investigations, however, indicate that there are positive correlations for some persuasive communications and negative correlations for others, depending upon the types of arguments and appeals that are used.

Evidence of an inverse relationship has been reported by Wegrocki [35]: a negative correlation was found between scores on the Otis Advanced Intelligence Test and amount of opinion change induced by a series of propagandistic statements which contained "specious" arguments. Working with high school students in a Catholic parochial institution, Wegrocki administered an initial attitude scale which required each subject to rate various social groups (nationalities, religious sects, and political parties) with respect to feelings of personal like or dislike. Three weeks later the students were exposed to crudely propagandistic statements concerning each of the groups that had been rated; e.g., ". . . when we hate Jews we hate Jesus." Retest results based on the original attitude scale showed that the most intelligent students were *least* influenced by the propaganda.

Studies of the effects of United States Army documentary films, reported by Hovland, Lumsdaine, and Sheffield ([*17*] pp. 147–175), provide evidence of positive correlations, the more intelligent men being *more* influenced than the less intelligent. Using level of terminal education (years of schooling completed) as an index of general intellectual ability, these authors noted that the general effects of the films on opinion tended to increase with higher intellectual ability. Further analysis revealed that while this was the dominant or average trend, the reverse relationship also occurred in the case of certain types of opinion items. Their data, all of which were derived from controlled exposure studies, suggest that over-all indices of general intelligence comprise several disparate, interacting components: *a) learning ability,* which enables the brighter people to learn and remember more from a given experience; *b) critical ability,* which predisposes the more intelligent to reject interpretations that are unsound or irrational, to be alert to signs of propagandistic intent, and to recognize bias in argumentation; *c) ability to draw inferences,* which enables the better educated to interpret and see the implications of the manifest and latent content of a communication. Since all three factors would enter into the relationship between general intelligence and the amount of opinion change produced by any given communication, the nature of the relationship would depend on the weighting to be given each factor according to the type of arguments contained in the communication. Hovland, Lumsdaine, and Sheffield summarize this point as follows: "Because of the heterogeneity of the relationships obtained with different [opinion] items, an over-all 'average' relationship between intellectual ability and opinion changes is relatively meaningless since it obscures the separate relations . . ." ([*17*] p. 267).

From the evidence presented by these authors, two general hypotheses can be inferred concerning the conditions under which general intelligence is predictive of responsiveness to persuasive communications:

1. Persons with high intelligence will tend—mainly because of their ability to draw valid inferences—to be *more* influenced than those with low intellectual ability when exposed to persuasive communications which rely primarily on impressive logical arguments.

2. Persons with high intelligence will tend—mainly because of their superior critical ability—to be *less* influenced than those with low intelligence when exposed to persuasive communications which rely primarily on unsupported generalities or false, illogical, irrelevant argumentation.

In the light of these two hypotheses the seemingly contradictory findings which have been cited are not necessarily inconsistent. Unlike the Army documentary films, the propaganda in Wegrocki's study [*35*] deliberately used slogan-like arguments of the sort that might be more readily rejected by individuals with greater critical abilities.

The various predispositional factors associated with intellectual ability are presumably intercorrelated to a high degree, and most persuasive communications in our society seem to contain mixed characteristics. Consequently, in order to predict the effectiveness of communications for audiences of high, low, or mixed intellectual ability, an elaborate weighting scheme would be required. This in turn would presuppose an elaborate set of propositions concerning the interactions among the various skill and capacity factors as a function of various patterns of communication characteristics.

By using simple communications for each of which only a single skill factor is predominant in determining the effects, it should be possible to study in detail the various communication characteristics that make for a positive or negative correlation. It seems likely that such research will help to illuminate our theoretical knowledge concerning the role of intellectual functions and higher mental processes in the modification of attitudes.

In further research, more refined measures of intellectual functioning might also help to isolate the critical components which are major determinants of persuasibility. Some of the evidence cited above clearly shows that when a single index of general intellectual ability is used the positive and negative relationships are likely to cancel each other out and thereby be obscured. Moreover, correlations based on IQ or on level of terminal education could sometimes be attributable to factors other than intellectual ability; these particular measures tend to be substantially correlated with demographic variables—occupation, income, and socio-economic status—which, in turn, might be associated with motivational predispositions. More refined measures which attempt to isolate the various types of abilities that enter into attention, comprehension, and acceptance would probably be less highly correlated with demographic variables and might highlight more clearly the role of intellectual factors in opinion change.

MOTIVE FACTORS ASSOCIATED WITH HIGH PERSUASIBILITY

It seems probable that there are certain types of individuals whose personality needs incline them to be highly gullible. Some clues as to motive factors which make for indiscriminate acceptance of persuasive communications can be found in a number of empirical studies which investigated the relationship between persuasibility and various indices of personal adjustment.

One of the studies in our research program was conducted by Janis [19] for the purpose of arriving at hypotheses concerning personality correlates of susceptibility to persuasion. It was carried out as a separate investigation which made use of data obtained from an experiment on the effects of active participation (cf. pp. 219–222). The experiment provides measures of the opinion changes induced in 78 male college students, each of whom was exposed to the same set of three persuasive communications. By obtaining additional information regarding personality characteristics of the subjects, it was possible to investigate the relationship between personality factors and opinion changes.

The communications were similar to ordinary magazine articles, editorials, or news commentaries of the sort that give a series of factual arguments in an attempt to convince the audience of a given belief or expectation. Since relatively simple language was used, it is probable that all of the subjects possessed the minimal skills necessary for absorbing the message. (One advantage of using well-educated subjects who are relatively homogeneous in intellectual capacities is that individual differences among them with respect to persuasibility would be especially likely to reflect differences in motivational predispositions rather than in abilities.)

A standardized exposure procedure was used which required each subject not only to read all three communications but also to present one of them orally and to listen to an oral presentation of the other two. Approximately four weeks earlier the subjects' initial opinions were ascertained by administering an opinion questionnaire which contained three key items focused directly on the issues subsequently dealt with by the communications: *a*) number of movie theaters in business three years from now; *b*) amount of meat available to the United States population two years from now; *c*) length of time before a cure is discovered for the common cold. None of the opinion estimates originally given by any of the subjects agreed with the extremely low estimates advocated by the communications.

The same three questionnaire items were repeated immediately after exposure, and it was found that on each item approximately two-thirds of the subjects lowered their opinion estimates, i.e., changed in the direction advocated by the corresponding communication. Some degree of consistency was noted with respect to individual differences in responsiveness to the communications. Opinion changes produced by the communications were found to be positively related on the basis of Chi-square analyses: Those who were influenced by Communication *A* were more likely to be influenced by Communication *B* and by Communication *C* ($p = .05$ and $.10$ respectively, using a one-tailed test). The relationship between changes on communications *B* and *C*, although nonsignificant, was in the same direction.

A persuasibility rating was assigned to each subject, representing the number of items on which he lowered his opinion estimates. The entire group was then divided into the following persuasibility categories: 1) "high," 32 cases who were influenced by all three communications; 2) "moderate," 21 cases who were influenced by two communications; 3) "low," 25 cases who were influenced by only one or by none of the communications. The three groups were then compared with respect to personality characteristics.

Personality data were obtained from two independent sources. The first was a set of detailed clinical reports available for 16 of the subjects who had voluntarily come to a clinic for psychological counseling. Although the number of cases for whom such information existed was too small to arrive at any definite conclusions, the clinical data nevertheless were found to suggest certain hypotheses concerning personality predispositions underlying low and high persuasibility. The hypotheses were tested systematically by making use of the second source of personality data, viz., a personality inventory given to all 78 subjects at the time of the precommunication questionnaire.

In addition to the main experimental group of 78 students exposed to the three communications, a small control group was used, consisting of 28 students who were given the same questionnaires (separated by the same time interval) but without being exposed to the three communications. The data from the control group were used to check on possible artifacts that might give rise to spurious correlations between opinion changes and personality inventory responses. The findings were also checked with respect to possible differences in initial opinion that could affect the observed relationships.

The results were first examined to see whether persuasibility was related to the presence or absence of emotional difficulties or to whatever other personality trends differentiated the small group, who sought psychological counseling, from the larger group who did not. The amount of opinion change shown by the 16 students who received counseling was compared with that shown by the other 62 students. No relationship was found.

Detailed analysis of the 16 case records, however, suggested that there were marked personality differences between men who were highly influenced and those who were relatively uninfluenced. The men who obtained low persuasibility ratings in the study had come for treatment mainly because of acute psychoneurotic symptoms, whereas those who showed most opinion change had sought psychological help primarily because of social inhibitions and feelings of personal inadequacy.

An outstanding feature in six of the seven cases in the highly influenced group was a subjective feeling of personal inadequacy in connection with everyday interpersonal relationships. Five of the seven cases were diagnosed by the psychiatric staff as "passive-dependent" personalities. By and large, the men in the highly influenced group were successful academically; their difficulties in social relationships rarely interfered with their studies. None of them showed any obvious manifestations of irritability or hostility of the sort noted among some of the resistant cases. The marked opinion changes displayed by these passive individuals seemed to be manifestations of a more general acquiescent tendency, perhaps reflecting a submissive attitude that is motivated by excessive fear of social disapproval. In other words, yielding readily to the arguments and conclusions presented in a persuasive communication might be interpreted as a form of social compliance stemming from an inability to tolerate anticipated disapproval for deviating from the opinions held by others. In any case, the clinical data suggest that persons who are chronically disturbed by feelings of shyness, personal inadequacy, and social inhibitions in coping with everyday situations are predisposed to change their opinions more readily than others when exposed to persuasive communications. A general hypothesis suggested by the particular constellation of personality factors involved is that persons with low self-esteem are predisposed to high persuasibility.

Data relevant for testing this hypothesis were obtained from the personality questionnaire, which was administered to all 78 men whose opinions had been measured before and after exposure to the three communications. The questionnaire contained 38 items selected from standard personality inventories which elicited self-ratings on emotional disturbances, interpersonal relationships, and behavioral symptoms. Figure 11 shows the results based on three different sets of items that are pertinent to the "self-esteem" hypothesis.

The first set consisted of nine items dealing with feelings of personal inadequacy and social inhibition, representing the essential characteristics mentioned in the case records. Included in this cluster were

self-ratings concerning feelings of shyness, lack of confidence in con-
versational abilities, high concern about the possibility that friends
may have a low opinion of one, and uneasiness at social gatherings.
It would be predicted from the "self-esteem" hypothesis that high
scores on this cluster would be associated with high persuasibility.

SELF–RATING SCORES ON PERSONAL ADJUSTMENT	PERSUASIBILITY		
	LOW	MODERATE	HIGH
A. SOCIAL INADEQUACY			
HIGH (N=28)	14%	29%	57%
LOW (N=50)	42%	26%	32%
B. INHIBITION OF AGGRESSION			
HIGH (N=31)	22½%	29%	48½%
LOW (N=47)	38½%	25½%	36%
C. DEPRESSIVE AFFECT			
HIGH (N=30)	30%	17%	53%
LOW (N=48)	33⅓%	33⅓%	33⅓%

FIGURE 11. Personal Adjustment Factors Related to High Persuasibility. *From Janis* [*19*].

This prediction is borne out by the results in the upper portion of
Figure 11. Subjects with high ratings on social inadequacy (four or
more positive responses to the nine items) were much more influenced
by the communications than those with low ratings. The difference
of 25 per cent in the percentage influenced by all three communications is statistically reliable at beyond the 2 per cent confidence level.

The second set consisted of six items dealing with inhibition of
aggression as manifested by the following characteristics: rarely criticizes others, rarely feels angry toward anyone, rarely feels like resisting
the demands of others, lack of oppositional feelings toward "bossy"

people, lack of distrust toward others, lack of resentment when deceived by others. These items deal with personality tendencies which are closely related to the excessive timidity noted in the case studies. On the assumption that personalities characterized by a sense of social inadequacy and low self-esteem tend to suppress or repress their aggressive impulses toward others, it would be predicted that inhibitions of aggression would be associated with high persuasibility.

As predicted, students with high ratings on inhibition of aggression (four or more positive responses to the six items) tended to be more influenced than those with low ratings. The difference between the percentages shown in the third and fourth rows of Figure 11 cannot be regarded as reliable; but an analysis of each of the six separate items yielded a highly reliable percentage difference on one of the items (rarely criticizes others) and smaller differences, consistently in the predicted direction, on the remaining ones. This consistent trend tends to support the "self-esteem" hypothesis.

Another indirect implication of the same hypothesis was tested by the third set of (three) items which dealt with depressive affect (often feel "blue," "unhappy," "discouraged"). One might expect the presence of depressive feelings to be at least a rough indicator of low self-esteem. Clinical studies of depressed patients indicate that subjective feelings of sadness and melancholia are associated with self-critical attitudes and low self-esteem ([7] pp. 392–397). Some case studies ([7] pp. 404–406; [*13*] pp. 298–306) also suggest that passive-dependent personalities tend to deflect their aggressive impulses away from others toward the self, and are especially prone to become depressed.

If one assumes that the same relationships observed among the mentally ill hold for personalities within the normal range, one would predict that persons who complain of depressive feelings will tend to be characterized by low esteem and hence be more readily influenced by persuasive communications than those who report a relative absence of such feelings. This prediction was tested by comparing subjects who reported that they frequently felt blue, unhappy, or discouraged with those who reported that they rarely experienced any such feelings. The 20 per cent difference shown in the last two rows of Figure 11 is reliable at beyond the 5 per cent confidence level (one tail).

In summary, feelings of social inadequacy, inhibition of aggression, and depressive affect were found to be associated with high persuasibility as measured by responsiveness to the three persuasive communications. The results based on the three pertinent sets of personality items provide some preliminary support for the "self-esteem" hypothesis.[4]

Findings from a number of other studies bearing on predispositional factors also tend to be consistent with the self-esteem hypothesis. Suggestive evidence is to be found in Robinson's study [33] in which scores on the Humm-Wadsworth temperament scale were studied in relation to opinion change scores obtained after exposure to group discussion on a controversial issue. The students who shifted their opinions most were found to have higher "Depressive" scores than those who shifted least.[5]

Some of the data from correlational studies, although subject to alternative interpretations, also seem to be in line with the self-esteem hypothesis. In Layman's study [23] of the intercorrelations among 67 self-ratings on personality characteristics there is some supporting evidence, though of questionable validity (cf. note 3, pp. 207–208). Upon examining her questionnaire, one finds two items which manifestly deal with deviations that imply excessively high responsiveness to social influence: 1) "Are you easily discouraged when the opinions of others differ from your own?" and 2) "Do you find it difficult to get rid of a salesman?" Both of these items were found to be positively correlated with items indicating feelings of personal inadequacy and feelings of inferiority: easily embarrassed, difficulty making conversation, self-conscious, high concern about social disapproval, doubts about one's own abilities, low self-confidence. A centroid factor analysis showed that both items had high positive loadings in the "inferiority" (lack of self-confidence) factor and sizable positive loadings in the "social inadequacy" factor. These correlational findings could be interpreted as being consistent with the self-esteem hypothesis.[6]

Suggestive evidence also comes from case study observations of change and persistence in the behavior and personality of young school children. McKinnon [27] observed a small number of cases in which conforming modes of behavior predominated (highly responsive to teacher's suggestions, to school requirements, etc.). She noted that they were excessively timid and inhibited, as compared with other children; one of their outstanding characteristics was lack of self-confidence.

From the various studies which have just been reviewed, it appears that the available evidence tends to support the "self-esteem" hypothesis. Nevertheless, the hypothesis should be regarded as highly tentative until tested further with other indices of self-esteem and with more extensive measures of persuasibility. The data from Janis' study, for example, involved a rough measure of persuasibility, based on responsiveness to a series of only three persuasive communications. In further research, it would be preferable to use a much larger series of communications which vary in subject matter, argumentation, source, and so on. In this way, it should be possible to determine whether the self-esteem hypothesis actually does provide a basis for predicting how different individuals react to persuasive communications and, if so, whether there are limiting conditions as to the type of persuasive communications to which they apply. It is quite possible, for example, that persons with low self-esteem would tend to be *less* influenceable than others when the source is perceived to be unpopular or socially disapproved by the community, even though such persons may be highly influenceable when communications come from neutral or prestigeful sources, as was the case in the studies which have been reported.

Where a significant relationship is observed between low self-esteem and persuasibility, there are a number of alternative explanations to be considered. For instance, excessive fear of social disapproval might give rise to strong facilitating motivations with respect to acceptance of persuasive communications. Persons who are exceptionally lacking in a sense of personal adequacy may have an exceptionally strong need for approval. They may tend to be indiscriminately influenced by anticipations of the *immediate* reward of approval from the communicator or from others who are assumed to share his point of view. Excessive compliance might therefore be a compensatory mechanism which leads to chameleon-like changes in response to any prestigeful communicator who attempts to influence them. Thus, the compliance manifested by people with low self-esteem might be a defensive form of behavior that permits the individual to agree with almost everyone in an attempt to guarantee that nobody will be displeased with him.

Other psychological factors might also be involved. For instance, any motives which interfere with group identification could give rise both to low self-esteem and to high persuasibility. In line with the discussion in the preceding chapter, one would expect that failure to become affiliated with primary and secondary groups in the community would leave the individual with "unanchored" attitudes and hence more amenable to change than persons who become strongly committed to the norms of various reference groups. The motivational patterns which could account for the observed relationship between self-esteem and persuasibility obviously require further investigation.

Motive Factors Associated with Low Persuasibility

The available evidence suggests that there are three major constellations of manifest personality traits which characterize persons who tend to resist social influence: a) persistent aggressiveness toward others, b) social withdrawal tendencies and c) acute psychoneurotic complaints. The first two constellations seem to reflect interfering adjustment factors associated with low motivation to accept the demands and suggestions of others, while the third constellation might be regarded as indicative of emotional disturbances which have an inhibiting effect on responsiveness to external symbol stimuli. We shall briefly review the evidence pertaining to each.

Overt Aggressiveness

From the evidence presented in Figure 11 we have seen that those persons whose self-ratings indicate *less* than the "average" amount of social aggressiveness were found to display *more* than the "average" amount of opinion change. The additional findings we are about to consider also point to a relationship between social aggressiveness and persuasibility. It seems that extreme deviations in the direction of strong hostility toward others make for low persuasibility, just as deviations in the opposite direction make for high. At the purely descriptive level, the available data support the following hypothesis: Persons who openly express hostility and display overt aggression toward others in everyday interpersonal relationships are predisposed to remain relatively uninfluenced by persuasive communications.

The most cogent evidence comes from one of the pioneering investigations of responsiveness to a series of persuasive communications —Barry's controlled exposure study [2] of susceptibility to majority opinion. The investigation was carried out with high school students and was replicated with other groups, including inmates in a penal institution. These groups were given a questionnaire consisting of 40 Yes-No items concerning a variety of attitudes and opinions, covering such diverse topics as race relations, government ownership of public utilities, trial marriage, bobbed hair, and card playing. One week later the same questionnaire was repeated but this time along with a series of communications which provided information concerning the answers given by the majority of the group. Changes in positive or negative responses to the questions, as well as certainty ratings, were taken into account in rating each individual's susceptibility to this series of communications.

On the basis of his observations of the subjects' overt behavior in various social situations, Barry noted that those with low susceptibility scores tended to be most irritable or easily annoyed. Pursuing this observation further, he obtained systematic evidence from one or more of the groups covering: *a*) average rating by associates of the individual's irritability; *b*) the degree to which the individual attributed irritability to his comrades; *c*) the expression of critical or hostile attitudes toward others in introspective reports by each individual; *d*) the omission of customary titles of respect in addressing superiors. The first measure was found to be unrelated to susceptibility, but the other three showed a significant inverse relationship. From these findings Barry concluded that low susceptibility is associated with critical, derogatory attitudes toward others. The correlations Barry reports, although subject to other interpretations, seem to be consistent with the hypothesis that there is an inverse relationship between susceptibility to social influence and aggressiveness toward others.

Further evidence comes from a number of studies which have made use of more indirect indicators of persuasibility. Newcomb ([30] *passim*) compared students who became more liberal in their attitudes with those who remained conservative during four years of college. He presents a detailed description of the liberal social atmosphere of the particular women's college where the study was carried out (Bennington), from which it seems likely that the students with persistent conservative attitudes were, by and large, less susceptible to community influences than those who changed in the liberal direction.[7] An intensive personality study was made of 19 resistant students, and these were compared with 24 others who had shown more than the average amount of attitude change. Newcomb noted that many of the resistant students manifested overt negativism in their classroom behavior, aloofness, and low capacity for social relationships. In some cases negativistic habits were of precollege standing while in others they apparently represented a reaction to frustrated hopes of social success in college. Fewer of the nonconservatives were considered aggressive, either by the faculty or by the other students.

The inverse relationship between overt aggressiveness and conformity to social influence is also supported by correlational data based on behavioral observations of nursery school children reported by Richards and Simons [32]. Low conformity to social demands was found to be associated with lack of emotional control, excitability, quarrelsomeness, and cruelty.

Distrust of others might be one of the critical factors that precludes persuasibility in the case of persons who show a generalized aggressive orientation toward others. Some suggestive results concerning distrust of others were reported by Coser [5]. On the basis of intensive interviews of 23 high school students concerning their interpersonal relationships, Coser divided them into a "tension" group and a "no tension" group; the former group was selected on the basis of expressing "uneasiness" and "hostility" toward others. Both groups were asked the following question: "Is there anyone whose opinions you particularly trust when it comes to politics?" Coser reports that fewer students in the "tension" group asserted that they trusted someone's opinions (age mates, friends, family members, teachers, etc.). This finding suggests that persons who are least able to maintain adequate interpersonal relationships may be comparatively resistant to social influence because they are inclined to distrust others.[8]

Social Withdrawal

In interpreting some of the findings which have just been cited, it is difficult to discriminate sharply between overt aggressiveness and social withdrawal tendencies, both of which may be manifested by generalized attitudes of indifference toward others. Psychoanalytic observations, particularly of persons with markedly schizoid and narcissistic tendencies, suggest that socially withdrawn persons, who are extremely indifferent toward others, are typically resistant to social influence. Thus Freud [11] asserts that the capacity to develop strong emotional attachments to other people ("object libido") is a necessary condition for responsiveness to therapeutic influence: "A human being is therefore on the whole only accessible to influence, even on the intellectual side, in so far as he is capable of investing objects with libido; and we have good cause to recognize, and to fear, in the measure of his narcissism a barrier to his susceptibility to influence, even by the best analytic technique" (p. 387).

Although far from conclusive, there is some systematic evidence of a relationship between sociometric status and conformity to social norms which supports the following hypothesis: Persons who display social withdrawal tendencies are less likely than others to be influenced by persuasive communications from sources in the community. Festinger, Schachter, and Back ([9] pp. 101–113) studied the relationship between conforming attitudes and group affiliations among people who resided in a large housing project. They found that those who held deviant opinions (whose views concerning various aspects of their community life were different from those of the majority of their associates) tended to be social isolates. These people were much less involved in community activities, had fewer friends in adjacent houses and had fewer social contacts with others in the entire neighborhood. On sociometric tests the deviates received fewer friendship choices from others in the project than did the conformers.

In some cases the relative isolation of the deviates may have been

an effect of nonconformity, inasmuch as failure to conform is likely
to elicit rejection by the group. In other cases, however, isolation may
have been a cause of nonconformity, i.e., the group exerted a weaker
influence upon the deviants because of their lack of group affiliation.
For some of the deviants, social life and group affiliation were centered
outside of the housing project, but in other cases their social isolation
may have been due to personal preference or personality defects. In
either case, nonconformity could arise from *a*) lack of awareness of
group pressures, because of infrequent social contact and nonexposure
to ordinary channels of communication; or *b*) low motivation to accept group norms and to be swayed by group opinion.

Further research is needed on both the causes and consequences of
social isolation. Various types of defensive personality needs might
prove to be underlying factors in the avoidance of social contacts. For
instance, phobic reactions toward others or excessive timidity may
be an extreme defense to bolster a person's precarious control over
his aggressive impulses. On the consequence side, it would be important to determine whether socially withdrawn personalities generally show a low degree of opinion change in response to persuasive
communications and, if so, whether it is mainly because of inadequate exposure or unresponsiveness to arguments, appeals, and other
incentive stimuli. It is possible that the attitudes of socially detached
personalities remain comparatively unaffected by anticipations of how
others will react toward them. If so, they may fail to respond to bandwagon appeals and to other forms of persuasion which, through calling attention to group consensus or to authoritative opinion, explicitly
or implicitly allude to the promise of social approval or the threat of
disapproval.

Acute Psychoneurotic Symptoms

One might expect to find that low persuasibility is associated with
personality factors which involve various types of inhibiting motivations—defense mechanisms, emotional blocks, and generalized avoidance tendencies which interfere with attention, comprehension, and
acceptance. There are, of course, no precise methods for discriminating among different types of interfering motivational factors. But
manifestations of acute psychoneurotic symptoms might be regarded

as a rough over-all indicator of the presence of underlying inhibitions that would interfere with the efficient use of intellectual capacities. As the psychoanalysts put it, acute neurotic conflicts have the effect of impairing "ego" functioning. Even among persons who fall well within the "normal" range of personal adjustment, those who display milder manifestations of acute neurotic anxiety would presumably be somewhat less likely than others to function efficiently in communication situations.

These assumptions are indirectly borne out by some of the investigations of personality correlates of persuasibility. The available observations provide preliminary support for the following hypothesis: Persons with acute psychoneurotic symptoms—notably obsessional ideas, hypochondriacal complaints, insomnia, and work inhibitions—are predisposed to be more resistant than others to persuasive communications. Pertinent evidence comes from Janis' study [*19*] which compared the personality characteristics of college students who displayed varying degrees of susceptibility to a series of persuasive communications (cf. pp. 184–189). Both the clinical records available for a small number of cases and the personality inventory data obtained from a larger group of students indicate that acute psychoneurotic complaints occurred predominantly among the men who were least influenced.

As we have mentioned, among the students who received psychological counseling those who had been highly influenced by exposure to the three persuasive communications had sought psychological aid primarily because of social inhibitions and feelings of personal inadequacy. But those who had remained uninfluenced by the communications had come for counseling mainly because of acute neurotic symptoms of the sort usually diagnosed as obsessional neurosis, hysteria or anxiety neurosis.

Confirmatory evidence was obtained from two sets of questions that had been included in a personality test administered to 78 men whose opinions had been measured before and after exposure to the three communications. One set consisted of 18 separate items from the Minnesota Multiphasic Personality Inventory ([*4*] #60) and from the U.S. Army Neuropsychiatric Screening Adjunct ([*34*] pp. 535–538). This combined set of items covered various symptoms of *neurotic anxiety,*

notably hypochondriacal complaints, morbid fears, insomnia, night-
mares, excessive perspiration, and chronic concern about possible body
injury. A second set consisted of two items pertinent to *obsessional
symptoms: a)* inability to get rid of some unimportant idea "which
comes to mind over and over again," and *b)* constant need to make up
rules of self-control so as to be sure to do the right thing at the right
time.

The results in Figure 12 show that on each of the two sets of items
students with high scores tended to be less influenced by the persuasive communications than those with low scores. A significant difference in the predicted direction was found when the small group who

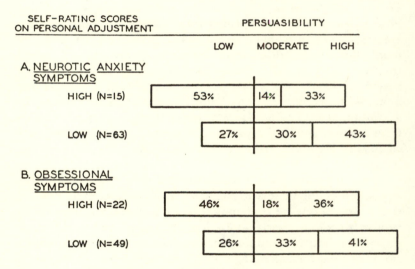

FIGURE 12. Personal Adjustment Factors Related to Low Persuasibility. *From Janis*
[*19*].

reported from 10 to 18 neurotic anxiety symptoms ("High") was compared with the group who reported fewer symptoms ("Low"). The
items dealing with obsessional symptoms also yielded reliable differences in the predicted direction, when those who gave positive responses to both items were compared with those who gave a negative
response to one or both items. (The same methodological checks used

in connection with the results in Figure 11 were also used for the results in Figure 12 [see note 4]). Hence, the findings on obsessional symptoms and those on neurotic anxiety symptoms suggest that persons with acute psychoneurotic symptoms tend to be less influenced than others.[9] If these findings are confirmed, additional research, using indices to separate attention, comprehension, and acceptance, will be needed in order to investigate underlying inhibitions that might account for the greater resistance to opinion change observed in persons who complain about acute neurotic symptoms.

IMPLICATIONS

In the preceding sections we have reviewed the available evidence on personality correlates of general persuasibility and have extracted several hypotheses which are partially confirmed. It now seems in order to raise a question as to the direction that future research in this area might take. A number of alternatives are open but one which seems especially likely to be productive is that of integrating predispositional research with research on hypotheses which specify the ways that externally controlled variables influence the effectiveness of communications.

INDIVIDUAL DIFFERENCES AND EXPERIMENTALLY CONTROLLED VARIATIONS

It would seem to be a fairly good working assumption that externally produced variations in such variables as suspicion toward the communicator, level of fear, salience of community norms, and so on have their counterpart in individual differences in predispositions among the members of an audience. In other words, it can be assumed that the very same factor that is varied by manipulations of the external environment can also be reflected, to varying degrees, by predispositional differences which are static individual constants. We further assume that these individual differences would have the same consequences as the corresponding externally controlled variations. Consider, for example, two groups who differ in some consistent way in their spontaneous level of suspicion toward a given type of communicator—in the readiness with which their suspicions are aroused by minimal cues of manipulative intent or in the limits of the range to which their suspiciousness can be raised or lowered. On the basis of the research findings on experimental variations of level of suspicion, it would follow that those persons who are chronically most suspicious would tend to be least influenced. By assessing the pertinent characteristics of the members of an audience, it should be possible to classify them according to high or low suspicion and to test various hypotheses under conditions where everybody is exposed to the same environmental stimuli.

The same assumptions would also be made for other externally manipulated variations—e.g., that there are individual differences in threshold of fear arousal, in spontaneous tendencies to be aware of community norms, in readiness to engage in role playing, and so on. The crucial point is that these individual differences in predispositional tendencies would affect the way people respond to communication stimuli and would be expected to show the same relationship to communication effectiveness as the corresponding manipulated variations in the stimuli.

The working assumptions which have just been proposed are intended primarily to be of heuristic value with respect to developing promising hypotheses and orienting predispositional research along lines that are likely to be most productive. Perhaps the greatest advantage of integrating research on predispositional characteristics with research on externally manipulated variations is that the two types of findings can be mutually confirmatory, and thereby greatly increase the weight of the evidence in favor of hypotheses about each.

What is meant by this is best clarified by an example of the combined approach used in one of the studies in our research program. In Chapter 3 an experiment on fear appeals by Janis and Feshbach [20] was described in detail. In addition to the findings on the effects of varying degrees of fear arousal, data were also obtained on the differential reactions of subjects who showed different predispositions with respect to anxiety (cf. p. 83 and note 6, pp. 93 f.). Thus, some evidence was provided on the *joint* effects of an experimentally manipulated variable (fear arousal) and a statistically controlled variable (individual level of fear or anxiety) that were studied in combination.

Comparisons of the effects of different intensities of fear appeals in a standard communication on dental hygiene indicated that under communication conditions of the sort represented in the experiment the use of a fear appeal which arouses a high degree of emotional tension tends to reduce the over-all effectiveness of a persuasive communication. From this finding, it would be predicted that the effects of a strong fear appeal would be most unfavorable on personalities who are most vulnerable to fear arousal. By making use of the personality data it was possible to confirm this prediction. The unfavorable effects of the strong appeal were found to occur predominantly among those persons who were chronically most anxious, as manifested by indices of emotional excitability and various neurotic anxiety symptoms [21]. Moreover, an analysis of second order differences indicated that this outcome could not be explained entirely in terms of the general relationship between psychoneurotic tendencies and persuasibility discussed in the present chapter (pp. 197–198). The difference in amount of opinion change between high and low anxiety subjects was found to depend upon the intensity of the fear appeal to which they were exposed: within the group which had received the minimal appeal the difference was markedly less than within the group which had received the strong appeal. Thus, the findings provide some empirical support for the hypothesis that when a strong fear appeal is used persons who chronically display a high level of anxiety are predisposed to be more defensive and hence to be less influenced than others.

In this study, the predispositional hypothesis investigated was deduced from the experimentally observed relationship between fear arousal and communication effects. By investigating individual differences with respect to level of anxiety in combination with experimentally manipulated anxiety arousal, two sets of data were obtained which mutually support each other. This illustrates the type of gain that one can hope to obtain by tying in predispositional research with investigations of theoretical propositions concerning manipulable variables. In general, a twofold gain can be expected. On the one hand, it should be possible to arrive at a more complete set of propositions concerning predispositional factors by taking account of what is already known about effective communication stimuli. On the other hand, the confirmation of predispositional hypotheses tells us something about the correctness of the dynamic relationship from which it was inferred.

The latter aspect of research on predispositional factors is often overlooked. In research on opinion change it is precisely this aspect of predispositional research that might prove to be of greatest value in the long run. There are many theoretical constructs concerning internal processes in opinion change which cannot be easily investigated by manipulating external stimuli. But some of the consequences of the theory might be tested by comparing people whose predispositional differences can be assessed. By noting which types of personalities are most influenced and which are least influenced after exposure to a given set of communications, one can make some inferences about mediating factors. Investigations oriented toward testing such inferences may prove to be of considerable value for evaluating theoretical hypotheses concerning the reinforcement mechanisms involved in acceptance, inasmuch as such hypotheses are exceedingly difficult to test in any direct fashion. In the section which follows we shall attempt to indicate the nature of this line of inquiry by discussing several theoretical hypotheses in terms of their consequences for predispositional relationships.

HYPOTHESES CONCERNING MEDIATING MECHANISMS

One of the major incentives that is assumed to foster attitude change in response to persuasive communications is the anticipation of social rewards and punishments. For instance, an important type of direct reward that a communicator can offer, if he is a respected authority figure or a representative of a group with which the communicatee is affiliated, is the implicit promise of subsequent approval and esteem for adopting the ideas, values, and preferences he is advocating. Moreover, anticipations of social rewards and punishments also are likely to be induced whenever a communicator predicts that conformity with his recommendations will elicit approval from others or that nonconformity will elicit disapproval.

If the above assumptions are correct, one would expect that those persons who for any reason are deficient in their motivation to develop a close relationship to others, and especially to authority figures or group leaders, will be only weakly motivated by anticipated approval for conformity and hence will tend to be less responsive to persuasion than others. The social withdrawal hypothesis discussed in the preceding section seems to be in line with this prediction. Seclusiveness and social isolation may often be indicators of low capacity to develop positive emotional attachments to others—attachments of the sort that would motivate striving for anticipated approval and avoidance of disapproval. The same motivational deficiency might also account for the overt aggressiveness hypothesis, inasmuch as manifestations of generalized hostility or irritability might be indicators of low motivation to secure the approval of others.

From the same assumptions, one would also expect that those personalities who are most strongly motivated to obtain the approval or to avoid the disapproval of others would be most likely to accept the demands or recommendations made by a persuasive communication, particularly when they are aware of the threat of social criticism or rejection for failing to conform. The self-esteem hypothesis, discussed earlier, can be viewed as being consistent with this expectation.

Another aspect of the reinforcing effects of anticipating future rewards and punishments may tie in with the inverse relationship between acute psychoneurotic symptoms and susceptibility to persuasion. Let us assume that when a communicator discusses the favorable or unfavorable consequences of behaving in a certain way, the recipient imaginatively rehearses the situation depicted by the communicator. Loosely speaking, he sees himself as doing or thinking what the communicator recommends and, at the same time, he imagines receiving the rewards or avoiding the punishments that are asserted to be consequences of this activity. Having vicariously experienced the anticipated reward predicted by the communicator, the individual supposedly would be more likely to accept the communicator's recommendation and to try it out in a real life situation.

Assuming that anticipated rewards operate in this way, one would expect to find a relatively low degree of persuasibility among those individuals who, because of some inhibition or emotional disturbance, have difficulty in anticipating accurately the rewarding or punishing situations depicted in persuasive communications. It seems probable that persons with acute psychoneurotic symptoms are especially likely to experience pronounced deficiencies in imaginative or apperceptive processes. We have already noted that such individuals may be unresponsive to social pressure because of rigid emotional defensiveness. In addition, many clinical investigations, including those based on intensive psychoanalytic interviews, suggest that psychoneurotic patients typically have great difficulty in imagining themselves into any future situation where important social rewards or punishments might ensue, without introducing spontaneous *distortions* that stem from their pervading neurotic conflicts (cf. Fenichel [7] pp. 43–53). Their apperceptions and their fantasies are filled with unrealistic anticipations which incline them to expect danger when they are assured that everything is safe, and conversely, secretly to expect some hidden form of reward (masochistic or guilt-reducing satisfactions) where others expect punishment. Thus the type of imaginative activity by which people normally are able to anticipate accurately what is being predicted by a communicator would presumably be subject to marked distortion in the case of many persons who suffer from acute neurotic conflicts.

It would be unwarranted, of course, to assume that the empirical findings concerning the relationship between acute psychoneurotic complaints and low persuasibility can only be explained in this particular way. Nevertheless, the assumption that neurotic conflicts interfere with symbolic mechanisms which facilitate acceptance would seem to be a promising lead.

By further intensive investigation of the special psychological disabilities of those personalities who are least capable of being influenced, it should be possible to arrive at more precise information concerning "what it takes" to be responsive to persuasive communications. Similarly, by studying the personality characteristics of individuals who deviate in the opposite direction, the mediating processes which make for discriminating acceptance or rejection of persuasive communications might be illuminated.

Notes

1. Although a great deal of evidence has accumulated concerning personality characteristics associated with anti-Semitic, anti-Negro, and other antiminority group attitudes (cf. the summary of the literature in Hartley and Hartley [15] pp. 710–740), most of it comes mainly from comparisons of college students with high and low "prejudice" scores on various opinion scales. Among the characteristics which have been found to be associated with antiminority group "prejudice" are the following: a) a high degree of concern about deviations from conventional moral standards and a tendency to project such deviations onto outgroups; b) limited imagination and rigidity of set in approach to problem-solving tasks; c) "passive-dependent" tendencies; d) diffuse anxiety and repression of sexual and aggressive impulses in everyday interpersonal relationships; e) a marked tendency to displace aggression toward remote external targets.

Only a few investigators have tested the assumption that persons with high or low degrees of one or another of the above traits are more likely to *change* their attitudes in the predicted direction, when exposed to propaganda or to other social influences that attempt to induce pro- or antiminority group attitudes. A pioneering investigation of this sort was carried out by Mussen [29]. Working in an interracial summer camp whose nonsegregation policy was intended to break down anti-Negro prejudice, Mussen assessed the effects of direct interracial contact on children's attitudes. He studied attitude changes, as measured by the Horowitz picture tests, in relation to personality data obtained from a modified form of the Thematic Apperception Test. His results suggest that the boys who increased in prejudice, as compared with those who decreased in prejudice, had a greater need to defy authority and to express strong hostile feelings, coupled with a high degree of concern about the consequences of aggressive behavior (expectation of punishment and retaliation). Thus his findings provide some support for a generalization that is implied by the static correlational studies: Persons with strong personality needs that are satisfied by a hostile attitude toward Negroes (or toward other minority groups) are less likely than others to respond favorably to environmental conditions which ordinarily foster prominority group attitudes.

In general, the available evidence seems consistent with the assumption that those persons who most readily adopt antiminority group attitudes and who most strongly resist changing toward a more tolerant point of view have strong aggressive motives that are satisfied by such attitudes. Presumably, the constellation of personality factors is such as to predispose them to displace hostility toward weak social targets and to project their own repressed impulses onto them.

The readiness to adopt pro or anti attitudes toward powerful social groups, toward various political leaders, and toward various institutions might be expected to involve diverse constellations of personality factors. But little research has been done on attitudes other than ethnocentrism and antiminority group prejudice. One would expect to find additional mechanisms, besides displacement and projection, involved in the acquisition of other need-satisfying beliefs and attitudes. For example, some social scientists have speculated that a strong tendency to develop reaction formations against aggressive impulses predisposes individuals to adopt a pacifist ideology, that reaction formations against sexual impulses incline a person to acceptance of antihedonistic (pro-ascetic) attitudes and values, and that the need for bolstering self-esteem via identification might make for readiness to support militaristic national policies (cf. Lasswell [22] pp. 52 ff.). Many predispositional tendencies of this sort remain to be investigated. Further research on other content areas will undoubtedly increase our knowledge about the ideological and personality factors that underlie susceptibility to specific types of beliefs and attitudes. For this purpose, many suggestive leads can be extracted from clinical investigations of people who appear to be highly susceptible to communications that foster distrust and derogation of authority figures, that oppose social innovations, that present pessimistic views about the future, and so on. Eventually, it should be possible to arrive at a fairly comprehensive set of generalizations concerning personality predispositions which incline people to develop favorable or unfavorable attitudes toward various classes of events and toward various classes of objects.

2. To clarify further the special sense in which the term "topic-free predispositions" is to be understood, it may be useful to consider a few additional examples which highlight the ways in which such factors can be "bound." One obvious, although trivial, example is the skill factor of literacy. Inability to read predisposes a person to remain uninfluenced by any printed or written communication, irrespective of the content of its conclusions. Thus, illiteracy meets the definition of a topic-free predisposition, even though it may provide little basis for predicting how a person will respond to communications via radio, television, or other media. Similarly, lack of familiarity with mathematical and engineering concepts would prevent a person from being influenced by those highly technical books on cybernetics which, like the more popular ones, attempt to influence the reader to accept various social attitudes and beliefs. This would be an extreme example of a predispositional factor which can be designated as topic-free but is nevertheless extremely limited in applicability since it can be used for predicting a person's responsiveness only to those few communications which contain key assertions that employ certain mathematical or engineering concepts.

Except for definitional purposes, the specific factors mentioned in the above illustrations are of relatively little interest. Obviously, in attempting to formulate general hypotheses concerning persuasibility, the more specific kinds of factors will be ignored and attention will be directed primarily to those which seem to have the greatest degree of generality.

3. Although subject to several potential sources of error, the findings based on behavioral ratings lend some empirical support to the assumption that there are general conformity tendencies. A study by Richards and Simons [*32*], which made use of behavioral observations of young children, reports high intercorrelations among ratings of "conformity," "obedience," "social suggestibility," and absence of "resistance"—all of which were found to have high loadings in a single factor. McKinnon's longitudinal case study of a small number of children [*27*] suggests that consistent individual differences in conformity may appear at an early age and remain fairly stable during later years.

Findings based on data from self-rating questionnaires also point to a general factor which seems to be pertinent to persuasibility. Layman [*23*] reports evidence (based on intercorrelations among personality inventory items) of a "self-sufficiency" factor, which is fairly well confirmed by Brogden and Thomas [*3*]: heavy loadings occur on items dealing with preference to plan, think, and arrive at decisions alone, without suggestions from others. But the validity of factors of this sort, extracted from self-rating responses, remains open to question. Hovland and Mandell [*18*] studied the opinion changes induced by a persuasive communication in relation to responses on personality test items (including some of the items that have high loadings in Layman's "self-sufficiency" factor). No significant relationships were found. Both when the communicator stated his conclusion explicitly and when he allowed the audience to draw its own conclusion, those who reported having a strong preference to make up their minds independently showed no less opinion change than those who reported being amenable to suggestion from others. Such evidence calls attention to the need for obtaining objective indices of persuasibility, rather than relying upon the subjective reports obtained from self-rating questionnaires.

While the various findings which have been cited above and in the text (pp. 177 ff.) suggest that there may be some consistent individual differences in responsiveness to social influence, there are additional findings which imply that there is no single, unitary factor of "general suggestibility" [*2, 6, 12*]. Barry [*2*], for instance, found that neither hypnotizability, nor susceptibility in the waking state to direct suggestion (of perceptual illusions, etc.), was significantly correlated with opinion change in response to information about majority opinion. Other investigators [*6, 12*] have shown that the wide variety of tests used to measure "suggestibility" (such as Binet's progressive weights, odor suggestion, heat illusion, body sway suggestion, etc.) involve at least two or more distinct factors. The conformity tendencies with which we are concerned, however, do not include ideomotor suggestibility and readiness to experience perceptual illusions in response to false or misleading cues. Rather, we are concerned with the readiness with which individuals undergo relatively sustained changes in their opinions and attitudes in response to persuasive communications. Even within this more circumscribed area of social conformity, however, there is probably no single general factor. Linton [*25*], for example, found only a small, nonsignificant correlation between two measures of experimentally induced conformity: *a*) amount of opinion change in response to three persuasive communications, each dealing with a different topic, and *b*) changes in autokinetic judgments as a result of hearing another person's judgments. It is noteworthy, however, that each of these conformity measures was found to be significantly correlated with scores on perception tests that are presumed to be indicative of personality tendencies.

4. The data in Figure 11, based on comparisons between subgroups sorted into high and low self-ratings on each personality factor, require careful checks to make sure that the observed relationships are not due to spurious factors. Two main types of checks were carried out [*19*], the results of which preclude the possibility that regression effects or other artifacts could account for the positive findings:

1. The various personality subgroups were compared with respect to initial (precommunication) opinions. No significant or consistent differences were found that could account for the observed differences in opinion change.

2. When the (unexposed) control group was sorted into the same subgroups (according to high and low self-ratings on each set of personality items) only very small and insignificant differences were found in opinion change. All subgroup differences reported as being significant were substantiated by recomputing the significance tests in terms of second order differences between experimental and control subgroups. Thus, the control data tend to rule out the possibility that the findings could be accounted for in terms of factors other than differential responsiveness to the communications.

5. In Robinson's study [*33*] the subjects were 336 sophomores in a college course on Argumentation. They were divided into 43 separate groups, where they discussed a controversial issue (either Capital Punishment or War). Before the group discussions were held, each subject was required to read pertinent discussions of the issue and to prepare a discussion outline which summarized his reading and his thinking. Attitude changes were measured by administering Thurstone Attitude Scales immediately before and after the two-hour discussion period. Students who made shifts of two or more units on the Thurstone Scales were compared with students who showed less attitude change. Those who shifted most were found to have lower "normal" scores and higher "manic," as well as higher "depressive" scores. Robinson interprets his findings as showing that persons who undergo large shifts of attitude have components of temperament which mark them as being "deficient in control and balance" and who characteristically manifest "emotional thinking" and "fluctuations of activity."

It is difficult to accept Robinson's interpretation when one makes a detailed examination of the specific items on which the normal, the depressive and the manic scores are based. Most of the items on the Humm-Wadsworth Depressive Scale deal with the characteristics specified by the self-esteem hypothesis—feelings of personal inadequacy, lack of self-confidence, and depressive affect. Consequently,

Robinson's finding that high depressive scores are associated with attitude change lends some additional support to the self-esteem hypothesis. But when we examine the items comprising the other two scales, we find that they are extremely heterogeneous in content and cannot be used to test any of the hypotheses with which we are concerned in the present chapter, nor do they directly suggest any of the personality factors mentioned in Robinson's interpretative statements. The manic scale, for example, includes items dealing with changeability of mood, worry, responsiveness to the moods of others, excitability, impatience, and other diverse characteristics.

Robinson obtained some additional data, however, that seem to have some bearing on the self-esteem hypothesis. He observed that although there was no correlation between changes in attitudes and the number of times a person participated in the discussion, those participants who were most "argumentative" and "dogmatic" during the discussion made slightly larger changes of opinion than did "cooperative" and "friendly" individuals. No systematic records or significance tests are reported for this observation, but it suggests that *overt* self-assertiveness may be positively correlated with persuasibility. If verified, this finding would imply that the subjective components of low self-esteem—including low self-ratings on assertiveness—may be unrelated to the individual's overt behavior in actual social situations. Further systematic research is obviously needed in order to ascertain the interrelations among low self-esteem, overt self-assertiveness, and persuasibility.

6. Lazarsfeld, Berelson, and Gaudet ([24] pp. 70 ff.) also present some pertinent observations. They compared the personality characteristics of people whose political opinions showed marked changes during a presidential election campaign with people whose opinions remained fairly constant. Whether the changes shown by the former groups were due to political propaganda or to any other form of social influence, however, remains open to question. If it is assumed that social pressures were responsible for the changes, their findings provide additional evidence relevant to high persuasibility. Personality traits of each member of the panel were rated by the interviewer after the fourth interview, by which time he had become fairly well acquainted with the respondent. Those who changed their intended votes during the campaign were reported to be less self-assured, narrower in their social interests, and more unhappy than those who did not change.

Although the authors interpret these results as reflecting "emotional maladjustment," the specific traits point more to low self-confidence and low self-esteem than to the acute psychoneurotic disturbances of the sort to be discussed in the next section of this chapter. But there are two major difficulties, from a methodological point of view, which prevent one from accepting the correlation observed by Lazarsfeld, Berelson, and Gaudet as clear-cut evidence of a relationship between personality factors and persuasibility: a) there is no evidence that the opinion fluctuations manifested by the "changers" were attributable to exposure to persuasive influence as against other causes of fluctuation (e.g., chronic uncertainty); and b) the personality ratings made by the interviewers may have been influenced by knowledge on the part of the interviewer as to whether or not each subject had shown opinion changes.

7. For each year over a four-year period, 250 students (representing the entire student body) filled out questionnaires concerning public issues. This panel study showed that the majority of students did, in fact, become less conservative. Newcomb [30] describes many sources of social influence, emanating from the community at large as well as from the classroom, which tended to change the conservative attitudes with which most of the students entered college. The small minority who clung to their conservative attitudes were presumably resistant to attitude change.

8. Further evidence concerning personality correlates of persuasibility comes from the small number of systematic studies on psychotherapy, psychiatric case work, and related forms of psychological treatment. Particularly pertinent are those on the effects of preventive or remedial treatment of the sort which uses a certain amount of directive or persuasive technique with more or less normal subjects. Such studies are relevant to our present inquiry in that the treatment relies on verbal communication to bring about sustained changes in attitudes toward others and toward the self. To be sure, there are numerous limitations to be taken into account when attempting to use such data for testing the hypotheses which we have been considering. For instance, the therapeutic techniques, and the skill with which they are applied, are likely to vary from one patient to another. As is generally recognized, it is unsafe to assume that failure to respond to verbal methods of treatment is always attributable to the patient rather than to the therapist. Moreover, the attitudes which psychotherapeutic treatment attempts to modify are generally linked with deep-seated personality disturbances, for which rational, intellectual insight has only very limited effects because of neurotic resistances, whereas the attitudes with which we have been primarily concerned are relatively "conflict-free," in the sense that they are not directly affected by neurotic defenses against anxiety which interfere with modification via the operation of higher mental processes. Despite this difference, however, there is evidence—such as that cited in the chapter on fear appeals (pp. 84–89) —which implies that some of the processes of attitude change in psychotherapy are essentially the same as in the more common communication situations of everyday life. Accordingly, one would expect some of the major predispositional factors that are determinants of responsiveness to psychotherapy also to be determinants of susceptibility to other types of attitude change. We shall briefly review the findings from four studies of psychological treatment which have some bearing on the "aggressiveness" hypothesis.

Willoughby [36] compared a group that had responded poorly with an equivalent group that had responded well. Five experienced case workers conducted the treatment and used similar criteria in their ratings. No appreciable differences were noted between the two groups with respect to medical history, family background, external stresses to which the families were exposed, or economic level. It was found that aggressive reactions and overt hostility were more often shown by the unsuccessfully treated than by the successfully treated group. It is possible, of course, that this finding was influenced by spurious "halo" effects due to the fact that the case workers made their clinical ratings at a time when they already knew what the outcome of treatment had been. Nevertheless, the evidence lends some additional support to the overt aggression hypothesis.

Similar findings were also reported by Lodgen [26]. She studied the personality characteristics of 30 mothers, all of whom were originally judged (by the clinical staff of a child guidance clinic) to have attitudes which interfered with the adjustment of their children. Fifteen mothers whose attitudes were changed by treatment were compared with 15 who remained unchanged. Most of the women in the unchanged group were rated as dominating, aggressive, and extremely irritable whereas those in the changed group were rated as predominantly insecure, conscientious, and troubled by feelings of inferiority.

Confirmatory findings, based on a study of a completely different age group, are also reported by Albright and Gambrell [1]. Seventy-nine adolescent children, all of whom had received the same type of psychiatric treatment, were rated on personality traits and on responsiveness to therapy. Those who were extremely aggressive and hostile in almost all situations proved to be most resistant to treatment. These cases are described as being openly defiant, ruthlessly disregarding others in pursuit of their own ends, and addicted to accusing, blaming, criticizing, and abusing others. Those who confined their aggression to certain areas or who were timid and retiring were found to be much more responsive to treatment, provided they did not show signs of social withdrawal. Thus, the inverse correlation between social aggressiveness and persuasibility, as predicted by the overt aggressiveness hypothesis, seems to be borne out by these observations.

The same type of attitudes observed by Albright and Gambrell in their study of resistant adolescents was also noted in a study of adults which made use of a standardized personality test. Harris and Christiansen [14] administered the Minnesota Multiphasic Personality Inventory to 53 medical patients who were given brief psychotherapy because of delayed convalescence from physical disease or injury. The test findings were used to compare the personality traits of those who responded well with those who responded poorly to psychotherapy. The traits that were found to characterize the latter, according to the authors, were the following: *a*) amorality or lax moral standards and rejection of parental authority; *b*) narcissism or ego inflation; *c*) ideas of external influence or of persecution. The authors point out that while such attitudes might be diagnostic of paranoid or other pathological tendencies, none of the patients displayed detectable signs of such pathology in their actual behavior. Hence, the test scores might represent personality tendencies that are not necessarily correlated with severity of mental disorder. In subsequent research on personality correlates of persuasibility it would seem worthwhile to explore the possibility that attitudes of this sort might underlie the generalized hostility and chronic irritability that have been observed to be associated with resistance to social influence.

9. Hoch [*16*] asserts that the neurotic individual lacks elasticity in coping with internal and external situations because the impact of emotional conflicts is so dominant and obsessive that, "like an intractable pain experience," he is unable to throw it off. The same type of emotional rigidity to which Hoch refers might also account for the relationship which emerged from the study of college students who were more or less "normal" individuals (Figure 12).

Newcomb ([*31*] p. 249) has called attention to the fact that despite wide divergences in theory and technique practically all schools of psychotherapy agree that attitudes cannot be changed unless the patient's defensiveness is reduced. Thus, direct clinical experience suggests that rigid defensiveness underlies the neurotic's excessive resistance to attitude change. In such cases, inhibitions in mental functioning, motivated by excessive anxiety or guilt, might continually interfere with responsiveness to the usual sources of social influence in everyday life.

References

1. Albright, Sue, and Gambrell, Helen. Personality traits as criteria for the psychiatric treatment of adolescents. *Smith College studies in social work,* 1938, *9,* 1–26.
2. Barry, H., Jr. A test for negativism and compliance. *J. Abnorm. Soc. Psychol.,* 1931, *25,* 373–381.
3. Brogden, H. E., and Thomas, W. F. The primary traits in personality items purporting to measure sociability. *J. Psychol.,* 1943, *16,* 85–97.
4. Buros, O. K., ed. *The third mental measurements yearbook.* New Brunswick, Rutgers Univ. Press, 1949.
5. Coser, Rose L. Political involvement and interpersonal relations. *Psychiatry,* 1951, *14,* 213–222.
6. Eysenck, H. J. *Dimensions of personality.* London, Routledge & Kegan Paul Ltd., 1947.
7. Fenichel, O. *The psychoanalytic theory of neurosis.* New York, Norton, 1945.
8. Ferguson, L. W. An analysis of the generality of suggestibility to group opinion. *Character & Pers.,* 1944, *12,* 237–244.
9. Festinger, L., Schachter, S. and Back, K. *Social pressures in informal groups.* New York, Harper, 1950.
10. Fiske, D. W. Consistency of the factorial structures of personality ratings from different sources. *J. Abnorm. Soc. Psychol.,* 1949, *44,* 329–344.
11. Freud, S. *A general introduction to psychoanalysis.* New York, Garden City Publishing Co., 1943. Trans. by Joan Riviere.
12. Furneaux, W. D. The prediction of susceptibility to hypnosis. *J. Personal.,* 1946, *14,* 281–294.
13. Grinker, R. R., and Spiegel, J. P. *Men under stress.* Philadelphia, Blakiston, 1945.
14. Harris, R. E., and Christiansen, Carole. Prediction of response to brief psychotherapy. *J. Psychol.,* 1946, *21,* 269–284.
15. Hartley, E. L., and Hartley, Ruth E. *Fundamentals of social psychology.* New York, Knopf, 1952.
16. Hoch, P. H. Biosocial aspects of anxiety. In P. H. Hoch and J. Zubin, eds., *Anxiety.* New York, Grune & Stratton, 1950, 105–116.
17. Hovland, C. I., Lumsdaine, A. A., and Sheffield, F. D. *Experiments on mass communication.* Princeton Univ. Press, 1949.
18. Hovland, C. I., and Mandell, W. An experimental comparison of conclusion-drawing by the communicator and by the audience. *J. Abnorm. Soc. Psychol.,* 1952, *47,* 581–588.
19. Janis, I. L. Personality correlates of susceptibility to persuasion. *J. Personal.,* 1954. (In press.)
20. Janis, I. L. and Feshbach, S. Effects of fear-arousing communications. *J. Abnorm. Soc. Psychol.,* 1953, *48,* 78–92.

21. Janis, I. L., and Feshbach, S. Personality differences associated with responsiveness to fear-arousing communications. 1953. (In preparation.)
22. Lasswell, H. D. *World politics and personal insecurity.* New York, McGraw-Hill, 1935.
23. Layman, Emma M. An item analysis of the adjustment questionnaire. *J. Psychol.,* 1940, *10,* 87–106.
24. Lazarsfeld, P. F., Berelson, B., and Gaudet, Hazel. *The people's choice.* New York, Duell, Sloan & Pearce, 1944.
25. Linton, Harriet B. Relations between mode of perception and the tendency to conform. Ph.D. dissertation, Yale Univ., 1952.
26. Lodgen, Pearl. Some criteria for the treatability of mothers and children by a child guidance clinic. *Smith College studies in social work,* 1937, *7,* 302–324.
27. McKinnon, Kathern Mae. *Consistency and change in behavior manifestations.* New York, Bureau of Publications. Teachers College, Columbia Univ., 1942.
28. Murphy, G., Murphy, Lois B., and Newcomb, T. M. *Experimental social psychology* (rev. ed.). New York, Harper, 1937.
29. Mussen, P. H. Some personality and social factors related to changes in children's attitudes toward Negroes. *J. Abnorm. Soc. Psychol.,* 1950, *45,* 423–441.
30. Newcomb, T. M. *Personality and social change.* New York, Dryden Press, 1943.
31. Newcomb, T. M. *Social psychology.* New York, Dryden Press, 1950.
32. Richards, T. W., and Simons, Marjorie P. The Fels Child Behavior Scales. *Genet. Psychol. Monogr.,* 1941, *24,* 259–309.
33. Robinson, K. F. An experimental study of the effects of group discussion upon the social attitudes of college students. *Speech Monogr.,* 1941, *8,* 34–57.
34. Stouffer, S. A., Guttman, L., Suchman, E. A., Lazarsfeld, P. F., Star, Shirley A., and Clausen, J. A. *Measurement and prediction.* Princeton Univ. Press, 1950.
35. Wegrocki, H. J. The effect of prestige suggestibility on emotional attitude. *J. Soc. Psychol.,* 1934, *5,* 384–394.
36. Willoughby, R. R. A note on personality factors affecting the rehabilitation of problem families. In McNemar, Q., and Merrill, Maud A., eds. *Studies in Personality,* New York, McGraw-Hill, 1942. Pp. 281–283.

CHAPTER 7: *Acquiring Conviction Through*
Active Participation

IN MANY everyday situations people are subjected to strong pressures to play a social role in which they are required to express ideas that are not necessarily in accord with their private convictions. For example, when a man begins his career as a business executive or in a profession, he is likely to become acutely aware of the necessity to express the "accepted" views that go along with his position in the community. Frequently the opinions that he overtly expresses come from various norm-setting communications, to which he is expected to conform. In order to live up to social role expectations, the individual will repeat the message to others as his own opinion, even though he may have inner reservations. When the person is induced to assert what has been said in a communication as if it represented his own opinion, we use the term "active participation."

That active participation induced through assuming a role can sometimes lead to changes in personal convictions has been suggested by numerous impressionistic observations. Myers [*17*], for example, claimed that a number of the "chronic kickers" at an Army camp during the first World War showed a marked improvement in morale as a result of their participation in a public speaking course, where they were under competitive pressure to invent speeches favorable to Army life: "They kept at this boosting for several class periods until they really began to believe what they were saying and to act accordingly" [*17*].

Role playing, as a device for inducing changes in attitude, has recently been introduced into adult education, leadership training programs, employee counseling, and group psychotherapy [*1, 14, 15, 16, 21*]. The usual procedure consists of applying psychodramatic techniques in which persons play specified roles in a simulated life situation. One of the main values of this device, according to its proponents, is that it has a corrective influence on beliefs and attitudes which underlie chronic difficulties in human relations (cf. Maier [*15*]).

In this chapter we shall examine hypotheses and experimental evidence bearing on the effects of one type of demand that is made upon a person when he is induced to play a social role—namely, the requirement that he actively participate in communicating various opinions to others as if he really accepted them. Our inquiry will be focused on one general problem which may have important implications for developing a sound theoretical account of the processes of attitude change: Under what conditions does overt verbal conformity facilitate or interfere with acceptance of the beliefs or opinions advocated by a communication?

Although investigations of the effects of active participation are pertinent to practical ways and means of increasing the effectiveness of persuasive communications, our interest is primarily in discovering the psychological mechanisms involved. Such discoveries could help to illuminate many aspects of social behavior that extend far beyond the field of mass communication. It is by no means improbable that active participation plays an important part in the socialization of children and in the acculturation of adults who find themselves under strong pressure to conform outwardly to social role expectations. Hence research on verbal conformity of the sort to be discussed here may ultimately help to increase our understanding of the conditions under which role playing experiences in daily life lead to important changes in beliefs, preferences, values, and attitudes.

BACKGROUND

We do not assume that all the various instances of active participation which occur in diverse communication situations form a homogeneous class of variables. A given method of eliciting overt verbal conformity may involve several different components, any one of which could exert some influence on the way the content of a communication is perceived, interpreted, assimilated, and reinforced. Until each variable is systematically investigated with respect to the ways it influences the effectiveness of persuasive communications, one cannot hope to predict the outcome of any given device.

Experimental evidence indicates that one of the effects of overt verbalization is to increase the rate of learning verbal material. A study on audience participation, reported by Hovland, Lumsdaine, and Sheffield ([6] pp. 228 ff.), showed that elicitation of overt verbal responses resulted in a marked gain in learning efficiency: the Army's phonetic alphabet, presented in a film strip, was learned more rapidly by an audience which was required to rehearse the names aloud than by an equivalent audience which merely saw and heard the communication. Studies of this kind indicate that audience participation augments the effectiveness of purely instructional communications.

Little prior research has been done on the parallel problem with which we are concerned in this chapter: Does active participation have any effect on the acquisition of *beliefs or opinions* from persuasive communications? A few experiments have been reported which suggest the possibility that acceptance, as well as learning, may be affected by eliciting overt verbalizations.

The device that has been most frequently investigated is that of eliciting overt verbal participation by using the discussion group method of teaching. Several studies present evidence showing that the discussion method produces greater changes in beliefs, preferences, and attitudes than the more passive types of exposure [4, 20, 22]. Hadley [4], for example, reports a greater positive change in appraisals of poems after classroom discussion than after silent reading. Studies of group decision show similar facilitating effects [2, 12, 13, 18]. Unfortunately, however, no clear-cut conclusions concerning the influence of active participation can be drawn from these studies because they lack controls on communication exposure. For instance, as Lewin has pointed out ([13] p. 337), the positive effects of group discussion could be due to the increased information about the opinions held by others in the group, which was not available to the "control" subjects.

In the sections which follow we shall examine a series of studies, conducted as part of our program, that were specifically designed to investigate the effects of active participation on opinion change. In a final section the theoretical implications will be highlighted by discussing alternative mediating mechanisms that may account for the experimental findings.

RESEARCH EVIDENCE

Influence of Role Playing on Acceptance

In our research program, interest in the effects of verbal conformity began with explorations of a phenomenon that seems to occur in many different social situations: namely, that when a person verbalizes an idea to others he becomes more inclined to accept it himself. It is often said, for example, that salesmen become convinced by their own salestalks and that political speakers tend to be swayed by their own improvised arguments.

As a preliminary step in exploring this phenomenon, Janis interviewed a group of collegiate debaters who, as members of an organized team, repeatedly were required to express publicly views that did not necessarily correspond to their personal convictions. Most of the debaters reported that they frequently ended up by accepting the conclusions which they had been arbitrarily assigned to defend. This phenomenon, like that noted earlier by Myers [17], suggests that "saying is believing"—that overtly expressing an opinion in conformity to social demands will influence the individual's private convictions.

The role-playing effects described above have not yet been verified by systematic research. If substantiated, they would still remain open to a variety of alternative explanations. For instance, inducing the individual to play a role in which he must publicly advocate a given position might guarantee exposure to one set of arguments to the exclusion of others. Thus, the apparent effect of active participation might merely be the result of concentrated exposure to persuasive material favoring only one side of the issue. If this is the case, the phenomenon under discussion might turn out to represent nothing more than a series of somewhat unusual illustrations of a rather obvious proposition, that increased exposure to arguments favoring a given position will generally tend to produce increased opinion change. On the other hand, it is possible that even when exposed to the same persuasive communications people who are required to verbalize the communications to others will tend to be more influenced than those who are only passively exposed. Consequently, it seemed worthwhile to attempt to investigate the effects of role playing in a controlled laboratory situation where, if the alleged gain from role playing occurs, it might be possible to isolate the critical factors and systematically explore the mediating mechanisms.

Janis and King [7] devised an experiment in which communication exposure was held constant. They compared the opinion changes of two experimental groups: a) "active participants" who were induced to play a role which required them to deliver a persuasive communication to others, and b) "passive controls" who merely read and listened to the same communication.

The experiment was conducted with male college students in a series of small group meetings. The students were given an "oral speaking test" which involved being exposed to three different communications. They were told that the purpose was to assess their ability to speak effectively in a group conference situation. At the end of the session they were told that, in order to study agreement among different judges, it was necessary to have their ratings on each speaker's performance and their answers to a series of questions concerning their interest in, and opinions on, the various topics covered. Opinion changes produced by the communications were measured by comparing each student's postcommunication answers with those he had given in a general opinion survey conducted approximately four weeks earlier.

In the experimental sessions the subjects were asked to give an informal talk based on a prepared outline. Each active participant was instructed to play the role of a sincere advocate of the given point of view, while the others listened to his talk and read the prepared outline. The three communications were presented by different speakers so that each subject in turn delivered one of the communications and was passively exposed to the other two. In order to prevent selective attention effects, none of the subjects was told what the topic of his talk would be until his turn came to present it.

Each of the communications took an extreme position on a controversial issue concerning future events. The arguments were logically relevant but highly biased in that they played up and interpreted "evidence" supporting only one side of the issue. Communication *A* predicted that as a result of television and other recent developments, "movie attendance will be hit so hard that *two out of every three* movie theaters will have to go out of business during the next three years." Communication *B* took the position that "within two years, the total meat supply available to the civilian population in this country will decline to the point where there will be only *50 per cent* of the amount that is currently available." Communication *C* argued that "a completely effective cure for the common cold will be discovered very soon—probably within the next year or so."

The results presented in Table 13 indicate that in the case of two of the three communications (*A* and *B*), the active participants were more influenced than the passive controls. In the case of the third communication (*C*) both groups showed approximately the same amount of opinion change. But additional findings showed that the active participants who presented Communication *C*, like those who presented the other two communications, expressed a higher level of *confidence* in their postcommunication opinions than the corresponding passive controls. The results indicate that active participation with respect to Communication *C*, while producing no increase in the incidence of opinion change, produced a significant net gain in confidence among those students whose opinion estimates were most influenced by the communication. Insofar as confidence ratings can be regarded as indicators of the degree of conviction with which the new opinions are held, the positive findings based on Communication *A* and *B* were partially confirmed by the findings based on Communication *C*. These findings, together with various methodological checks on potential sources of spurious differences, support the following conclusion: Active participation induced by role playing tends to augment the effectiveness of a persuasive communication.

Additional observations were made by the same authors to explore possible psychological mechanisms underlying the gain from active participation. Their further inquiry took account of the fact that under certain stimulus conditions (represented by Communications *A* and *B*) a clear-cut gain from active participation was manifested by increased opinion change, whereas under other conditions (represented by Communication *C*) the gain was manifested only in the form of higher confidence ratings. They examined the experimenter's records on each subject's behavior during the session and the responses

TABLE 13. *Comparison of Active Participants with Passive Controls: Changes in Opinion Estimates following Exposure to Persuasive Communications*

Experimental Groups	Change in Opinion Estimates * Net Change (Slight or Sizable)	Net Change (Sizable)	
Communication *A:* (Movie Theaters)			
Active participants (N = 31)	71%	45%	
			$p = .01$
Passive controls (N = 57)	58%	21%	
Communication *B:* (Meat Shortage)			
Active participants (N = 29)	62%	41½%	
			$p = .01$
Passive controls (N = 57)	52%	17%	
Communication *C:* (Cold Cure)			
Active participants (N = 30)	53%	40%	
			$p > .30$
Passive controls (N = 53)	51%	45%	

* The "net change (slight or sizable)" is defined as the percentage changing in the direction advocated by the communication minus the percentage changing in the opposite direction. The "net sizable change" in the case of Communication *A* was the difference between the percentage who lowered or raised their estimate by 5,000 or more. For Communication *B,* a sizable change was 25 or more; for Communication *C* it was 5 or more.

From Janis and King [7]

given to a standard interview conducted at the end of the session. Two suggestive leads emerged:

1. The active participants who presented Communication *C* seemed to engage in *less improvisation* than those who presented the other two communications. The Communication *C* group appeared to adhere much more closely to the prepared outline, making little attempt

to reformulate the main points, to insert illustrative examples, or to invent additional arguments.

2. Subjects in the Communication *C* group seemed to experience much more difficulty than the other groups in presenting their talks. During their performance they appeared to be more hesitant and tense. Afterward they expressed many more complaints about the task, claiming that their topic (the prospects of developing a cure for the common cold) was more difficult to present than either of the other two. In general, these subjects seemed *less satisfied* with their performance than those who presented the other two communications.

The improvisation factor could not be investigated further with the data at hand, but additional evidence pertinent to the satisfaction factor was available. Noting that there may have been an objective basis for the greater dissatisfaction experienced on Communication *C* (because of the greater amount of unfamiliar technical material it contained), the authors investigated the subjects' own appraisals of their performance by making use of a self-rating questionnaire which had been filled out by all students after exposure to the three communications. The results showed that the active participants who presented Communication *C* rated themselves lower than those who presented either of the other two communications. Further evidence was then obtained by subdividing each group of active participants according to the self-ratings. The greatest amount of opinion change was found among those who rated their speaking performance as satisfactory or better. Active participants who felt that they performed poorly, on the other hand, failed to show any more opinion change than the passive controls, and on one of the communications (*C*) showed reliably less change than the passive controls. These supplementary observations suggested that *satisfaction with one's own performance* may be an important factor that influences the magnitude and direction of participation effects.

IMPROVISATION VERSUS SATISFACTION

Both the improvisation factor and the satisfaction factor were investigated experimentally in another study on the effects of role playing. The second experiment was designed by King and Janis [*9*] for the purpose of determining *a*) whether the main findings on the gain from role playing would be confirmed when a much more familiar and more ego-involving topic is used, and *b*) whether either improvisation or satisfaction is critical in producing participation effects.

The persuasive communication used in the second experiment dealt with the prospects of military service for college students. It contained arguments in support of two main conclusions: 1) that *over 90 per cent* of college students will be drafted within one year after their graduation, and 2) that the length of military service required of the majority of college students will be at least *three* years, i.e., one or more years longer than the current official requirement.

All of the subjects were college students of draft age who were free from any possible physical defect that might enable them to be deferred on medical grounds. Accordingly, it was anticipated that the communication would be of considerable personal concern to them and that initial opinions would be well structured because the subjects had acquired a good deal of information about this topic, had thought about it frequently, and were well aware of the pertinent factors involved.

The same role-playing instructions were used as in the first experiment, requiring the active participants to give a convincing oral presentation. The purpose was again described as assessing oral speaking ability. But in this experiment the active participants, instead of talking to a small group, made a tape-recording (which they were told would be presented later to a group of judges) with only the experimenter present at the time. The passive controls read the same communication silently but did not present it orally. In order to control the level of attention and other factors associated with the "set" to give an oral presentation, a special procedure was introduced which involved using an irrelevant communication in addition to the critical one. All subjects, including the passive controls, were initially told that they would be asked to give an oral presentation of one or the other communication. After having silently read both communications, the subjects in the experimental groups were asked to make an oral presentation based on the critical communication, whereas the control subjects were asked to give a talk based on the irrelevant one.

For the purpose of investigating the improvisation and satisfaction factors, two experimental groups were used: Group A, the main experimental group, was given a comparatively *difficult* task which required a *high degree of improvisation*—presenting the talk without the script, shortly after having silently read it; Group B, the supplementary experimental group, was given a much easier task which required *no improvisation*—reading the talk from a completely prepared script. The main experimental group was further subdivided with respect to being given favorable ratings, unfavorable ratings, or no ratings on their speaking performance.

It will be noted that comparison of Group A with Group B pits the improvisation factor against the satisfaction factor. The subjects' self-ratings concerning their performance were found to be markedly influenced by the more difficult task, Group A showing significantly lower satisfaction ratings than Group B. The subdivisions of Group A were designed to provide additional observations as to the effects of different degrees of satisfaction induced by social rewards, when improvisation is held constant. As expected, self-ratings were found to be significantly affected by the communicator's ratings.

Opinion changes were studied by comparing responses on a post-communication questionnaire with those obtained from an opinion survey conducted several months earlier. The main results, shown in Table 14, support the improvisation hypothesis in that they bear out the prediction that subjects who give an improvised talk (Group A) will be more influenced by the persuasive communication than those who engage in oral reading (Group B) or in silent reading (the passive control group). Group A consistently showed more opinion change than Group B. This trend is apparent on all five items as well as on the combined index. Group A showed more opinion change than the passive control group on four out of the five items and differed reliably on the combined index. Thus the results indicate that there is a significant gain from active participation when the individual is required to engage in improvised role playing.

Comparison of Group B with the passive control group, on the other hand, indicates that there was no consistent gain from oral reading. In general, the results fail to support the satisfaction hypothesis. A markedly higher degree of satisfaction was expressed in the self-

TABLE 14. *Effect of Role Playing on Opinion Changes following Exposure to a Communication concerning the Prospects of Military Service for College Students*

Opinion Items	Net Percentage Who Changed in the Direction Advocated by the Communication		
	Improvisation Group A (N = 32)	Oral Reading Group B (N = 23)	Silent Reading Control Group (N = 20)
1. Estimates of required length of service for draftees	41	27	5
2. Estimates of percentage of college students who will be deferred	44	26	25
3. Estimates of percentage of college students who will become officers	70	47	45
4. Personal expectations of length of military service	59	46	50
5. Personal expectations of being drafted	50	26	55
6. Combined index: per cent influenced on three or more of the five opinion items	87½	54½	65

$p = .01$

$p = .03$

From King and Janis [9]

ratings obtained from Group B than in those from Group A; accordingly, the satisfaction hypothesis would predict more opinion change in Group B than in Group A. This prediction is definitely not borne out by the evidence in Table 14. Furthermore, the supplementary data based on the comparisons of the subdivisions of Group A failed to show any sizable or consistent differences in the direction predicted by the satisfaction hypothesis: The subjects who received favorable ratings from the experimenter on their improvised talks had manifested a relatively high degree of satisfaction in their self-ratings, but showed approximately the same amount of opinion change as those who received unfavorable ratings or no ratings.

Thus the second experiment [9] supports the observations on the improvisation differential noted in the first experiment [7] but fails to confirm the correlational findings based on self-ratings. More weight is probably to be given to the findings of the second study, since the experimental conditions successfully *induced* alterations in the level of satisfaction (as shown by significant differences in self-ratings). If the findings are confirmed in further replications of the second experiment, the satisfaction hypothesis cannot be regarded as an adequate explanation of the experimental findings on the effects of role playing. The possibility remains, however, that in the second experiment some unknown factor may have obscured or counteracted the positive effects of enhancing the subjects' satisfaction with their performance. For instance, boredom on the part of those who performed the easy task—or (secret) pride on the part of those who performed the more difficult task—might have operated to some extent in the second experiment but not in the first.

For the present it can be said that the weight of the evidence clearly favors the improvisation factor as the more important one in mediating the observed effects of active participation. Obviously, further research on the improvisation factor will be required in order to investigate alternative mediating mechanisms of the sort to be discussed in the final section of this chapter.

Further evidence suggesting that overt verbalization which stimulates thinking about convincing arguments tends to augment opinion change comes from another study in the present research program, carried out by Kelman [8]. Seventh grade students were given a talk in which the speaker asserted that jungle comic books are more suitable reading than fantastic hero books. Immediately afterward they were asked to write essays in support of one or the other type of comic book. Three experimental variations were introduced by offering different incentives for writing in favor of the speaker's position: 1) the high incentive group was told that *every* student who conformed would be given both a small and a large prize; 2) the low incentive group was told that if they conformed they would be *eligible* for the large prize (which would be awarded, however, only to a few of the members of their class) and that if they chose the *opposite* position on the issue they would *definitely* be given the small prize; 3) the control group was offered no special incentive. Opinion changes in all three groups were measured by comparing postcommunication responses on an opinion questionnaire with those given one week earlier, before exposure to the communication.

As expected, the control group had the smallest and the high incentive group the largest percentage of subjects whose essays conformed with the communicator's position. The amount of opinion change, however, did not vary directly with the degree of conformity: significantly more change was found in the low incentive group than in the other two. Thus the results indicate that, at least with the essay-writing type of verbal response, opinion change is not a simple function of verbal conformity with the communicator's position but varies with the incentive conditions under which conformity is elicited.

Having arrived at this finding, Kelman sought to determine in what way the high and low incentive conditions produced different reactions. One of the outstanding findings was that the verbalizations elicited by the high and low incentive conditions were not of equal quality. The essays written by the low incentive group tended to be longer, to include more improvisation, and to be of better over-all quality (as rated by several judges) than those written by the high incentive group (cf. Table 15). Moreover, when the subjects who wrote conforming essays were asked a series of questions concerning their subjective thoughts and feelings, those in the high incentive group reported somewhat more resentment and more negativism than those in the low incentive group (e.g., thoughts about how wrong the speaker was and how unpleasant it was to be writing the essay).

Kelman interprets his results as supporting the hypothesis that the

TABLE 15. *Mean Scores on Three Measures of the Quality of Essays Written by Conformists under Three Different Incentive Conditions*

	EXPERIMENTAL GROUPS		
	No Incentive: Control (N = 32)	Low Incentive (N = 49)	High Incentive (N = 61)	*p* for Low vs. High Incentive Comparisons
1. Number of words in essay	102.34	118.63	95.43	<.001
2. Ratings of over-all quality	2.61	3.34	2.66	<.001
3. Ratings on production of new arguments	2.33	3.12	2.72	.06

From Kelman [8]

gain in attitude change depends upon whether the implicit verbal responses accompanying the essay writing are of a supporting or an interfering nature. He points out that the higher incidence of supporting material in the essays of the low incentive group may have been due to *a*) greater need to make a choice (because of the conflicting incentives offered), which may have stimulated the subjects to think through their position; *b*) the increased effort to do a convincing job (because of the competition stimulated by offering a large prize to be awarded to a chosen few); or *c*) less awareness of pressure to conform, with correspondingly less interference from antagonistic thoughts. In any case Kelman's findings, like those from the role-playing experiments [7, 9], suggest that eliciting overt verbalization tends to augment opinion change if it stimulates active rehearsal of convincing arguments.

IMPLICATIONS

From the preceding review of the experimental evidence that has accumulated so far, we have seen that under certain conditions active participation induced by role playing (or by other devices) tends to augment the effectiveness of persuasive communications. In this section we shall discuss various psychological factors that may determine the way in which verbal conformity influences the processes of opinion change. An attempt will be made to specify a number of alternative mediating mechanisms and to formulate theoretical implications which pose important problems for subsequent research in this area. For this purpose, various leads will be highlighted which are tentatively suggested by one or another of the experimental studies described in the preceding sections. Although some of the leads appear to be much more promising than others, too little research has been done as yet to warrant any definite conclusions concerning the key factors which determine the attitude effects of role playing. One of the values of exploring the possible implications of the preliminary research findings on verbal conformity is that it focuses attention on psychological mechanisms of opinion change which might otherwise be neglected.

EXTRANEOUS REWARDS

When a persuasive communication is effective, one might expect that it is because the content of the communication in one way or another provides intrinsic rewards—for instance, by evoking satisfying anticipations of attaining a goal or of averting a threat. But before examining the possible effects of verbal conformity on the complex processes involved in intrinsic rewards, we shall consider a somewhat simpler mechanism based on purely *extraneous* rewards (which have no relation to the content of the communication). The latter might operate in such a way as to reinforce whatever belief happens to be verbalized at the time the rewarding experience occurs.

Razran [*19*] has reported experimental findings which suggest that extraneous situational factors (such as an enjoyable meal or an unpleasant odor) can influence the acceptance of a communication. A similar type of effect might be produced by the social reactions that are evoked when one overtly verbalizes a communication in the presence of others. For instance, when a person expresses his *own* opinion to others, social approval or disapproval of what he says may facilitate its acceptance or motivate its rejection. But another sort of social effect of a purely extraneous character might also be postulated: approval of a person's *performance* in the role of communicator could reinforce whatever ideas he happens to be expressing, whether or not he initially believes what he is saying. One hypothesis that would follow from this assumption is that when a person conforms outwardly to social demands by playing a role which requires him to advocate a given opinion, he will begin to believe what he is saying if he is made to feel that he says it well. According to this hypothesis, extraneous social reinforcements would have an important influence on the transformation of outer conformity to inner conformity.

Results from one of the studies suggest that there might be a mechanism of this kind. In the first experiment by Janis and King [7], the analysis of self-ratings in relation to opinion changes suggested that when communicatees are induced to play a role which requires overt verbalization of a persuasive communication the effectiveness of the communication will be increased or decreased depending upon whether the communicatees feel satisfied or dissatisfied with their performance. During the experimental sessions there were no apparent sources of extraneous social rewards from the environment. (Since the others present remained silent, the active participant had no opportunity to know how they were reacting to his talk, except possibly by subtle signs from their facial expressions or from their body movements.) But even in the absence of any obvious external cues to social approval, it seems probable that *anticipations* of such approval would occur if the individual felt he was performing well. Hence, self-delivered cues could conceivably provide the basis for extraneous rewards.

In the light of the evidence from the second experiment by King and Janis [9], however, any explanation of the experimental results which postulates an extraneous reinforcement mechanism becomes questionable. The second study (on improvisation versus satisfaction) showed that when feelings of satisfaction were experimentally varied there were no apparent differences in amount of opinion change. Despite this negative evidence, it would nevertheless seem premature to discard the hypothesis suggested by the first experiment until other implications of the extraneous reward mechanism have been investigated.

ATTENTION EFFECTS

Experimental data on rote verbal learning, as noted earlier, show that overt verbalization facilitates learning of the informational content of a communication. The increase in learning efficiency may come about partly through heightening the listener's attention to the content of the communication. If so, this could be one of the factors that helps to explain the gain in effectiveness of persuasive communications produced by active participation. The ego-involving task of verbalizing a communication to others probably induces greater attention to the content, which may increase the chances that one will think about it and be influenced by it.

In the experiments on role playing, however, attention effects do not seem to be crucial. If increased attention due to active participation were responsible for the increased opinion change, one would expect to find a similar effect from any other device which evokes increased attention to the content. One such device would be to require the communicatees to take careful notes on the main arguments contained in the communication. This device was applied to a supplementary group of passive controls, in the first experiment by Janis and King [7]. The supplementary group did *not* give an oral presentation but was asked to follow each of the three communications carefully and to take notes on the main arguments given in each of the three speeches. Despite the fact that their notes were fairly complete and indicated a relatively high degree of attention to the content of all three communications, the subjects in the supplementary group showed approximately the same amount of opinion change as those in the original group of passive controls, whose attention level was presumably lower. Consequently, the supplementary findings suggest that variations in attention level probably were not a crucial factor that could account for the observed gain in opinion change produced by active participation.[1]

In the second experiment by King and Janis [9] an immediate recall test was given to the active participants who had presented an improvised talk and to those who had read aloud from the script, as well as to the passive controls. The test consisted of seven questions covering some of the main items of information presented in the communication. It was found that the improvisation group did *not* obtain higher information scores than the oral reading group or the passive control group. Hence it seems unlikely that learning factors could account for the greater amount of opinion change shown by the improvisation group.

Despite the negative evidence which has just been cited, there is some reason to expect that under certain conditions the heightened attention produced by eliciting overt verbal conformity may prove to be an important factor. For instance, in circumstances where there is some source of distraction which interferes with attention to a persuasive communication, or where the communicatees have very low motivation to expose themselves to the content of the communication, eliciting overt verbalization of the content may have considerable effect on the level of attention and thereby increase the chances that the communication will be influential.

SELECTIVE RETENTION EFFECTS

By facilitating verbal learning, active participation may increase the amount of informational content that is retained during the post-communication period. A study by Kurtz and Hovland [*11*] has shown that overt verbalization at the time of observation of stimulus objects will significantly improve the subsequent recall of the objects. Seventy-two elementary school children observed an array of 16 familiar objects. Half of them were given a sheet of names of the objects and the other half a sheet of pictures. As the experimenter indicated each of the objects, the subjects found and circled on their sheet the name or picture of the object. The group that had printed names was asked to pronounce each name aloud as the experimenter pointed to the object. Without prior announcement all subjects were tested for retention a week later. Both on recognition and on recall tests there was a clear superiority for the verbalization condition. Results from the recall test, as shown in Table 16, indicate that the subjects who had verbalized at the time of initial observation recalled more items correctly and made fewer incorrect responses than the subjects in the control group.

TABLE 16. *Mean Number of Correct and Incorrect Recall Responses by Verbalization and Control Groups*

Group	A. Correct Responses	B. Incorrect Responses
Overt verbalization	7.33	0.25
Control (no overt verbalization)	5.00	1.17
p	<.01	<.01

From Kurtz and Hovland [11]

If there is greater retention from overt verbalization, there would be a greater chance that the arguments and conclusions presented in a persuasive communication would "come to mind" on future occasions when the same topic is again brought to the focus of attention. The selective recall of contents which were previously verbalized may set the stage for *subsequent reinforcements* by influencing what the person will think and say in subsequent situations. For example, if the communicatee later repeats to others some of the arguments and conclusions which he recalls from a persuasive communication, he may elicit social approval or disapproval which could facilitate or interfere with acceptance. Or the subsequent reinforcement may come about when, upon further reflection, the individual selectively recalls the crucial arguments or motivating appeals that had been actively rehearsed at the time of exposure to the antecedent communication. Thus, any active participation device which augments retention of the content of a communication may ultimately influence acceptance by increasing the chances that the content subsequently will be thought about or expressed under conditions where reinforcements can occur. One would expect this type of carry-over effect to be especially prominent in the case of persuasive communications which deal with opinions that are contingent upon retention of a high degree of informational content—for example, the evaluation of a complicated plan or policy which one would be unlikely to think about or to discuss unless one could recall the details.

In the experiments on verbal conformity conducted so far, opinion changes were measured within a short time after exposure to the persuasive communication. Further studies on the persistence of opinion changes induced through active participation are needed in order to take account of possible gains in acceptance due to selective retention effects.

IMPROVISATION FACTORS

All of the experimental evidence available at present points to the improvisation factor as a crucial one in determining the effects of active participation. Mere repetition of the original communication has little or no effect as compared with an improvised restatement of the communication. It will be recalled that this was clearly shown by the King and Janis experiment [9] in which oral reading of a prepared script was compared with an extemporaneous oral presentation (Table 14). Supporting evidence also came from Kelman's experiment [8], which pointed to the importance of the quality of the conforming essays that the subjects had been induced to write.

One of the salient characteristics of improvisation is that the individual *reformulates the communication in his own words*. It is possible that reformulation per se may give rise to a marked gain in *comprehension* of the content and thereby augment the chances that the persuasive communication will be influential. Opinion change may be facilitated by the mere act of translating the content into a more familiar vocabulary—perhaps by making it more meaningful in that the implications of the arguments become more apparent and the conclusions more easily assimilated into the person's existing cognitive framework of beliefs, expectations, and values.

That this particular aspect of improvisation might account for the experimental results on active participation does not seem very probable in the light of the available evidence. The differences in quality of verbalization noted among the experimental groups in Kelman's study probably did not involve any marked differences with respect to reformulation since all of the subjects wrote their essays from memory and were instructed to write them in their own words. The high incentive condition presumably induced a higher percentage of subjects to write essays in which they reformulated the communication in their own words than was the case with the control condition, which allowed the students more freedom to choose the alternative position. Since Kelman found no significant difference in the amount of opinion change resulting from these two conditions, it would appear that reformulation had no effect (or so little effect as to be overridden by the mild resentment that might have been evoked by stimulating the subjects to misrepresent their own position).

Insofar as the reformulation factor is assumed to exert its influence solely by facilitating the individual's ability to comprehend the communication, it would not seem to offer a likely explanation for the outcome of the experiments by Janis and King on role playing. The communications on which the active participants based their improvised talks contained relatively obvious arguments that could be readily comprehended by the college students who served as subjects. There was only one communication (the prospects of discovering a cure for the common cold) which contained difficult technical material such that some beneficial effect might be expected from stimulating the students to reformulate it in their own words. And yet it was precisely on this communication that active participation had the least effect.[2]

Thus the reformulation factor does not appear to account for the available experimental findings on the gain in communication effectiveness produced by active participation. There may be other types of communication situations, however, in which this factor could become an extremely important one. For instance, the cognitive gain from reformulation might markedly augment the effectiveness of persuasive communications which attempt to induce conformity to a complicated series of instructions, especially when the audience does not readily grasp the purpose of each of the important steps. Further systematic research is obviously required in order to determine the conditions under which reformulation influences acceptance of persuasive communications.

If we tentatively assume that reformulation is not the essential characteristic which accounts for the observed effects of inducing an improvised restatement of a communication, we are led to seek for other characteristics of improvisation which may prove to be of greater importance. Accordingly, we shall examine the possible implications of another feature of improvisation: the spontaneous additions and elaborations of the arguments contained in the original communication. This characteristic consistently appeared to be associated with amount of opinion change induced by active participation in the role-playing experiments [7, 9] and in the essay-writing experiment [8]. We shall briefly consider some of the ways in which this factor might have the effect of augmenting the influence of a persuasive communication.

Hollingworth [5] points out that the strength of a suggestion depends in part on the degree to which it seems to be of spontaneous origin: resentment and negativism will often interfere with the acceptance of a *direct* suggestion, whereas the subject's impression that he is acting on his own initiative will enhance the effectiveness of an indirect suggestion. Discussions of the principles of nondirective psychotherapy also imply that sustained attitude changes are most likely to occur when a person believes his ideas and decisions to be of spontaneous origin.

In the case of overt verbalizations induced by role playing, the person's performance might be accompanied by silent thoughts such as "This is my own idea"; "I arrived at this argument by myself"; "This is somebody else's idea which I am now expressing." We shall use the term "implicit labeling responses" to refer to any thoughts of this type. The essential feature of these uncommunicated (implicit) responses is that they label the source or origin of the arguments and conclusions that are being rehearsed—whether one is listening to someone else or to one's own overt verbalizations.

It seems plausible to assume that when a person is induced to improvise new arguments, there will be a higher frequency of implicit labeling responses which refer to oneself as the source than would be the case if one were passively exposed to a communication from someone else. Under certain conditions, particularly when the individual does not feel capable of arriving at his own judgments, these implicit labeling responses may have little or no effect on opinion change (cf. the discussion of explicit versus implicit conclusion drawing, pp. 100 ff.). Under other conditions, however, awareness that a given conclusion comes from somebody else may interfere with its acceptance. For example, when a person feels that he is relatively well informed about the issue, he may show a greater tendency to accept a new idea —or less tendency to react negativistically—if he attributes the idea to himself rather than to someone else. Thus the implicit labeling responses induced by improvisation might sometimes be a key mediating factor that helps to explain why certain methods of eliciting overt verbalization facilitate opinion change whereas other methods fail to do so. In the case of the King and Janis experiment [9], those subjects who were induced to improvise new arguments while presenting their talks would presumably have many more of the facilitating type of implicit labeling responses than those who were required to read aloud from a prepared script. In Kelman's experiment [8], one would also expect the essay writing induced under the low incentive condition to be more successful in this respect than under the high incentive condition.

In addition to implicit labeling responses, there are other types of implicit responses that might also be affected when people are induced to give an improvised presentation of a persuasive communication. Kelman observed that the comparatively high frequency of interfering responses which accompanied the essay writing of the high incentive group was associated with a low degree of opinion change. In general, one would expect to find that acceptance of a communicator's conclusions is inversely related to the incidence of various types of implicit interfering responses, including thoughts about opposing arguments, doubts about the communicator's veracity, and various kinds of conflicting anticipations as to the consequences of adopting the recommended opinion. Acceptance of a persuasive communication would presumably be greatly augmented by any device which successfully reduces the total incidence of all such interfering responses (cf. Krugman [10]). Perhaps it is in this respect that the improvisation factor facilitates acceptance.

Let us suppose that a person who is passively exposed to a communication fails to be convinced by many of the arguments because, although he comprehends their meaning, he fails to have the sort of anticipations which would motivate him to change his mind. Let us say that the communication is the one which deals with prospects of military service, used in one of the active participation experiments. When the communicatee rehearses the argument that there is a critical shortage of skilled personnel in the military services, he may think of this in purely abstract terms, wonder whether it is really true, and remain unconvinced. But when the same person is required "to put this idea across" in an informal talk, he may become motivated to think up a variety of vivid illustrations and elaborations which make it a much more impressive argument.

This last hypothesis assumes that when a person is induced to improvise his own ideas in support of a communicator's conclusions the chances are increased that he will experience the types of anticipations which make for acceptance. Improvised role playing could be viewed as a technique whereby the communicatee is stimulated to help make the communication as effective as possible, to think up exactly the kinds of arguments, illustrations, and motivating appeals that he regards as being most convincing. In effect, the communicatee is induced to "hand-tailor" the content so as to take account of the unique motives and predispositions of one particular person—namely, himself.

Notes

1. It is conceivable, of course, that the activity of taking notes on a communication might have interfered in some way with responsiveness to the persuasive content of the message. While this possibility cannot be excluded, it seems implausible inasmuch as the subjects were college students who had had considerable practice in taking notes during lectures. Educational research on the effects of notetaking (e.g., Crawford [3]) indicates that this form of activity generally has a beneficial rather than a detrimental effect on the student's ability to absorb the content of an oral communication.

2. It was mentioned earlier that clear-cut reformulation of the material in the outline occurred among a somewhat smaller percentage of active participants who presented this topic than among those who presented the other two topics. But this fact is irrelevant to the comparison under discussion. A sizable percentage of the active participants who presented this topic reformulated the arguments from the outline, whereas none of the passive controls were induced to do so. There was no significant difference in opinion change for these two groups; the gain from active participation showed up only in the form of increased confidence.

References

1. Bavelas, A. Role-playing and management training. *Sociatry*, 1947, *1*, 183–191.
2. Coch, L., and French, J. R. P., Jr. Overcoming resistance to change. *Hum. Rel.*, 1948, *1*, 512–532.
3. Crawford, C. E. Some experimental studies of the results of college note taking. *J. Educ. Res.*, 1925, *12*, 379–386.
4. Hadley, J. E. Teaching poetry appreciation. *Studies in higher education, Bulletin of Purdue University*, 1936, *37*, 52–54.
5. Hollingworth, H. L. *The psychology of the audience.* New York, American Book Co., 1935.
6. Hovland, C. I., Lumsdaine, A. A., and Sheffield, F. D. *Experiments on mass communication.* Princeton Univ. Press, 1949.
7. Janis, I. L., and King, B. T. The influence of role-playing on opinion-change. *J. Abnorm. Soc. Psychol.* (In press.)
8. Kelman, H. C. Attitude change as a function of response restriction. *Hum. Rel.* 1953, *6*, 185–214.
9. King, B. T., and Janis, I. L. Comparison of the effectiveness of improvised versus non-improvised role playing in producing opinion changes. Paper presented before the Eastern Psychological Association, April 1953.
10. Krugman, H. E. The role of resistance in propaganda. *Int. J. Opin. and Attitude Res.*, 1949, *3*, 235–250.
11. Kurtz, K. H., and Hovland, C. I. The effect of verbalization during observation of stimulus objects upon accuracy of recognition and recall. *J. Exp. Psychol.*, 1953, *45*, 157–164.
12. Lewin, K. Forces behind food habits and methods of change. In Report of the Committee on Food Habits, 1941–1943, *The Problem of Changing Food Habits*, Bull. of the National Research Council, No. 108, 1943, pp. 35–65.
13. Lewin, K. Group decision and social change. In T. M. Newcomb and E. L. Hartley, eds., *Readings in social psychology.* New York, Holt, 1947. Pp. 330–344.
14. Lippitt, R. The psychodrama in leadership training. *Sociometry*, 1943, *6*, 286–292.
15. Maier, N. R. F. *Principles of human relations.* New York, John Wiley, 1952.
16. Moreno, J. L. *Psychodrama.* Vol. 1. New York, Beacon House, 1946.
17. Myers, G. C. Control of conduct by suggestion: an experiment in Americanization. *J. Appl. Psychol.*, 1921, *5*, 26–31.
18. Radke, Marian, and Klisurich, Dayna. Experiments in changing food habits. *J. Am. Dietetic Assoc.*, 1947, *23*, 403–409.
19. Razran, G. H. S. Conditioned response changes in rating and appraising sociopolitical slogans. *Psychol. Bull.*, 1940, *37*, 481.

20. Timmons, W. M. Can the product superiority of discussors be attributed to averaging or majority influences? *J. Soc. Psychol.*, 1942, *15*, 23–32.
21. Zander, A., and Lippitt, R. Reality-practice as educational method. *Sociometry*, 1944, 7, 129–151.
22. Zeleny, L. D. Experimental appraisal of a group learning plan. *J. Educ. Res.*, 1940, *34*, 37–42.

CHAPTER 8: *Retention of Opinion Change*

ONCE attitudes and opinions are changed by a communication what is the course of subsequent change? What types of communications create opinions that are enduring and resistant to change once they have been altered? Under what conditions are opinions transient, easily changed in one direction but then reverting quickly to their initial position? What are the main determinants of the persistence or retention of opinion change? Studies to date do not provide complete answers to these questions but do suggest some of the factors which must be considered. In general the prior studies indicate a sizable carry-over effect of communications over a considerable period of time. But they also indicate marked variability in retention of effect. In some studies individuals quickly revert to their precommunication attitudes, while in others the effects of a communication may be even greater after an interval of time than immediately after the presentation.

The wide range of outcomes with respect to the extent of retention of opinion change over time suggests the importance of a careful analysis of the factors influencing the amount retained. Accordingly, the present chapter is devoted to a review of studies of retention which have a bearing on the permanence of changes in opinion produced by communication. Two principal sets of factors are considered: 1) those having to do with learning and remembering the content of the communication, and 2) those involved in the persistence of acceptance of the conclusions advocated by the communicator. As a background for this analysis we shall first review briefly the major past researches on the retention of opinion change following communications.

BACKGROUND

An important early study of the effect of communications on attitude and opinion is that of Peterson and Thurstone [*28*]. Motion pictures (silent) shown to school children of the seventh through the twelfth grades were used as the communications. The immediate and retained effects were studied by means of attitude scales administered before the film, immediately after the film, and after periods of delay ranging from two and a half months to a year and a half. Attitudes were measured by the Thurstone attitude scale method or by the method of paired comparisons. The issues studied were attitudes toward nationality and race, crime, punishment of criminals, capital punishment, and prohibition. Some of the results obtained with different films are shown in Table 17. On the basis of these data the

TABLE 17. *Per Cent of Initial Attitude Change Produced by Films, Remaining at Various Time Intervals*

Film	Number in Experimental Group	Interval	Scale Values			Per Cent of Effect Remaining
			Pre-film	Immediate Post-film	Delayed Post-film	
"The Criminal Code"	257	2½ months	5.33	4.78	4.85	87
"The Criminal Code"	195	9 months	5.42	4.84	4.97	78
"Son of the Gods"	117	5 months	6.57	5.26	5.76	62
"Son of the Gods"	76	19 months	6.61	5.19	5.76	60
"The Birth of a Nation"	350	5 months	7.46	5.93	6.51	62
"Four Sons"	87	6 months	5.74	5.27	5.16	123
"All Quiet on the Western Front"	138	8 months	4.34	3.74	4.64	−50 *

* Here the attitude toward the topic (pacifism) was less favorable than it was before the film.

Based on Studies by Peterson and Thurstone [28]

authors concluded that the effect of motion pictures on children's attitudes "persists for a considerable period of time" (p. 62). Differences between the precommunication attitude scale and the second postcommunication test indicate significant change. Characteristically the effect remaining at the second postcommunication test is less than that obtained at the time of the first communication but in the same direction. There were several exceptions to this, however. In one of the series of seven experiments listed in Table 17, the effect of the film *increased* with time (producing a value above 100 per cent retention). In another instance the attitude after the lapse of time was in a direction opposite to that produced initially by the film (giving a negative change value in the table). Other studies on films, summarized by Hoban and van Ormer [*16*], typically show gradual loss of opinion changes with time.

Complete loss over a five-month period of the change in opinion produced by a communication was reported by Chen [*7*]. He tested college students' attitudes toward the Japanese and Chinese positions in the Manchurian crisis. Opinions were measured before, immediately after, and five months after oral communications. The speeches produced a significant effect in the direction of the communication immediately afterward. But by the time of the second test there was an almost complete reversion to the subjects' initial opinions. Chen's finding is contrary to the majority of other studies in this field, which characteristically show sizable changes in opinion up to a year or more after the communication.[1]

Changes in opinion induced by direct personal experience are thought to be even more lasting than those produced by mass media, although systematic comparisons are not available. A study by Zeligs [*39*] indicated that contact with a visiting Chinese woman produced marked changes in her twelve-year-old subjects, and the effects were still pronounced three months later. But the lack of a control group makes it difficult to know whether these results are attributable to the effects of personal contact or to other influences occurring simultaneously or during the period of delay. A more significant study of the retention of changes in opinion produced by personal experience is that of Smith [*34*]. The effects on attitudes toward Negroes of two week ends spent in a guided tour through Harlem were studied. Negro history, culture, and accomplishments were discussed with Negroes of superior education and social status. The 40 experimental and 40 control subjects were graduate students in education matched with respect to initial opinion, sex, and geographical background. The personal contact with Negro institutions produced a sizable immediate effect in a positive direction, and 83 per cent of the initial effect was still present ten months later.

A major exception to the typical phenomenon of gradual forgetting was reported in a study by Hovland, Lumsdaine, and Sheffield ([*20*] pp. 182–200). These experimenters chose for their communication "The Battle of Britain," a film produced by the Army to show the accomplishment of the British. This film was selected because it had previously been found to elicit large opinion changes. The experimental design involved four groups of soldiers (two experimental and two control). All were initially given an opinion questionnaire. Subsequently the two experimental groups were shown the film. One pair of experimental and control groups was given a second questionnaire five days after the film presentation. A second pair received the after-questionnaire nine weeks after the film was shown. It will be noted that each group of men received the after-questionnaire only once.

Memory of factual information conveyed by the film showed a characteristic decrease with time. However, opinion changes showed an average *increase* with the passage of time for the opinion items of the questionnaire as a whole. The increase in effect was not found in all items, but there was a reliable increase with time in the effects on a number of opinions. The investigators named this phenomenon the "sleeper effect" and suggested a number of hypotheses as to factors which could account for it. These will be considered below.

In summary, the preceding studies tend to show moderately high retention of opinion changes over a period of time even in the case of rather brief communications. But in some studies little effect appears to be retained, while in several investigations there is an apparent increase in the extent of change with the passage of time. Factors which may be responsible for these differences in outcome will be discussed in this chapter.

RESEARCH EVIDENCE AND ANALYSIS

In analyzing the diversity in results of prior studies we find it useful to employ the distinction used in previous chapters between the *learning* of the content of the communication and the *motivation to accept* its conclusions. If one remembers none of the arguments from the communication, one's opinion about the issue may revert to its initial level. Or if one is no longer motivated to accept what was said, the opinion change will not persist. Thus, opinion change following exposure to a communication depends on retention both of the informational content and of the incentives for acceptance.

Forgetting of the Content of the Communication

With respect to the factors affecting the forgetting of content a considerable body of evidence is available, derived for the most part from laboratory studies of the processes of learning and forgetting. In many instances repetitions of these studies are needed under naturalistic communication conditions.

Most studies indicate that there is an initial period of rapid forgetting of verbal material, followed by a more gradual decrease until an asymptote is reached where little further loss occurs. A typical result is that of Dietze and Jones [*10*]. These investigators presented to

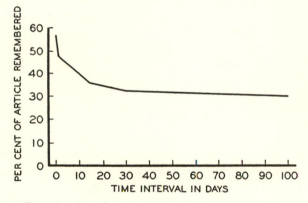

FIGURE 13. Forgetting Curve for a Single Presentation of Meaningful Prose Material. *From Dietze and Jones [10].*

school children a series of articles dealing with radium, the Germans, and Sir Richard Arkwright, the English inventor. Memory tests were then administered immediately after the reading and at intervals of 1, 14, 30, and 100 days. The curve of retention is presented in Figure 13. It follows closely the form obtained by Ebbinghaus and other investigators for more artificial material. When Dietze's and Jones' data are plotted using logarithmic coordinates, a straight line relationship emerges, showing that the amount remembered is inversely proportional to the logarithm of the time elapsed.

In some studies, however, there is a paradoxical increase in what is remembered over time. Results from an early study by Ballard [3] showed a gradual rise in the amount of material reproduced over a three-day period, followed by the usual subsequent decline. The initial increase in retention was labeled "reminiscence." Our knowledge about the factors affecting reminiscence is far from adequate, but it appears to be due most frequently to removal of interferences occurring in initial learning which serve to depress the observed effect immediately after the learning. These interferences frequently disappear with time and make later performances superior to the initial ones. A discussion of the factors will be found in a review by Hovland ([18] pp. 651–657).

Whether the form of the forgetting curve is one showing a gradual loss with time or one with a period of initial increase appears to depend upon the nature of the material, the amount of learning, the way in which retention is elicited, as well as upon the personality predispositions of the communicatee. Each of these factors will now be considered briefly.

1. Nature of Material

Users of mass communications are well aware that some messages are grasped better and retained longer than others. Some of the factors affecting retention of different content are the degree of meaning the communication has for the listener, its vividness, and its emotional tone.

It is a matter of common knowledge that more meaningful material is better retained than less well understood material. This has frequently been demonstrated with verbal learning in the laboratory ([18] pp. 645–646) and is also found with classroom learning (e.g., [10]).

Another closely related factor has to do with the vividness of the material. Laboratory experimentation clearly indicates that materials which "stand out" are better retained (Van Buskirk [35] and von Restorff [31]). Experiments by Jersild [23] and Ehrensberger [13] indicate that various means of emphasizing a portion of prose material (e.g., communicator saying "Now get this.") are effective in increasing the retention of material. But it is conceivable that the overuse of such emphasis devices can backfire. If too many points are emphasized they will lose their distinctiveness. Similarly, if emphasis is not carefully placed, the wrong points may stand out. This is the well-known phenomenon of "remembering the joke but not what it was supposed to illustrate."

While human learning experiments show that the meaningfulness of the material and its vividness or emphasis influence the retention of the material, there are relatively few studies dealing with these variables on the level of complex prose material. Thus there is still a gap in the generalization of simple learning data to problems in opinion change.

2. Degree of Learning

The more completely material is initially learned the longer it will be remembered. This has important implications with respect to repeating major points if it is desired that they be retained. Data from laboratory studies indicate that a higher number of repetitions increases the degree of retention (Krueger [25]). Of more direct relevance to communication are the results of Jersild on the effect of repeating certain sentences in the communication. His results show improvement in retention with increasing repetition up to about three or four times. Thereafter the effect of additional repetitions is slight.

Repetition does not influence the retention of the information content of a communication in a simple manner. While the usual effect is to increase retention under some circumstances, too frequent repetition without any reward leads to loss of attention, boredom, and disregard of the communication. The latter phenomenon is closely analagous to "extinction" in conditioned response learning (for further discussion cf. [19]). Variation in form, style, and expression, together with repetition of the major points, is cited by Hollingworth ([17] pp. 143-144) as a particularly effective solution to this problem.

3. Type of Retention Required

Remembering something to the point of being able to recognize that you have seen or heard it before is much easier than remembering the message verbatim. So it is natural to expect that the rate of forgetting will depend on the criterion used in evaluating retention. In some types of communication it is important that considerable detail be remembered; in others familiarity with the general idea is sufficient. An example of the former would be a situation where individuals are being persuaded to adopt a position to which there are many objections. The aim of the communication may then be to get the audience to learn the entire set of supporting arguments so that they can answer opposing points. Other communications may merely indicate the position of some esteemed group on an issue. Here only recognition memory is required: when the same question is subsequently discussed one has only to recognize that the position is one supported by the group.

Laboratory studies have compared three different methods of evaluating what is remembered: 1) recognition, where the subject has only to indicate whether he can identify the material presented; 2) recall, where the individual has to reproduce exactly what he learned; 3) "relearning," which requires the subject to learn the material a second time and considers the "savings" he makes in learning it again (this is frequently involved when a series of communications are presented). Comparisons of retention measured in each of these ways are presented in Figure 14 (from a study by Luh [27]). The extent of advantage when one is required only to recognize the material is shown by the fact that after two days retention is 72 per cent by this criterion but only 11 per cent when exact recall of the items (nonsense syllables) is tested.

Results obtained under conditions more nearly typical of those involved in communication were reported by English, Welborn, and Killian [*14*]. These researchers found that school subjects are rapidly forgotten when the retention is measured by the number of details retained. But they are well retained when the basis of evaluation is whether the general idea or gist of the material presented is remembered.

Results of this kind suggest the possibility that in the case of persuasive communications the conclusions are better retained than the detailed arguments used in support of the conclusions. Individuals may have a tendency to remember only the summary statements or generalizations rather than the specific reasons or arguments. However, a study by Bell [*5*] on the retention of a persuasive talk on the possible contributions of "Cybernetics" indicates that when other factors were controlled and the same type of retention tests used, arguments and conclusions were equally well retained.

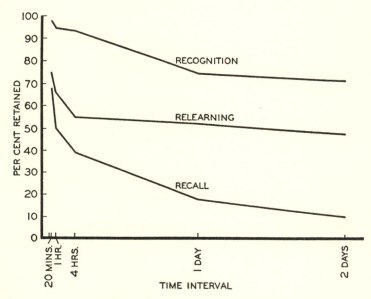

FIGURE 14. Retention Curves Obtained with Three Different Methods of Measuring Retention. *From Luh* [27].

Consideration of the type of retention that will be required may sometimes be of major importance in planning communications. Where only general familiarity with the content will be necessary a single presentation of the arguments may suffice. On the other hand, where detailed knowledge is needed (as when an individual must be able to meet arguments presented by others) thorough coverage and repeated presentation may be necessary to insure complete recall at the time of delayed elicitation.

4. Predispositions of the Audience

The extent to which communications will be retained would be expected to be affected to a significant extent by the motivations and interests of the audience. These will affect not only the quantity of material which will be retained but also certain of the qualitative features of what is retained.

One of the simplest phenomena in verbal learning is that the degree of interest in material affects the extent to which the individual will learn the content of the communication. How well it has been learned will then affect how well it will be retained. This is a phenomenon with which we are all familiar: we learn what we are interested in. Even when no attempt is made to learn and very weak motives are present, "incidental learning" sometimes occurs. This is of considerable interest in relation to persuasive communication because frequently an individual is not "set" to try to remember what is communicated (cf. Berlyne [6]). Characteristically when exposed to advertisements, lengthy political speeches, educational programs, and the like, the audience initially has only a rather passive interest, and hence the arousal of motivation to learn the message is essential for success. Retention may also be affected by the degree to which the person is motivated on subsequent occasions to try to recall the material learned. Degree of motivation frequently affects the degree to which the individual will rehearse the material he has learned.

One of the pioneer studies of the effect of motivation on recall is that of Bartlett [4]. He presented to his subjects a complicated story taken from an unfamiliar culture. The forgetting of this story took the direction of changing the material in a way compatible with the subjects' motives and biases. Unfamiliar details dropped out and what remained constituted an organized, understandable arrangement of material. Many similar phenomena have been found to operate in rumor transmission, where the same message is communicated from individual to individual (Allport and Postman [1]).

Rapaport ([29] pp. 41–110) reviews experiments showing a tendency for material experienced by subjects as unpleasant to be forgotten more rapidly than material considered pleasant. Experimentation on this problem was conducted primarily to investigate the psychoanalytic concept of "repression" which implies that forgetting can sometimes be motivated by a wish to avoid painful subjective experiences. One hypothesis which derives from this research is that when the content of the material conflicts with the individual's wishes, values, and motives, forgetting proceeds more rapidly than when the material is nonconflictful. Sharp [32] has shown that "acceptable" phrases (e.g., "securing justice," "feeling better") are retained better than "unacceptable" phrases (e.g., "fearing poison," "disliking folks") even though they were more difficult to learn.

The line of research concerning the learning and memory of prose materials which are compatible with or in conflict with the subject's values or frame of reference can appropriately be considered here. These studies assume the audience has an initial opinion on a given issue, and communications are presented in accordance with or in opposition to this opinion. One of the first systematic studies of the relationship between the initial attitudes of the learner and the extent of recall is that of Clark [9]. He presented 271 high school boys and girls with a communication involving conflict between the sexes. Tests for memory of the material were made one, two, three, and four weeks after the presentation of the communication. In general, his results showed that males and females change or distort the communication in different ways characteristic of their sex. For example, boys "tended toward personalization—to identify themselves with the man of the situation and make their recalls in terms of the 'affective' dynamics of the situation, particularly as related to the potential or actual damage to the prestige of the man" (p. 61). Similar tendencies toward personalization in recall were found when comparison was made of the reproduction by college students and WPA workers of a communication concerning WPA workers. Clark concludes that an individual's sentiments, anxieties, and attitudes all play an important role in influencing the recall of meaningful prose material. Similar results were obtained by Watson and Hartmann [36] on retention of material about religion by students with theistic and atheistic positions: ". . . material which *supported* the subject's attitudinal frame was *retained* better than material which opposed it" (p. 330).

An extensive investigation of this problem was conducted by Edwards [12]. His hypothesis states that experiences which coincide with an individual's frame of reference will be learned and remembered better than those which conflict with it. His subjects were given a passage about the Roosevelt New Deal administration which contained statements both favorable and unfavorable to it. Test items to measure retention consisted of two sets, one favorable to the New Deal and the other unfavorable. Tests were administered both immediately and after three weeks. Subjects with different initial positions judged the same speech differently: pro-New Deal subjects considered the speech pro-New Deal while those with an anti-New Deal attitude considered it unfavorable to the New Deal. The subjects tended to remember the arguments which agreed with their political position better than those opposed to it. Edwards concludes that initial attitude is not only a determining factor in initial perception and learning but also has a persisting effect on the remembering process.

In a more recent study Levine and Murphy [26] gave subjects both an anti-Soviet and a pro-Soviet article to read. After the learning session the subjects were asked to reproduce the material. Subjects were used who were known to have pro- and anti-Soviet positions respectively. In both groups of subjects the material which was in line with their beliefs and attitudes was learned more readily and retained better. Retention of learning was measured over five days and four weeks respectively. The curve of retention of learning for each group of subjects on each type of communication showed clearly significant differences between the two groups.

In the above-mentioned studies it is difficult to know whether the more rapid forgetting is the result of less complete initial learning. This point was systematically explored in an experiment by Weiss [37]. He attempted to control the degree of initial learning by having subjects learn (to a uniform criterion of accuracy) statements associated with a true or false label. The statements, which consisted of arguments about the undesirability of smoking, were learned equally well by the last learning trial, regardless of the subjects' initial attitudes toward smoking. However retention of the statement-label association was found to be affected differentially by a combination of the subjects' attitudes before and after the communication. Weiss found that the individuals who were most favorable toward the arguments were most likely to retain the learned associations.

The results of Doob [11] on the retention of a series of assertions about different issues suggest that it is not necessarily the direction of the subject's opinion which is correlated with high retention but rather the intensity with which the opinion is held. Subjects who indicated either strong agreement or strong disagreement with a position were more inclined to remember the communication. It is likely that individuals who feel strongly one way or the other are more inclined to pay close attention to the communication and afterward to rehearse the arguments to themselves.

Subsequent Experiences

In laboratory studies of retention one can employ stimulus materials, such as nonsense syllables or maze patterns, which are unrelated to the stimuli with which the individual will subsequently come in contact. In naturalistic communications, however, the material learned is frequently encountered in many different contexts which may counteract the original learning experiences. The retention of communicated material is thus affected to a considerable extent by subsequent exposure.

The effect of subsequent learning on the retention of the material already acquired is labeled *reproductive facilitation or interference*. This concept assumes considerable significance in Chapter 4, which deals with the structure of the communication, because the order in which various arguments are presented can have some effect on the extent to which arguments learned early in the communication are interfered with by those learned at the end (cf. also below, pp. 260–264).

THE "PERSISTENCE" OF ACCEPTANCE

In addition to the forgetting of the content of the communication, there are changes over time in the degree to which the communicator's message is accepted. Observations of ordinary life situations, like the experimental results cited at the beginning of this chapter, reveal two opposing phenomena. On the one hand, an individual may be exposed to a communication and accept the communicator's point of view but after a period of time may revert to his previous attitude. On the other hand, an individual may at first reject the communicator's point of view but after a period of time "come around" to the communicator's position. The present discussion is concerned with the conditions and factors which make one or the other outcome occur.

1. The Communicator

One of the most important factors affecting the extent to which a message in a communication is accepted is the attitude of the audience toward the communicator. The enhancement of effects attributable to the communicator is usually labeled the "prestige effect" and is discussed earlier, in Chapter 2, pp. 19 ff. In the present discussion the implications of this factor for retention are analyzed.

To explain the finding by Hovland, Lumsdaine, and Sheffield [20] of a sleeper effect, discussed at the beginning of this chapter, one of the hypotheses advanced was that the increase in agreement with the communication might be due to the disappearance of initial skepticism with the passage of time. This hypothesis assumes that forgetting arguments and other content which support the communicator's conclusion is the general rule. Consequently agreement with the recommended opinion may be fairly high immediately after exposure but will show a gradual decline with the passage of time. If it should happen, however, that the source of the communication is regarded with skepticism or antipathy, there may be little initial agreement with the communicator's position. If, then, the discounted source is forgotten more quickly than the content (or "dissociated" from the content) agreement with the recommended opinion should increase with time.

The first experiment to investigate these hypotheses was that of Hovland and Weiss [21]. They used identical communications on four different topics. To half the subjects these were presented by sources considered trustworthy and to half by sources considered untrustworthy. The topics were "The Future of Movie Theaters," "Atomic Submarines," "The Steel Shortage" and "Antihistamine Drugs." Opinion questionnaires were presented to the subjects before the communication, immediately after the communication, and four weeks afterward. Items on the questionnaire included measures of factual material as well as measures of opinion. Measures were also taken of the subject's memory of the source of the communication. The communications were presented to undergraduate college students, who read them without knowledge that tests of retention would be administered. Initially the communications presented by the untrustworthy sources were "discounted" by the audience and had less effect on opinion than those presented by the trustworthy sources. With the passage of time, however, the initial differences attributable to source disappeared, so that when the subjects were retested after a period of four weeks the amount of opinion change retained from the two sources was approximately equal. It was above the point initially obtained for the negative source and below that for the positive source. Thus there was a forgetting effect when the presentation was by a trustworthy communicator and a sleeper effect when the communication was presented by a negative communicator. The results, which are presented in Figure 15,

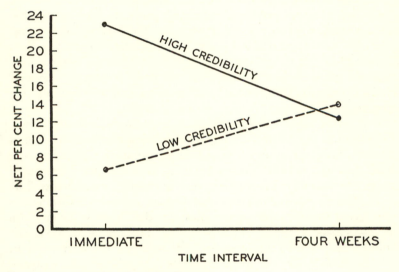

FIGURE 15.   Retention of Opinion Change.

Changes in extent of agreement with position advocated by high credibility and low credibility sources immediately after exposure to communication and four weeks later. *From Hovland and Weiss* [21].

can be interpreted to mean that the contents of both the trustworthy and untrustworthy communications were learned and forgotten at the same rate, but that the trustworthy communicator produced an initially positive prestige effect and the untrustworthy communicator a negative prestige effect, both of which tended to disappear with time.

The original hypothesis in this study was that the cause of the sleeper effect was the forgetting with time of the source of the communication. This hypothesis does not seem to be borne out by the data. The subjects in the low credibility group who showed increased belief (sleeper effect) were found to be able to name the source of the communication to about the same extent as those who showed decreased belief. Hovland and Weiss's results clearly show, however, that there is a decreased tendency over time to reject the material presented by an untrustworthy source. The authors point out that "This may or may not require that the source be forgotten. But the individual must be less likely with the passage of time to *associate spontaneously* the content with the source. Thus the passage of time serves to remove recall of the source as a mediating cue that leads to rejection" (p. 648; italics ours). In other words, while the subjects were able to recall the source when questioned about it directly, they may not have thought of it when they were merely asked their opinion concerning the issue.

This formulation was further tested in an experiment by Kelman and Hovland [24] where the source was "reinstated" at the time of delayed testing for opinion. A total of 330 summer high school students were the subjects. Three different communicators were used to present a plea for lenient treatment of juvenile delinquents. The communications were identical except that different introductions were given for the three communicators: the "positive" communicator was made to appear as competent and fair, the "neutral" as fair but uninformed, and the "negative" as biased and uninformed. This was accomplished by playing a transcribed, experimentally arranged "radio interview" to the subjects. For each of the three experimental groups the "announcer" varied the introduction of the speaker in such a way as to modify his prestige value in the desired direction. At the time of delayed testing, the source was "reinstated" for half of each experimental group, and not reinstated for the other half. "Reinstatement" consisted of playing back the introduction of the communicator, before passing out the delayed after-questionnaire. Initially, the greatest change in attitude was produced by the positive communicator and the least by the negative, with the neutral in between. After three weeks, the time of delayed testing, the opinion change retained was approximately equal for the positive and negative communicator, under nonreinstatement conditions—which supported the above-mentioned results of Hovland and Weiss. That is, those exposed to the communication from a low prestige source showed more opinion change three weeks later than immediately after the communication (the sleeper effect). The subjects exposed to the positive prestige communicator showed a decrease in change of attitude with time. These results are shown in Figure 16.

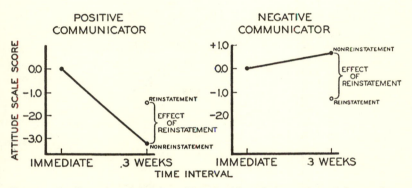

FIGURE 16. Retention of Opinion with and without Reinstatement of Source. *Data from Kelman and Hovland* [24].

That the influence of the communicator was an important factor was shown by the effects of reinstating the communicator. The retained change under reinstatement conditions was higher for the positive communicator and lower for the negative communicator than when no reinstatement was involved.

The foregoing results suggest that one can separate the effects of the communicator's prestige from the over-all effects, in the way represented in Figure 17. Let the initial effect of the communication content be represented by C. With the passage of time there will be a decline in the amount of the content remembered, and hence in the amount of influence C exerts on opinion change. This is shown in the diagram as C'. The effect of the communicator is to boost or depress the original value of C. If a positive communicator is employed there will be a positive prestige effect which we will label +P. A negative communicator will have a negative prestige effect which we can label —P. So the initial total effect will be C + P for the positive communicator and C —P for the negative. The retained effect of the positive communicator will be labeled +P' and that for the negative —P'. At the time of delayed testing the retention of the prestige effects has been

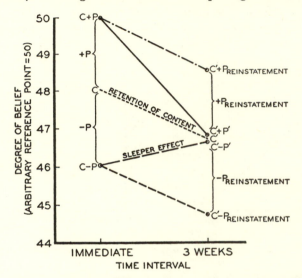

FIGURE 17. Effects of Content and Prestige Factors on Degree of Belief Immediately after the Communication and Three Weeks Later, with and without Reinstatement of the Communicator.

Values are all shown relative to C + P, which is given the arbitrary value of 50. Distances between circled points are based on empirical data from Kelman and Hovland [24]. Other values are hypothetical. Explanation of symbols in text.

found to be significantly less for the nonreinstated group than for the reinstated group. Without reinstatement the values of P' will approach zero; so that the C' + P' and the C' — P' values will tend to coincide. But if the source is reintroduced there will be an additional effect which will reinstate the initial effects of the communicator, boosting the positive and reducing the negative. These values are indicated as C' + P$_{\text{reinstatement}}$ and C' — P$_{\text{reinstatement}}$ in the figure.

In the experiments to date the loss of prestige effects over a three- or four-week period was almost complete. It also appears that the effect of reminding the audience of the communicator is to bring back the prestige effects to their initial value. An important research problem is to explain the loss in the effects of prestige with time. One possibility which we have suggested is that the loss is due to dissociation between the content and the source. Hence the prestige effects are eliminated. The evidence fails to support the alternative assumption that the individuals who show the sleeper effect would be the ones who fail to recall the source at the time their opinion is elicited.

In summary, the available evidence indicates that both positive and negative prestige effects tend to be lost over a period of time; the degree to which an audience accepts a persuasive communication that is attributed to a prestigeful (respected or trustworthy) source tends to be comparatively high at first but gradually declines, whereas the degree to which an audience accepts a persuasive communication attributed to a nonprestigeful source tends to be comparatively low at first but gradually increases. These effects seem to be due to the fact that with the passage of time the *content* of a statement is less likely to be spontaneously associated with the source; i.e., people often remember what was said without thinking about who said it. (Cf. related discussion of hypotheses in Chapter 2, pp. 41 ff.).

2. Predispositional Factors

The manner in which motivation influences the retention of factual material has already been discussed. It is probable that motivation is also significant in affecting the persistence of acceptance, but there are to date no definitive studies of this factor. It is commonly observed that individuals will appear adamant in their opinion while in the heat of argument, only to use the adversary's arguments completely on a subsequent occasion. But there are also instances where the individual is motivated to maintain his new position after he has been influenced (cf. discussion pp. 127 f.).

Closely related are other predispositions which make an individual inclined to accept a position after he has been exposed to it even though he shows little immediate effect. Data bearing on this problem are found in the study of the retention of opinion change by Hovland, Lumsdaine, and Sheffield [20]. According to their hypothesis, a person soon forgets the ideas he has learned which are not consonant with those of the socioeconomic and educational group to which he belongs. But he retains without loss or even with an increment those ideas consonant with his predispositions (i.e., those of his social or educational stratum). They assumed that an opinion which is very infrequent in a particular subgroup (e.g., the uneducated) is one which that subgroup is predisposed against, whereas an opinion held by the great majority of the subgroup is one toward which they are predisposed. They found clear evidence that the opinion changes during a seven-week period following exposure to the communication showed increments or decrements corresponding to the direction of the dominant opinion of the educational stratum of the population to which the individual belonged. Thus the results of their analysis tended to confirm the expectations from the predisposition hypothesis, although, as will be seen shortly, the data can also be interpreted in terms of subsequent intercommunication.

3. Subsequent Experiences

We have already referred to the fact that real life situations differ sharply from laboratory learning, where the entire experience is confined to a single occasion. In the former the material is frequently recalled later and is often discussed with others. Depending on how other individuals react who are told about the material, the original acceptance may be either augmented or diminished. The importance of subsequent events is indirectly referred to by Peterson and Thurstone [28] in explaining the unusually high retention of one of the attitudes changed by a film: "We suggest as an explanation [for the high retention] the fact that there was no theater in Genoa [Illinois] regularly showing pictures and that the motion picture "Four Sons" was probably the subject of considerable comment and discussion among the children because a motion picture was a relatively rare occurrence for this group" (p. 52).

Subsequent experiences possibly played a part in producing the high degree of forgetting in the Chen [7] study and the high retention in the Zeligs [39] study. These studies both dealt with "hot" social issues. The prevailing social trends quite possibly led to group discussions and also provided a context for additional communications to fit into. Where the communication concurs with the prevailing social trends, it tends to be reinforced, and one would expect large amounts of retention. Where the communication is such that it is followed by a barrage of countercommunications, the measured retention would be small. Only a control group would enable one to evaluate these influences.

The results of Hovland, Lumsdaine, and Sheffield [20] mentioned in the preceding discussion may also be interpreted as due to differential experiences after the communication. The individuals who changed their opinions further in the direction of the communication belonged to socioeducational groups whose prevailing opinion was favorable to the communication, while those who changed negatively belonged to groupings with negative attitudes toward the issue presented. The explanation might be that many individuals had never thought about the topic presented until the film showing. This event set the stage for their thinking about it and talking about it. The group to which they belonged then determined whether the repeating of the message of the film would be rewarded or punished.

A related aspect of this problem is discussed in Chapter 5 on the effect of group affiliation factors. It is suggested there that while attitudes which go counter to the norms of one's group may frequently be changed more effectively by minimizing the conflict with the norms, the delayed effect of conflict between the norm and one's newly formed belief may produce a great weakening of the retention of the attitude fostered by the counternorm communication.

Subsequent experiences affect the retention of communications, but subsequent experiences are also differently perceived as a result of prior communications. The retained effects of a prior communication may sometimes be seen dramatically in terms of the way they modify the influence of a new communication or event. An experimental study of this type is represented by the investigation of Janis, Lumsdaine, and Gladstone [22]. A communication dealing with Russia's ability to produce atomic bombs was presented in June 1949. The opportunity to study retention of the communication after exposure to a major event arose unexpectedly when President Truman announced in September 1949 that Russia had set off its first atomic explosion.

Fifty-five subjects from a Connecticut high school were used in the experimental group given the communication and 55 were used as controls. The groups were matched with respect to age, grade, and intelligence. The experimental subjects were exposed to a radio talk which presented the view that Russia would be unable to produce atomic weapons in large quantities for at least five years. The commentator stressed the Soviet Union's industrial and technological weaknesses and lack of natural resources, as well as the difficulty of constructing atomic bombs in mass quantities. Several weeks before this communication was given, a general current events questionnaire was administered. Embedded in it were questions designed to test the subjects' opinions concerning atomic developments in the Soviet Union. A week after the communication a questionnaire which contained the crucial questions about atomic developments in Russia was again administered to all subjects. The control group received the before- and after-questionnaires but no communication. The third questionnaire was administered to both groups about three months later, a few days after the news of Russia's first A-bomb was released.

The retention effects of the communication are indicated by the percentage of subjects believing, after the announcement of the A-bomb explosion, that it would be five years or more before Russia will have large numbers of A-bombs. The difference between the estimates of subjects who were exposed to the preliminary communication and those who were not provides a measure of the effect of the communication over time.

Table 18 presents some of the results obtained by Janis, Lumsdaine,

TABLE 18. *Retention of Opinion Change after a Counteracting News Event: Per Cent of Subjects Believing It Will Take Five Years or More for the Soviet Union to Have Large Numbers of Atomic Bombs*

	Precommunication	Immediate Post-communication	Delayed (Post Event)
Control	60	67	18.5
Experimental	56	94	34.5
Difference	−4	+27	+16
p		<.01	<.05

(N = 55 for each group)

From Janis, Lumsdaine, and Gladstone [22]

and Gladstone. The data indicate that the percentage difference between experimental and control subjects' opinions was negligible before the communication was heard, but that 27 per cent more of the experimental group held the advocated position *after* the communication. The difference created by the communication still remained to a significant degree three months later despite the fact that an important event had occurred which countered the content of the communication.

The authors conclude from this finding that the communication "which had been presented three months earlier had an observable carry-over effect, producing a significant degree of *resistance* to the opinion-impact of [a subsequent] event" (p. 499). The results thus support the hypothesis they discuss, that *once a belief is modified by an effective communication there will be a tendency for the newly acquired opinion responses to interfere with the subsequent acquisition of any incompatible opinion responses.* The opposite outcome would have been expected on the basis of an overcompensation hypothesis. If a person feels that he has been taken in by erroneous propaganda, he may discount *all* of the arguments as untrustworthy or he may discharge his annoyance by shifting to the opposite position. The results indicate that overcompensation factors, if present, were overridden by interference factors.

The authors also consider the possibility that resistance to the opinion impact of a subsequent event could be due primarily to certain "sophistication" effects produced by the preparatory communication, irrespective of the *direction* or *content* of the particular beliefs that are created. Merely presenting a series of relevant arguments, on either side of the issue, may serve to teach the audience something about the nature of the problem and call their attention to the various factors to be taken into account that might otherwise be ignored. Increased familiarity with the issue could create a more sophisticated frame of reference that would enable the audience to make a more critical (and perhaps a more rational) assessment of the implications of the event, weighed in the light of other relevant considerations.

Data were available to test the sophistication hypothesis. The original experiment carried out in the spring of 1949 had also included, in addition to the control group and the main experimental group, a *third* equated group of 55 students. In June this supplementary group was exposed to the same radio program as the regular experimental group, but one week later the group was exposed to a different radio transcription. The new communication dealt with exactly the same topic but was designed to serve as counterpropaganda. In this second program the commentator argued in favor of the position that *Russia already had developed the A-bomb* and within two years would be producing it in large numbers. This supplementary group (the "double-communication" group) differed from the main experimental group only in that it was exposed to two opposing communications on the topic rather than a single one. The additional communication given to this group contradicted specific arguments of the original communication but would not tend to reduce sophistication effects in any way. On the contrary, it raised the issue a second time and referred to some of the same factors as being relevant in making a sound judgment on the issue. Thus the students in the double-communication group had *more* opportunity than the regular experimental group to develop a sophisticated frame of reference.

The results did *not* confirm the sophistication hypothesis. On the main question dealing with Russia's potential A-bomb supply, the double-communication group failed to differ significantly from the control group.

While replication with other types of groups, issues, and events will be needed, the findings do carry the implication that once a communication succeeds in modifying a belief the newly acquired opinion change will tend to persist even under conditions where the individual is exposed to other impressive communications or events which go counter to the original communication. In this experiment, one exposure to a brief communication was found to be capable of producing a substantial carry-over effect that was sustained over a period of at least several months. The interference effect created by the communication clearly emerges as a dominant tendency, powerful enough to reduce the influence of a dramatic news event.

IMPLICATIONS

Throughout the chapter it has been found useful to discuss the persistence of opinion changes induced by communications in terms of a separation of factors influencing the retention of *what was said* by the communicator and the continuation of *acceptance of the conclusions*. This distinction, used in other chapters, is not an absolute one, but does call attention to different phenomena which need further investigation. Almost all the studies of retention of content have been carried out under laboratory-type conditions, usually with artificial incentives and often with nonmeaningful material. The studies of persistence of opinion change, on the other hand, have involved live and meaningful issues but have seldom provided information as to the factors responsible for good or poor retention of the changes produced by the communication. Both have limitations for the present purposes. A number of basic studies are needed in which retention of content is studied under naturalistic conditions and with typical communications, to supplement laboratory studies. At the same time, controlled and analytic procedures need to be introduced more widely in the investigation of the persistence of opinion change produced by mass media. Integration of the results from these two sources will enable us to understand much more clearly the factors influencing the persistence of opinion change.

Notes

1. An extensive series of studies on the retention of opinion change produced by written communications was carried out at Purdue University in the middle 'thirties by Remmers and his associates (Remmers [30]; Hall [15]; Williamson and Remmers [38]). Even brief communications on a variety of topics, such as the relation of government to farming, had effects which lasted a year or more.

Sims [33] employed written propaganda to study changes in attitude toward the TVA among college students. Pronounced changes were still present three months after exposure to the communication. A high proportion of the students whose opinions were significantly changed immediately after exposure continued to show effects three months later.

Cherrington and Miller [8] studied the effects of a communication on attitudes toward pacifism, measured three days before a communication, 24 hours after, and six months after, on equivalent forms of an attitude scale. Two groups of subjects (totaling 85 college freshmen) were used. One group was presented with a lecture, the other with written materials. Both groups retained approximately 50 per cent of the initial attitude change after six months.

Annis and Meier [2] were concerned with change of attitude brought about in a naturalistic setting by having subjects read newspapers with planted editorials. One hundred and ninety-five subjects were instructed to read the editorials in a college newspaper. They were told the departments of journalism and psychology were interested in their reading habits. The subjects consisted of two groups: one group was given favorable planted editorials about an unknown Australian statesman and the other was exposed to unfavorable editorial comment. Within each group there were two subgroups, one required to read seven planted editorials, the other fifteen. Two editorials were read per week. Tests of attitude change were given immediately after the series and four months afterward. The results showed significant differential attitudes toward the person in question. These results remained substantially the same four months later: there were no significant differences between the attitudes determined immediately after the series and those four months afterward, except for one of the four subgroups of subjects.

References

1. Allport, G. W., and Postman, L. *The psychology of rumor.* New York, Holt, 1947.
2. Annis, A. D., and Meier, N. C. The induction of opinion through suggestion by means of "planted content." *J. Soc. Psychol.,* 1934, *5,* 65–81.
3. Ballard, P. B. Obliviscence and reminiscence. *Brit. J. Psychol. Monogr. Suppl.* 1913, *1,* No. 2., Cambridge Univ. Press.
4. Bartlett, F. C. *Remembering.* New York, Macmillan, 1932.
5. Bell, Elaine. An exploratory study of the recall of "arguments" and "conclusions." Unpublished study.
6. Berlyne, D. E. *An experimental study of human curiosity.* Ph.D. dissertation, Yale Univ., 1953.
7. Chen, W. K. C. Retention of the effect of oral propaganda. *J. Soc. Psychol.,* 1936, *7,* 479–483.
8. Cherrington, B. M., and Miller, L. W. Changes in attitude as a result of a lecture and of reading similar materials. *J. Soc. Psychol.,* 1933, *4,* 479–484.
9. Clark, K. B. Some factors influencing the remembering of prose materials. *Arch. Psychol.,* New York, 1940, *36,* No. 253.
10. Dietze, A. G., and Jones, G. E. Factual memory of secondary school pupils for a short article which they read a single time. *J. Educ. Psychol.* 1931, *22,* 586–598, 667–676.
11. Doob, L. W. Effects of initial serial position and attitude upon recall under conditions of low motivation. *J. Abnorm. Soc. Psychol.,* 1953, *48,* 199–205.
12. Edwards, A. L. Political frames of reference as a factor influencing recognition. *J. Abnorm. Soc. Psychol.,* 1941, *36,* 34–50.
13. Ehrensberger, R. An experimental study of the relative effectiveness of certain forms of emphasis in public speaking. *Speech Monogr.,* 1945, *12,* 94–111.
14. English, H. B., Welborn, E. L., and Killian, C. D. Studies in substance memorization. *J. Gen. Psychol.,* 1934, *11,* 233–260.
15. Hall, W. The effect of defined social stimulus material upon the stability of attitudes toward labor unions, capital punishment, social insurance, and Negroes. *Studies in higher education.* Purdue Univ., 1938, No. 34, 7–19.
16. Hoban, C. F., and van Ormer, E. B. Instructional film research (Rapid mass learning) 1918–1950, Technical report No. SDC 269-7-19, Washington, D.C.: Dept. of Commerce, Office of Technical Services, 1951.
17. Hollingworth, H. L. *The psychology of the audience.* New York, American Book Co., 1935.
18. Hovland, C. I. Human learning and retention. In S. S. Stevens, ed., *Handbook of experimental psychology.* New York, John Wiley, 1951. Pp. 613–689.
19. Hovland, C. I. Psychology of the communication process. In W. Schramm ed., *Communications in modern society.* Urbana, Univ. of Illinois Press, 1948. Pp. 59–65.

20. Hovland, C. I., Lumsdaine, A. A., and Sheffield, F. D. *Experiments on mass communication.* Princeton Univ. Press, 1949.
21. Hovland, C. I., and Weiss, W. The influence of source credibility on communication effectiveness. *Publ. Opin. Quart.,* 1951, *15,* 635–650.
22. Janis, I. L., Lumsdaine, A. A., and Gladstone, A. I. Effects of preparatory communications on reactions to a subsequent news event. *Publ. Opin. Quart.,* 1951, *15,* 487–518.
23. Jersild, A. Primacy, recency, frequency, and vividness. *J. Exp. Psychol.,* 1929, *12,* 58–70.
24. Kelman, H. C., and Hovland, C. I. "Reinstatement" of the communicator in delayed measurement of opinion change. *J. Abnorm. Soc. Psychol.,* 1953, *48,* 327–335.
25. Krueger, W. C. F. The effect of overlearning on retention. *J. Exp. Psychol.,* 1929, *12,* 71–78.
26. Levine, J. M., and Murphy, G. The learning and forgetting of controversial material. *J. Abnorm. Soc. Psychol.,* 1943, *38,* 507–517.
27. Luh, C. W. The conditions of retention. *Psychol. Monogr.,* 1922, *31,* No. 3.
28. Peterson, Ruth C., and Thurstone, L. L. *Motion pictures and the social attitudes of children.* New York, Macmillan, 1933.
29. Rapaport, D. *Emotions and memory.* Baltimore, Williams & Wilkins, 1942.
30. Remmers, H. H. An experiment on the retention of attitudes as changed by instructional material. *Studies in higher education.* Purdue Univ., 1938, No. 34, 20–22.
31. Restorff, H. von. I. Über die Wirkung von Bereichsbildungen im Spurenfeld. In W. Köhler and H. von Restorff, Analyse von Vorgängen im Spurenfeld. *Psychol. Forsch.,* 1933, *18,* 299–342.
32. Sharp, Agnes Arminda. An experimental test of Freud's doctrine of the relation of hedonic tone to memory revival. *J. Exp. Psychol.,* 1938, *22,* 395–418.
33. Sims, V. M. Factors influencing attitude toward the TVA. *J. Abnorm. Soc. Psychol.,* 1938, *33,* 34–56.
34. Smith, F. T. An experiment in modifying attitudes toward the Negro. *Teachers College, Columbia University, contributions to education, No. 887.* New York, Bureau of Publications, Teachers College, Columbia Univ., 1943.
35. Van Buskirk, W. L. An experimental study of vividness in learning and retention. *J. Exp. Psychol.,* 1932, *15,* 563–573.
36. Watson, W. S., and Hartmann, G. W. The rigidity of a basic attitudinal frame. *J. Abnorm. Soc. Psychol.,* 1939, *34,* 314–335.
37. Weiss, W. A "sleeper" effect in opinion change. *J. Abnorm. Soc. Psychol.,* 1953, *48,* 173–180.
38. Williamson, A. C., and Remmers, H. H. Persistence of attitudes concerning conservation issues. *J. Exp. Educ.,* 1940, *8,* 354–361.
39. Zeligs, Rose. Influencing children's attitudes toward the Chinese. *Sociol. & Soc. Res.,* 1941, *26,* 126–138.

CHAPTER 9: *Summary and Emerging Problems*

THE present volume reports the results of a continuing program of research designed to investigate how opinions and beliefs are modified by persuasive communications. In this chapter the main findings will be briefly reviewed first, and then some of the emerging problems will be delineated. In the final section an attempt will be made to indicate some of the implications of the studies for a theoretical analysis of persuasion.

SUMMARY OF RESULTS

Most of the results can be viewed as specifying the effects of a communication according to the nature of 1) the communicator (*who* says it), 2) the communication (*what* is said), and 3) the audience (*to whom* is it said). Within each of these three areas selected topics have been investigated, primarily by controlled experimental studies on classroom audiences. We shall indicate the generalizations which are beginning to emerge, but again remind the reader that a great deal of replication and systematic variation, both in our own and in other cultures, will be required before comprehensive propositions can be conclusively established.

A. THE COMMUNICATOR

Several of our studies analyze the effects upon opinion of varying the expertness and trustworthiness of the communicator. In the experiment by Hovland and Weiss [7] identical newspaper and magazine articles were attributed to various high credibility sources (like Robert Oppenheimer) in one group and to low credibility sources (like *Pravda*) in another. The results of this and supplementary investigations [4, 21, 28] indicated:

1) Communications attributed to low credibility sources tended to be considered more biased and unfair in presentation than identical ones attributed to high credibility sources.

2) High credibility sources had a substantially greater immediate effect on the audience's *opinions* than low credibility sources.

3) The effects on opinion were not the result of differences in the amount of attention or comprehension, since information tests reveal equally good learning of what was said regardless of the credibility of the communicator; variations in source credibility seem to influence primarily the audience's motivation to accept the conclusions advocated.

4) The positive effect of the high credibility sources and the negative effect of the low credibility sources tended to disappear after a period of several weeks.

B. The Communication

When a communicator attempts to persuade people to adopt his conclusions he usually employs arguments and appeals which function as incentives. Among the major classes of such incentives are *a*) substantiating arguments, which may lead the audience to judge the conclusion as "true" or "correct"; *b*) "positive" appeals, which call attention to the rewards to be gained from acceptance; and *c*) "negative" appeals, including fear-arousing contents, which depict the unpleasant consequences of failure to accept the conclusion.

Some of our experimental studies highlight the ways in which symbols operate as effective incentives, while others stress factors involved in the effective organization of arguments.

1. *Fear appeals.* One way a communication can reinforce the acceptance of new beliefs is to arouse and then alleviate emotional tension. When an emotional appeal is successful, it may be assumed that the communication not only produces strong emotional reactions but also insures that emotional tension will be reduced at the time the recommended belief is rehearsed. When a communication relies on fear appeals, its effectiveness in arousing emotional tension depends upon such factors as explicitness, source, and prior communication experiences. The content usually is directed toward depicting a state of affairs in which the goals, security, or values of the audience are threatened.

Some of the factors which determine whether or not a fear-arousing communication will be effective were investigated in an experiment by Janis and Feshbach [*10*]. The study involved the arousal of fear by depicting potential dangers to which the audience might be exposed. Three different forms of an illustrated lecture on dental hygiene, representing three different intensities of fear appeal, were given to high school students. It was found that the strong appeal produced greater emotional tension than the moderate appeal, which in turn produced greater tension than did the minimal appeal. However, the greatest change in conformity to the communicator's recommendations was produced by the minimal appeal. The strong appeal failed to produce any significant change in dental hygiene practices and was less effective than the minimal appeal in producing resistance to counterpropaganda.

These findings suggest that the use of strong fear appeals will interfere with the over-all effectiveness of a persuasive communication if such appeals evoke a high degree of emotional tension without adequately providing for reassurance. The evidence is consistent with the following two hypotheses:

a. The use of a strong fear appeal, as against a milder one, increases the likelihood that the audience will be left in a state of emotional tension which is not fully relieved when the reassuring recommendations contained in the communication are rehearsed.

b. When fear is strongly aroused but not fully relieved by the reassurances contained in a persuasive communication, the audience will become motivated to ignore or to minimize the importance of the threat.

2. *Salience of group norms.* Various types of communication content having to do with group norms may function as powerful incentives for the acceptance or rejection of new opinions. Some inferences about relevant types of content can be drawn from the discussion of predispositional factors underlying conformity to group norms (cf. pp. 155 ff.). For instance, communications which call attention to group membership may prompt the individual to take account of group norms in forming his opinion on a given issue. This effect has been described as the "salience" of the group.

A study by Kelley [*16*] sought to ascertain whether the salience of group membership has any direct effect upon the resistance to change

of group-anchored attitudes. The principal subjects were Catholic
students in a public high school and in a nondenominational college.
Students of other religious faiths were also included for purposes of
comparison. During the regular class sessions, when the salience of
any particular religious affiliation could be expected to be low, some
of the students received reading material intended to heighten the
salience of Catholic Church membership and others received unrelated "neutral" material. The students were then given statements
intended to modify their opinions in a direction away from Catholic
norms. For the high school students, when salience of the church was
high, the Catholics tended to show greater resistance to change than
when salience was low. Thus the findings suggest that the use of contents which arouse awareness of a reference group can have a marked
effect on the audience's tendency to accept or reject the recommended
opinion. The absence of a similar effect for the college students, however, raises some question as to whether the phenomenon is a general
one or occurs only for persons who are strongly attached to a group
but have relatively little understanding of its norms.

Preliminary evidence was also obtained on the retention of opinion
changes produced under high and low salience. Under the particular
conditions investigated, the low salience sample continued to show
more effect at the time of a delayed test. This problem should be investigated further, particularly under conditions where, as suggested by
various theoretical considerations, the retention of change produced
under high salience is likely to be superior (cf. pp. 161–165).

3. *Conclusion drawing.* A recurrent problem in preparing communications is whether to state the conclusion explicitly or to leave
it to be drawn by the audience. There are theoretical considerations
favoring each alternative. A study to determine the effectiveness of
conclusion drawing with respect to a typical social issue was conducted
by Hovland and Mandell [4]. Two groups of college students listened
to a transcribed talk on "Devaluation of Currency." In one group
the appropriate conclusion was drawn by the speaker while in the
other group the conclusion was left up to the audience. Under the
conditions of this experiment, conclusion drawing by the communicator produced significantly more opinion change. The following general hypothesis is suggested: In communications which deal with com-

plicated issues, it is generally more effective to state the conclusion explicitly than to rely upon the audience to draw its own conclusions. With less complex issues, however, one would expect more members of the audience to be able to derive the appropriate conclusion independently. Similarly the superiority of conclusion drawing by the communicator would be expected to be less pronounced with more intelligent persons than with less intelligent—although within the narrow range of ability represented by college students in this experiment, no such relationship was found.

The extent to which the topic produces "ego involvement" might also be a factor that determines the relative effectiveness of explicit conclusion drawing. On topics where the individual is less inclined to be dependent upon experts and more likely to resist the influence of others, implicit treatment may be more effective. This may be characteristic of problems discussed in psychotherapy, for which "nondirective" techniques are frequently advocated. Conditions under which implicit presentation is more effective with mass communications remain to be investigated.

4. *Preparation for future experiences.* Special problems arise in planning the content of a communication when the task is that of preparing an individual or an audience for some future event or communication. As yet, little is known about the conditions under which preparatory communications diminish or augment the psychological impact of later events. When people have been given reassuring or optimistic communications beforehand, are they less likely to develop pessimistic attitudes in response to subsequent "bad" news? What types of preparatory communications will mitigate the effects of subsequent experiences of failure or disappointment? Such problems not only are of practical importance but also involve a number of general theoretical issues concerning the way in which persuasive communications can predispose an audience to interpret and react to subsequent life experiences.

Three experiments on the effects of preparatory communications have been undertaken in our research program. One of these was the study by Lumsdaine and Janis [24] on the effectiveness of different types of content in preparing individuals to resist the influence of subsequent counterpropaganda. Two versions of a recorded radio

program were used, in both of which the commentator advocated the
view that it would be at least five years before Russia could produce
A-bombs in quantity. One group of high school subjects received a
one-sided version, which presented only the arguments that supported
the speaker's conclusion. Another group was given a two-sided version, which contained the same arguments and the same conclusion
but in addition discussed the main arguments on the opposite side
of the question. Half the subjects in each group were subsequently
given a second communication in which a different speaker advocated
an opinion opposed to that presented in the initial communication.

Under conditions where there was no exposure to counterpropaganda, the two versions were found to be about equally effective in
modifying opinion. But for the subjects subsequently exposed to the
counterpropaganda, the two-sided version proved to be markedly
more effective in producing sustained opinion change. It appears that
when a two-sided presentation is used the hearer is led to the recommended opinion in a context which takes account of opposing arguments. In this way he is given an advance basis for ignoring or discounting the opposing arguments and is thus "innoculated" against
subsequent communications which advocate a contradictory point of
view.

A second experiment, which used some of the same subjects as in
the preceding experiment, was carried out by Janis, Lumsdaine, and
Gladstone [*15*]. The opportunity to study the effects of a preparatory communication arose unexpectedly when President Truman announced that an atomic explosion had occurred in Russia. It was
possible to observe the effects of an "optimistic" communication in
preparing the audience for an unfavorable news event, inasmuch as
the subjects had been exposed three months earlier to the radio program (described above) which took the position that Russia would
be unable to produce large numbers of A-bombs for many years to
come. Following the President's announcement, those subjects who
had received the optimistic program were compared with an equivalent control group which had not. It was found that the control subjects were much more likely to develop the expectation that Russia
would soon have a large supply of A-bombs and that war would be
imminent. Thus preparatory communication produced resistance to

the impact of the subsequent news event. The findings are consistent with the hypothesis that once a belief is modified by an effective communication there will be a tendency for the newly acquired opinions to interfere with the subsequent acquisition of any incompatible opinions.

A third ·type of problem concerns the use of communications to prepare individuals for experiences of failure. Subsequent events become especially important whenever a communication makes use of incentives which involve predictions about the future (e.g., statements to the effect that acceptance of the recommended opinion will lead to successful attainment of some specific goal.) If the predictions are contradicted by subsequent events, or if the individual acts upon these predictions and experiences failure, the degree of acceptance will tend to be markedly reduced. Whenever new beliefs are likely to be followed by initial experiences of failure, it may be necessary for the communicator to prepare the audience for such results, by apprising them of the possibility of subsequent failure in such a way that failures will be discounted and produce minimal frustration. A preliminary investigation by Janis and Herz [*12*], the results of which became available while the present volume was in preparation, indicates the role of prior communications in "innoculating" individuals for failure experiences. Their findings suggest that preparatory communications may teach the individual to anticipate that he will ultimately be rewarded if he "sticks with" the communicator's recommendations, and give him a basis for discounting failures, so that he will be less likely to experience frustration or to interpret subsequent failures as a sign that he is behaving incorrectly.*

* A game of chance similar to a pinball machine was used. The experimenters recommended a particular system of play, predicting that it was the best system in the long run. One group of subjects was given special preparation for discounting subsequent failures, while the other group was not. The prepared group was told that some practice was necessary before the system would yield successful results, and that at times the machine might operate so erratically that, for a series of trials, no system would work. The apparatus was set up so that whenever the game was played both groups would experience identical sequences of success and failure.

The results indicated that the prepared subjects showed significantly more conformity to the recommended system than the unprepared subjects. The verbal

C. The Audience

It is generally recognized that people will react differently to the same social pressures: incentives can function adequately only insofar as the individual has the necessary motivational predispositions. By taking account of such factors it should be possible to arrive at a more comprehensive set of general principles for predicting opinion changes.

1. *Group conformity motives.* Some of the most important predispositions are those related to the groups in which the person holds membership. During the past decade there has been increasing research into the development of norms within groups and the degree of conformity to them exhibited by various members (e.g., [25]). Some of the evidence from these studies suggests that persons who are most highly motivated to maintain their membership tend to be most susceptible to influence by other members within the group.

The discussion of group membership factors in the present volume has dealt primarily with the resistance that group members offer to communications which advocate views contrary to the group's norms. Kelley and Volkart [17] investigated the resistance to change of group-anchored attitudes as a function of the members' valuation of the group. Boy Scouts' attitudes toward camping and woodcraft activities were studied both before and after a speech by an outside adult who criticized the Scouts' emphasis upon these activities and recommended instead various activities in the city. The amount of change induced by this counternorm communication was studied in relation to an index of how much each Scout valued his membership in the troop. Under conditions where opinions were expressed privately, boys who

---

preparation resulted in continued acceptance of the communicator's recommendations not only during the initial trials, which were uniformly failures, but also during the later trials when successes were interspersed with failures. The effectiveness of the preparation was also a function of the ratio of success to failure. The preparation was effective for those subjects who were given a fair proportion of success experience, but had no effect upon those who were given success experiences very infrequently. Thus it appears that prior preparation can be effective provided the individual is not exposed to an inordinately high degree of failure.

most highly valued their membership were least influenced by the communication. Thus, the findings support the general hypothesis that persons who are most strongly motivated to retain their membership in a group will be most resistant to communications contrary to the standards of that group.

2. *Individual differences in persuasibility.* In addition to the motives stemming from group membership there are other sources of individual differences in responsiveness to communications. For example, prior research has indicated that differences in mental ability may affect the extent to which the individual is susceptible to persuasion. But there is a complex relationship involved: persons with higher intellectual ability would be expected to be able to learn what is presented more readily and to draw appropriate inferences more effectively; but they are also likely to be more critical in accepting arguments and conclusions than persons with lesser ability.

Differences in persuasibility associated with motivational aspects of personality would also be anticipated. Relevant data are provided in a study by Janis [9]. On the basis of the degree of change following three communications, subjects (undergraduates) were divided into categories of high, moderate, and low persuasibility. Personality data were obtained from detailed clinical reports on a small number of subjects who received psychological counseling, and from a personality inventory given to a larger group of subjects.

Both sets of data provided evidence in support of the hypothesis that persons with low self-esteem are predisposed to be highly influenced by persuasive communications. Students who manifested social inadequacy, inhibition of aggression, and depressive tendencies showed the greatest opinion change.

A second hypothesis suggested by the results is that persons with acute psychoneurotic symptoms are predisposed to be resistant to persuasive communications. The students who were most resistant to change had come for counseling largely because of acute neurotic symtoms similar to those of patients diagnosed as having obsessional neurosis, hysteria, or anxiety neurosis. The hypothesis was supported by the personality inventory results: students who remained relatively uninfluenced had higher scores than others on items indicative of neurotic anxiety and obsessional symptoms.

D. Response Factors

In all of our studies we have been concerned with the *effects* of communications, and hence with the responses of the audience. But in several investigations special aspects of response have been analyzed. One set of problems has to do with the effects of active participation, and another with the duration of the changes in response produced by persuasive communication.

1. *Active participation.* It frequently happens that an individual is induced to conform overtly before he has come to accept a norm or belief as his own. In the socialization of the child and in situations of entering a new community or social group, verbal conformity to normative beliefs is often required. In most cases these beliefs are eventually internalized; in many cases they are not. It would be important to investigate the factors leading to these alternative outcomes.

Some research on this problem [*13, 20, 22, 23*] was described in Chapter 7. Janis and King [*13*] designed an experiment to test the following hypothesis: When exposure to the same persuasive communication is held constant, individuals who are required to verbalize the communication aloud to others will tend to be more influenced than those who are passively exposed. The experiment involved the comparison of opinion changes in two experimental groups of college students: 1) "active participants" who were induced to play a role which required them to deliver a talk in a group situation and 2) "passive controls" who merely read and listened to the same communication.

The findings, based on three different communications concerning expectations about the future, support the conclusion that spoken agreement induced by role playing tends to increase the effectiveness of persuasive communication. The investigators then proceeded to explore the possible psychological mechanisms underlying the gain from active participation. Two suggestive leads emerged: 1) the amount of opinion change occurring with active participation may depend upon the amount of improvisation, i.e., the extent to which the main points are reformulated and illustrative examples are inserted or additional arguments invented; 2) the amount of opinion change is a function of the degree to which the individual feels satisfied with his performance in giving the talk.

A second experiment by King and Janis [22], using a more ego-involving topic, was designed to determine whether either of the two factors suggested by the first experiment is critical in producing participation effects. To test the effects of improvisation, some subjects were required to present the talk without a script, after having read it silently, while others were permitted to read directly from the script. Experimental variations were introduced in order to produce varying degrees of satisfaction and dissatisfaction with respect to the individual's speaking performance. The results consistently indicate that the amount of opinion change produced through active participation is dependent upon the amount of improvisation but is not related to the amount of satisfaction. Improvised role playing could be viewed as a technique whereby the individual is stimulated to make the communication as effective as possible, devising exactly the kind of arguments, illustrations, and motivating appeals that are most likely to be convincing to himself.

Further data on verbal conformity were obtained by Kelman [20] in an experiment in which various types of incentives were compared. Immediately after hearing a talk, school children were asked to write essays on the issue in question. Three experimental variations were introduced by offering different incentives for writing essays conforming to the communicator's position: the control group was offered no special incentive; a second group (high incentive) was told that every student who conformed would receive a prize; a third group (low incentive) was told that every student who conformed would be eligible for the prize but that only a few would receive it. The results showed the control group to have the lowest and the high incentive group the highest degree of conformity. The amount of opinion change, however, did not vary directly with the degree of conformity: significantly more change was found in the low incentive group than in either of the other two groups. The essays produced under the low incentive condition were found to be of superior quality and to contain a higher frequency of new arguments. The findings provide additional support for the improvisation hypothesis and suggest that the effects of active participation depend upon whether the act of overt conformity is accompanied by inner responses of a supporting or of an interfering nature.

It seems likely that under certain conditions role playing and other means of producing verbal conformity may *interfere* with acceptance. This is suggested by some of the incidental findings in the experimental studies. For instance, Kelman observed signs of resentment among subjects who were given a strong incentive to conform. In the Janis and King experiment, it was noted that a group of subjects who experienced dissatisfaction with their role-playing performance showed significantly less opinion change than the passive controls who did not engage in role playing. Systematic exploration is needed to discover the conditions under which active participation has negative or boomerang effects.

2. *Duration of effects.* Prior research has indicated considerable variability in the extent to which changes in opinion produced by communication are maintained over time. Several of our studies have been concerned with the paradoxical increase in opinion change which sometimes appears after a lapse of time (the "sleeper effect"). The study by Hovland and Weiss [7] suggests one possible explanation of the effect. They found that when a low credibility communicator presented the communication very small initial changes in opinion were obtained. But after a delay of four weeks the "negative prestige" tended to disappear while the conclusion was still remembered. This could account for the increased opinion change in the direction advocated in the communication. Their analysis suggests that people may initially resist accepting material presented by a low credibility source, but after a period they may no longer associate the conclusion with the source. This dissociation tendency would be maximal when the communication contains arguments and evidence which can be evaluated on their own merits and are likely to be recalled without bringing the source to mind. However, when the source and content are intimately related the tendency to dissociate them should be much less.

This line of reasoning would suggest that the sleeper effect will occur only when cues as to the source are absent. The effect should disappear if the audience is reminded of a low credibility source at the time of later testing. A study to test this prediction was carried out by Kelman and Hovland [21]. Separate experimental groups were exposed to the same talk on juvenile delinquency, preceded by an introduction in which either "positive" or "negative" characteristics were attributed to the speaker. Three weeks later, at the time of a follow-up test, the source was "reinstated" for half the subjects by reminding them who the speaker had been. The results showed that the positive communicator had the greatest initial effect and the negative communicator the smallest initial effect on the subjects' opinions. Subsequently, under nonreinstatement conditions, there was a decline in agreement with the positive speaker and an increase in agreement with the negative, as was found in the Hovland and Weiss study. Reinstatement of the source, however, increased the extent of agreement with the positive communicator and decreased the agreement with the negative. The reinstated sources produced effects approximately equal to those obtained at the time of the initial communication.

These experiments indicate, then, that delayed effects can be explained by the absence of the communicator as a cue for acceptance or rejection. However, the evidence fails to support the hypothesis that the opinion changes over time are a function of simple *forgetting* of the source. The critical difference seems to be contingent upon whether or not the source and the content are recalled at the same time. If the audience is reminded of the source, there is relatively little change over time. But normally there seems to be a tendency to dissociate the content from the source and consequently the positive (or negative) influence of the source declines with time.

EMERGING AREAS OF RESEARCH

One of the most interesting aspects of any research program is the discovery of new problems which must be attacked before further progress can be made. They are the topics which one feels afterward he should have been concentrating on from the start. Three such topics, which cut across the usual categories of communication research, are discussed in the following section. In these areas our research has not yet been published or has only recently begun.

INTERNALIZATION PROCESSES

The transformation of outer conformity into inner conformity—a phenomenon observed in the active participation experiments—poses a number of important theoretical problems. When people are under external constraint to adhere to the demands of authorities they sometimes conform only when they know that their deviant behavior will be detected and punished. Frequently, however, attitudes and behavior initially prescribed by an external authority or group become "internalized," i.e., genuinely accepted by the person and adhered to even in the absence of surveillance. The purpose of examining opinion change in terms of internalization processes is to focus upon situations where opinions are adhered to exclusively on the overt level at first and to analyze the conditions under which this conformity is changed into inner belief.

A variety of psychological mechanisms have been suggested to explain internalization. Of the various explanations advanced, the most general one, perhaps, is that the individual finds satisfaction in adopting the advocated view, even in the absence of the advocate. For example, an individual may take over the behavior of another person for whom he feels strong affection, as a means of maintaining feelings of security by keeping him, symbolically, close at hand. The need to resort to this form of behavior may perhaps be even greater in the absence of the loved person than in his presence. A similar mechanism may be operative when a person is highly dependent upon a group for satisfaction of his emotional needs. Here internalization may appear as conforming behavior which persists in private situations not under the surveillance of the group. Some evidence from our program tends to support the hypothesis that internalization of norms is a function of positive attachment to the group (cf. pp. 139 ff.).

Sometimes external social pressure may act in direct opposition to the individual's basic impulses. When the clash between the antagonistic pressures becomes intolerable, he may "disown" his impulses and apply the originally external standards to himself. A similar process may mediate the acceptance of new opinions when a person is forced to express them as if they represented his own position. It can be assumed that such expression, when it is contrary to deeply rooted attitudes, creates sharp awareness of being inconsistent. As a result, those persons who have strong self-consistency motives or highly integrated self-images which are threatened by "hypocritical" behavior will be strongly motivated to adopt the enforced expressions as their own.

While extensive work has been done on the processes of internalization in clinical studies, there is a great need for further systematic analysis of the implications of internalization processes as they occur in communication situations involving both mass media and face-to-face interactions.

CONFLICT AND OPINION CHANGE

Another important research task is the extension of conflict theory to problems of opinion change. A persuasive communication will often create a conflict between the motives aroused by the new incentives it offers on the one hand and whatever motives the individual may have for holding his initial opinions on the other. For instance, the continual demands of a boy's gang that one display his manhood by heavy smoking may be in direct conflict with anticipations of harmful physiological consequences which an antitobacco communication predicts will result from constant use of tobacco. Sometimes a single communication arouses two competing sets of motives within the individual. Communications which give two sides of a controversy deliberately expose the audience to conflicting arguments and evidence. On other occasions, the initial reactions to the source and to the content of the communication may be incompatible; the communicator may be highly respected but his proposals may be quite objectionable to the audience. From these examples it can be seen that in order to understand the outcome of many attempts at opinion change various kinds of conflict situations must be thoroughly explored.

There already exists a considerable body of behavioral data and psychological theory about the major types of conflicts (e.g., approach-avoidance, avoidance-avoidance) and their different consequences. In addition, the general effects of conflicting social influences have been investigated in studies of "cross pressures." The available evidence bears out some of the predictions from theories about conflict behavior: there have been observations of vacillation, apathy, and loss of interest in conflict-laden issues, of attempts to avoid conflictful communications, to attribute them to spurious sources, and to distort their meaning. For example, a recent study by Kelley and Woodruff [18] indicates that listeners tend to report an inaccurate impression of the speaker's point of view when there is an incompatibility between what he actually says (e.g., his proposals are contrary to their group's norms) and the approval he apparently receives from other members of their group. These effects should be investigated in their own right and in terms of their consequences for opinion change rather than as incidental by-products of communication situations. Detailed studies are needed to determine the conditions under which one or another of the various types of conflict solution is likely to occur.

Some especially interesting questions arise when one considers stability of opinion change in relation to the kind and degree of conflict created by the communication situation. Relatively little persistence is to be expected when the changes produced by the communication are subsequently brought into conflict with other motives or pressures. Some of our studies of situations of this kind suggest that resistance to these counterpressures can be heightened by placing the person in a similar conflict at the time of the communication. The techniques of presenting the opposing side of the issue as well as the one advocated, delivering a communication when the opposing norms are highly salient, warning the person that adhering to the recommendation will entail a certain number of failure experiences in the future —all these tend to increase the degree of conflict at the time of the communication. The greater persistence apparently produced by some of these methods suggests that heightened conflict at the time of the communication can lead to certain types of resolution which increase long-term effectiveness. The general problem revolves around the conditions under which there is a gain from having the conflict occur when the outcome can be influenced by the communication as compared with allowing it to occur later under conditions where the communicator is not present. Systematic investigation should be made of the sustained effects of communication techniques which force the individual to face and deal with conflicting pressures.

PERCEPTION, JUDGMENT, AND CONCEPT
FORMATION

Our experience in the field of persuasion emphasizes the extent to which progress in this area is dependent upon further advances in basic theory in psychology as a whole. Particularly relevant are developments in the area of the higher thought processes. While the intimate relationship between perception and attitude has frequently been noted, relatively little research has been directed toward integrating the two fields. One bridge between them may be found in the study of language. Linguists and anthropologists have reported interesting observations and have suggested a number of valuable hypotheses, but little systematic research on these problems has been undertaken. Accordingly it seems important to examine, with experimental methods, the role of language in the shaping of perception and in the assimilating of information (cf. Hovland [2], p. 431).

The problems of "frames of reference" and "reference groups" point to the necessity of more extensive study of judgmental phenomena. Statements made in the field of attitude measurement have implicitly contradicted generalizations derived from experiments on judgment. The latter assert that categorizing is markedly affected by the individual's own "anchorage" point, while discussions of attitude measurement state that the scaling of items is independent of the position of the person who makes the judgment. Several of our recent studies have attempted to resolve this contradiction. The results indicate that when individuals have strong positions on an issue their judgments *are* significantly affected (Hovland and Sherif [6]). This is shown even more markedly when an individual is allowed to choose the number of categories which he considers necessary to express the various shades of difference in opinion. An assessment of an individual's attitude is possible from the number of categories he uses and the way in which he distributes the items into the categories (Sherif and Hovland [26]). The differences in categorization appear to be due to different ways of viewing the issue rather than to an inability to discriminate among the items. When the method of paired comparisons is used, the discrepancies among individuals with different views are greatly reduced (Kelley, Hovland, Schwartz, and Abelson [19]).

Another relationship between judgment and attitude change is being explored in connection with the following phenomenon: a communication only slightly removed from the individual's position will sometimes influence him positively while one far removed will affect him negatively (boomerang effect). Experiments with simple psychophysical judgments indicate that a similar phenomenon occurs in this area, such that an anchor only slightly removed from the stimulus series yields an "assimilation effect" but one too far removed produces "contrast" (Sherif, Taub, and Hovland [27]). Further research is needed with complex verbal material to determine the way in which communications may serve as anchors to which an individual's position is referred. A related experiment now under way involves communications on the issue of prohibition which are directed at individuals whose initial opinions differ in varying degrees from the speaker's position.

A more substantial basis is also needed for understanding the nature of concept formation as it relates to communication and opinion change. Characteristically an individual is bombarded with a host of diverse and often contradictory points of view which must somehow be integrated in arriving at an opinion. This represents an important type of concept formation but one about which we know very little. One phase of the problem involves the relative roles of "positive instances" and "negative instances" in deriving concepts. This problem has been analyzed theoretically (Hovland [3]) and investigated experimentally (Hovland and Weiss [8]). Many further problems remain. When does the individual "compartmentalize" the information received, so that contradictory materials are retained without being integrated? When are compromise solutions taken, and when are there true integrations of disparate data? Answers to these questions will require both laboratory research and controlled field experiments under naturalistic conditions of communication.

PROBLEMS IN THE THEORETICAL ANALYSIS OF PERSUASION

The summaries given in this chapter have indicated the diversity of topics investigated and types of approach employed. Running through the studies, however, is one common emphasis—the necessity of isolating the critical factors involved in communication effects. Sometimes experimental analysis reveals uniformities which had not heretofore been observed. But at other times relationships which have been thought to be general "laws" are found to hold only under certain limited conditions, and the search must begin for the factors which determine whether one or another outcome will be obtained.

SEPARATING ATTENTION, COMPREHENSION, AND ACCEPTANCE

The need for isolating the critical variables is illustrated by experiments on primacy reported in the chapter on the organization of content (cf. pp. 120 ff.). The first investigator in this field (Lund) had found—and stated as the law of primacy—that whichever side of an issue is presented first will have greater influence on belief than the side presented second. An opposite outcome was obtained by a later investigator (Cromwell), who found results favoring recency (the communication presented last had more effect). The study by Hovland and Mandell [5] has indicated that the outcome will not always be the same: whether primacy or recency effects (or neither) will occur depends upon the conditions of the communication situation. The factors which were found to be most useful in analyzing the problem were those of attention, comprehension, and acceptance: 1) Variations in attention may determine whether the first or second communication on an issue will be more effective. For example, if the issue is an unfamiliar one and the audience only becomes aware of its importance late in the communication, the second one is in the favored position because it will receive greater attention right from the start. 2) Understanding and assimilating the first communication may increase the effectiveness of the second (e.g., if the material is complicated and requires prior familiarity for its full implications to be grasped). But sometimes the second one may be at a disadvantage with respect to comprehension (e.g., if the first side is barely assimilated and the person is then confronted with new and contradictory ideas in the second). 3) When both attention and comprehension factors are held constant, the outcome will depend upon a third set of factors which affect acceptance of the two opposed sides. For example, if the audience feels highly uncertain about an issue but is under pressure to make a decision, the first persuasive communication may have a disproportionate influence.

The distinction between attention, comprehension, and acceptance which was found useful in the analysis of primacy has been used throughout the volume. This differentiation is important because the variables which determine the effectiveness of a communication may affect these three phases of the influence process in varying ways and to different degrees. For example, in analyzing the persistence of opinion change over time as related to the credibility of the source, it was necessary to separate the effects attributable to the learning and retention of the content (determined by attention and comprehension) from those attributable to loss of the motivation to accept or reject the source's influence. This separation made it possible to explain the paradoxical increase in opinion change over time (sleeper effect).

A separation of the three phases of the influence process was also relevant in analyzing the effects of fear appeals. For example, it appeared that a strong appeal, which aroused fear of disease and suffering, increased *attention* to the content dealing with potential threats (Janis and Milholland [*14*]) but was self-defeating because it tended to reduce *acceptance* of the hygienic measures that were recommended by the communicator (Janis and Feshbach [*10, 11*]).

While numerous writers have utilized similar distinctions between various phases of the persuasive process, little research has been systematically directed toward disentangling them. Thus an important problem for future investigation is the analysis of factors which differentially affect attention, comprehension, and acceptance in complex communication situations.

This approach may be useful for research not only on the effects of communication stimuli but also on personality predispositions. With respect to each of the three phases of communication, there are likely to be individual differences in ability factors and in motive factors. One would expect to find that among the major sources of low persuasibility are deficiencies in one or another of the essential abilities. Some individuals might generally fail to be influenced by communications because of lack of ability to direct and sustain attention; others primarily because of a low degree of ability to grasp explicit and implicit verbal meanings, resulting in poor comprehension; and still others because of deficiencies in other types of intellectual skills that are directly related to acceptance, as when they have difficulty in responding to verbal incentives with appropriate anticipations of rewards or punishment. In this last example we have in mind the skills involved in the imaginative rehearsal that is assumed to be necessary if the individual is to be motivated by the communicator's promises, threats, and predictions.

Even when a person possesses the essential abilities, however, lack of responsiveness might occur as a result of motivational deficiencies. For example, an individual may be inattentive because of general lack of interest in what other people say or because he has developed involuntary defenses against anxiety which inhibit or interfere with sustained attention to communication stimuli. In some persons who are able and motivated to attend, poor comprehension may occur because of emotional inhibitions or defense mechanisms which result in evading or distorting the meaning of unfamiliar or disturbing ideas. Finally, a variety of personality tendencies, such as generalized suspiciousness, might be found to have an inhibiting effect on acceptance.

It seems likely that there are also some personality factors which make for deviations in the direction of *high* persuasibility. For example, high persuasibility might result from lack of critical ability. Persons who are relatively low in ability to engage in critical thinking, to discern fallacious arguments, and to discount propagandistic devices would tend to be highly gullible, readily accepting conclusions that others with a higher level of critical ability would tend to reject. Differences in motivation might also give rise to deviations in the direction of indiscriminate acceptance (cf. discussion of the relationship between low self-esteem and high persuasibility, pp. 187 ff.). Before clear-cut answers can be provided within this area, considerable methodological development will be required. Procedures must be devised to analyze both ability and motive factors in terms of the attention, comprehension, and acceptance phases of responsiveness to persuasion.

KEY FACTORS IN INSTRUCTION AND PERSUASION

For the purpose of highlighting some of the broader theoretical issues that are involved in the study of communication factors underlying attention, comprehension, and acceptance, it is useful to return to a problem which was briefly discussed at the beginning of this book: What are the similarities and differences between verbal instruction and verbal persuasion? In Chapter 1 we pointed out that when an instructor presents a strictly factual communication on a scientific or technological topic the main problem, from the standpoint of the communicator, is to elicit adequate rehearsal or practice of the content, so that the essential points will be correctly grasped and retained. In terms of the three phases of the communication process, it could be said that the major factors in successful instruction tend to be those involving the *attention* and the *comprehension* phases. Typically the classroom audience has initial expectations that the communicator's conclusions will be the "correct answers." Hence, *acceptance* can usually be taken for granted and the primary problems are those of maintaining attention and insuring comprehension. In the case of persuasive communications, however, motivation to accept or reject becomes a major consideration, and may sometimes even influence the degree of attention and comprehension.

By and large, the general principles of learning concerned with attention and comprehension are assumed to operate in persuasion in the same manner as in instruction. Hence, many of the hypotheses which bear on the attention or comprehension phase of effective persuasion will also apply to effective instruction. Consider, for example, an hypothesis discussed earlier concerning the arrangement of arguments: When an audience has a low degree of interest in a communication, an anticlimax order of the content elements will be more effective than a climax order (cf. pp. 114 ff.). When the members of the audience are relatively uninterested to begin with, placing the most impressive and interesting material at the beginning rather than at the end of the communication would have the effect of motivating them to pay more attention to what is being said, resulting in better comprehension and more complete learning of the content. If this explanation is correct, the outcome, according to the general assumption under discussion, would hold true for purely educational material as well as for propaganda and other types of persuasive communications.

Another hypothesis, suggested by the experimental evidence on the effects of conclusion drawing, might also be placed in the same category: Other things being equal, a communication which presents a series of arguments on a complex issue will generally be more effective when the conclusion is stated explicitly (as against allowing the audience to draw its own conclusion). Here the essential mediating factor seems to involve adequate rehearsal of the verbal material that the audience is expected to learn and retain. If the conclusion is not stated explicitly, the audience may "miss the point" of the arguments and learn something different from what was intended. We would expect this factor to operate in the case of complex instructional communications in the same way as in persuasive communications. In the latter case, however, other factors—involving motivation to accept —might often operate in the opposite direction, and sometimes override the learning gain to be expected from an explicit statement of the conclusion (cf. pp. 102–105).

In order to delineate the special problems involved in acceptance, let us compare two typical instances of instruction and persuasion. Suppose that in both instances the audience consists of a group of Air Force fighter pilots who are undergoing the last stages of their training. On one occasion, a superior officer gives a lecture on how to estimate the altitude of one's plane under conditions where the standard altimeter cannot be used; on another occasion the same officer gives a lecture on leadership practices and advocates his own view that in order to maintain good discipline the pilot should avoid any off-duty contact or fraternization with the ground crew men responsible for the maintenance of his plane. If we assume that on both occasions almost everyone in the audience pays close attention to what the speaker says and understands his exposition fully, the content of both lectures presumably will be learned equally well. In the first case, having learned the recommended method of estimating altitude, the members of the audience are likely to make use of this knowledge whenever it becomes relevant to do so. Whenever the appropriate question arises, whether in a conversation with a co-worker or in an actual flying situation, the individual will be inclined to take account of and to adhere to the instructor's conclusions, insofar as he remembers them. But the outcome would generally be quite different in the case of the second lecture. When a pertinent question arises concerning personal relationships with ground crew personnel, only a small percentage of the audience is likely to adhere to the speaker's conclusion, despite the fact that a very high percentage might be capable of recalling exactly what had been recommended.

What are the main psychological factors that make for this difference? Why is it that in the one case people are likely to accept the recommended conclusions whereas in the other case they frequently fail to do so?

An essential difference between instruction and persuasion involves the expectations or anticipations that affect a person's motivation to accept or reject the communication. In the case of the lecture on estimating altitude, we can assume that the pilots are likely to perceive the information as authentic and of potential utility. On the other hand, most members of the audience will realize that the issue being discussed in the lecture on relations with ground personnel is a controversial one. They will be aware that others who are at least as well qualified as their instructor hold antithetical views and that it is extremely difficult to arrive at any definitive conclusions on such matters. We assume that these and related expectations interfere with acceptance.

The various findings that have emerged from the research reported in this volume seem to converge upon three types of expectations that operate to increase or decrease the degree of acceptance: 1) expectations of being "right" or "wrong"; 2) expectations of being impartially advised, or of being manipulated by the communications 3) expectations of being approved or disapproved by others. It seems likely that such expectations are capable of arousing strong motives which have been acquired on the basis of prior experiences in which the individual has been rewarded (correctly advised, benefited, and socially approved) or punished (misled, exploited, and socially disapproved) as a consequence of believing and accepting what other people have told him. Shortly after a child learns to understand language, he probably begins to experience differential rewards and punishments which foster the development of some degree of discrimination, so that he does not always believe everything he hears. Certain discriminations of this sort are likely to be repeatedly reinforced throughout the individual's life and would presumably form the basis for differential reactions to persuasion and instruction.

We assume, of course, that each of the three types of mediating expectations involves a continuum, ranging from strongly facilitating expectations which motivate acceptance to strongly interfering expectations which motivate rejection. Those instruction situations in which high acceptance is readily produced seem to elicit faciliating expectations to the effect that the conclusions are incontrovertible, the purpose of the communication is to benefit the recipient, and he will be socially rewarded rather than punished for adhering to the conclusions. Persuasion situations, on the other hand, ordinarily contain cues which evoke one or another expectation of the opposite type, at the interfering end of the continuum. Many of the hypotheses derived from the results presented in this volume can be interpreted as specifying the conditions under which such expectations are shifted toward the facilitating end of the continuum. Such shifts could be described as reducing or minimizing the negative motivational effects of interfering expectations. We shall briefly review from this standpoint a number of the main hypotheses discussed earlier.

ANALYSIS OF INTERFERING EXPECTATIONS

1. *Expectations of being wrong.* Even in the case of the most impressive persuasive communications, people are apt to display at least some minimal degree of resistance if they anticipate that the issue is one which cannot be settled in any definite way or that there are grounds for adopting a position different from the one being advocated by the communicator. Any cue to the fact that the communication deals with a controversial issue would prevent a person from regarding the conclusions as incontrovertible, and would create some degree of hesitancy and caution. If the issue is of great importance to the person, his awareness that others hold a conflicting view, even without his knowing exactly what it is or why it is held, would ordinarily be sufficient to motivate him to be cautious.

The factor of communicator "expertness" would obviously be related to this type of interference. Expectations of being given false arguments or incorrect judgments are least likely to occur when the communicator is perceived as being highly expert. The relationship between expertness and acceptance would be particularly pronounced whenever the issue is perceived to be one that can be fairly well settled by making special kinds of observations or by making a skilled judgment. But when the audience believes that the issue discussed in the communication cannot be settled in this way, the relationship between expertness and acceptance might become attenuated and even disappear.

The hypotheses on one-sided versus two-sided presentations also appear to bear on the conditions under which interfering expectations of error, associated with awareness of conflicting viewpoints, can be minimized. We have seen that the evidence indicates that a two-sided presentation is more effective than a one-sided presentation under conditions where *a)* the recipient is initially opposed to the communicator's position, or *b)* the recipient has relatively high intellectual ability, or *c)* the recipient is subsequently exposed to a counter-communication which presents opposing arguments. In all three of these conditions the chances are relatively great that the recipient will be aware of conflicting viewpoints. One would surmise that the interfering expectations of potential error engendered by such awareness tend to be minimized when the communicator provides some basis for discounting or refuting the competing arguments. But this gain in effectiveness would not be expected among those recipients who are not familiar with the existence of opposing points of view. In such cases, calling attention to a conflicting set of arguments would have the reverse effect, in that it would arouse expectations of potential error and would therefore motivate greater caution with respect to accepting the communicator's conclusions. In this connection, it will be recalled that the evidence indicates that a two-sided presentation tends to be *less* effective than a one-sided one among those members of the audience who are initially *in agreement* with the communicator's position.

At the time of exposure to a given communication, interfering expectations of potential error would presumably be increased if the recipients had recently been exposed to other communications which had advocated a different position. Even when a highly impressive communication is presented, members of an audience would be more cautious and less likely to adopt the new conclusion if they had previously learned that there are grounds for maintaining a different position. These assumptions seem to be consonant with the hypothesis derived from a study of the effects of preparatory communication: When exposed to a dramatic news event which induces pessimistic opinions about the future, an audience will be more resistant to change if previously exposed to a communication that presents grounds for maintaining the opposite opinions. In general, persons who have previously received antithetical information and arguments would be least likely to regard the views suggested by the new communication as incontrovertible and would be most highly motivated to be cautious and critical.

2. *Expectations of manipulative intent.* When an adult wants children to do something for his own convenience, he is likely to speak and to argue in quite a different way than when he is attempting to induce them to carry out some action entirely for their own benefit. As a result of repeated instances in which they are misled, disappointed, or exploited, children are apt to become highly sensitive to cues to manipulative intent. Sometimes they even receive specific training in this respect from their parents and, later on, from their age-mates (e.g., "don't be a sucker"). As a result of learning experiences of this kind, most individuals acquire strong motives which incline them to notice signs of communicator intent and to avoid being influenced when they expect that the communicator is attempting to manipulate them. Although such expectations may have the same general effect as expectations of potential error, the psychological mechanisms involved are likely to be somewhat different. The motives aroused by expectations of manipulative intent seem to be closely linked with feelings of humiliation and with various types of noncompliant behavior that are sometimes described in terms of "need for autonomy." Consequently, expectations of manipulative intent are likely to give rise to strong resisting tendencies that extend beyond the motivation to avoid adopting an erroneous belief.

Numerous experiments on persuasion suggest that this particular source of interference is a major determinant of resistance. For instance, the finding that cues to the "trustworthiness" of the source will affect the way in which the audience judges the content of a communication would seem to involve this type of interference. In the experimental investigations on "source trustworthiness," the same communication is presented as coming from two different sources, one of which is represented as being impartial while the other is represented as having ulterior personal motives for trying to persuade others to adopt his view. The available evidence from such studies tends to be consistent with the general hypothesis that the less "trustworthy" a communicator is perceived to be, the greater the likelihood that his presentation will be judged as biased and distorted and the greater the tendency to reject his conclusions. Whenever the source is perceived to be trustworthy, expectations of manipulative intent would be absent.

Under conditions where the audience has little or no prior basis for judging the trustworthiness of the communicator, expectations of manipulative intent would be highly dependent upon the content of the message. In this respect, the effectiveness of the content would be maximal when the communicator avoids saying anything that could be interpreted as a sign that he has something to gain from inducing acceptance of his conclusions. Some of the hypotheses presented in earlier chapters could be interpreted as specifying content cues which are especially likely to evoke expectations of manipulative intent. One such hypothesis was suggested in the chapter on fear-arousing appeals: The effectiveness of a threat appeal in arousing emotional tension will be reduced if the communicator frequently emphasizes and elaborates on dangers which are perceived by the audience to be exaggerated. Such treatment is likely to be interpreted by the recipients as a sign that the speaker is attempting to manipulate them (e.g., "he is trying to scare us into doing what he wants"). Some of the evidence from exploratory interviews provided examples of interfering responses of this kind and suggested that expectations of manipulative intent are less likely to occur when a threat appeal employs objective, impersonal language to convey the implications of the threat.

Another finding which bears on cues to manipulative intent was derived from a War Department study of one-sided versus two-sided presentation. On the one hand, there was a significant gain from presenting both sides when the communication was given to an audience initially opposed to the communicator's position—a gain which we have interpreted as being mainly due to overcoming the interfering effects of expectations of potential error. On the other hand, there was a boomerang effect from presenting both sides when the communication omitted an important argument of which the recipient was aware. The latter finding suggests that when the communicator explicitly or implicitly conveys the expectation that he is examining both sides of the issue, the omission or soft-pedaling of any important argument will become highly noticeable and stimulate expectations of manipulative intent. Even when a persuasive communication is given to a relatively sympathetic audience, a perceptible omission is likely to be interpreted as a sign that the communicator is deceitfully concealing his true purposes.

The gain in acceptance from active participation induced through role playing might also be due, at least in part, to desensitization with respect to expectations of manipulative intent. That the amount of gain was found to depend upon the amount of improvisation suggests a lowering of psychological resistance when the individual regards the arguments as being his "own" ideas. One explanation advanced earlier (cf. pp. 235 ff.) was that while restating the message and improvising new arguments the recipient is less likely to experience interfering thoughts about the intentions of the original communicator. We have also pointed out that the "hand-tailored" arguments invented by the active participant may be more convincing to him than the "ready-made" arguments contained in the original communication. Insofar as the arguments produced by the active participant are more likely to meet his own criteria of "truth," there would be a reduction of interferences from expectations of being wrong.

3. *Expectations of social disapproval.* We have repeatedly noted that one of the major incentives in persuasion involves the anticipation of social rewards. A prestigeful communicator is often perceived as a barometer of the social climate within a given organization or community, and even when he does not make any explicit predictions concerning social approval the audience may anticipate receiving approval if his position is adopted. On the other hand, when the listen-

ers are sharply aware of the fact that others disapprove of the communicator's position, they are likely to become motivated to reject his conclusion. Expectations of social disapproval would tend to interfere with acceptance even when the audience attributes a fairly high degree of credibility to the communicator's statements and is not suspicious about his intentions. Much of the research literature bearing on the relationship between communicator prestige and acceptance could probably be interpreted as specifying cues which arouse facilitating expectations of social approval or interfering expectations of social disapproval. Similarly, the power of statements about majority opinion to shift an individual's opinions probably involves the same sort of expectations.

Quite aside from formal sanctions that are applied to violators, the mere perception that the vast majority of people in one's community accepts a given norm seems to operate as a powerful force on the individual to conform to it. The more closely the consensus of opinion within a community approaches unanimity on a given issue, the greater the likelihood that any individual will anticipate social disapproval for deviating and hence the stronger will be his resistance to communications which present a counternorm position on that issue. One of the implications of these considerations is that any counternorm communication will be less likely to evoke interfering expectations of social disapproval—and hence will exert more influence—if it calls attention to facts which reveal a lack of community consensus on the particular issue. The same considerations could account for the increased effectiveness of pro-norm communications resulting from "bandwagon" appeals which call attention to community consensus.

What has just been said about the effects of community consensus would also apply to any membership group. Many of the specific findings bearing on group membership factors in relation to resistance to counternorm communications could be readily interpreted in terms of expectations of social disapproval. One of the main hypotheses supported by our research evidence is that those individuals who place the highest valuation on their membership in a group will tend to be more resistant than others to any counternorm communication. It is the high valuation members who are most vulnerable to social punishment from the group, inasmuch as they are usually the ones who have the strongest motivation to maintain friendly relationships with fellow members, to secure the prestige and to retain the special privileges associated with their membership status. It seems probable that when these individuals are exposed to a counternorm communication they are most likely to anticipate the possible social dangers of deviating from the group norm and to be most strongly motivated to ward off any such dangers.

The occurrence of such anticipations would depend, in part, upon whether or not any specific cues are presented in the communication situations which remind the individual of his group's norms. We have seen that evidence concerning the effects of high and low salience conditions suggested that persuasive arguments contained in a counternorm communication will be more effective, at least in the short run, if presented when group symbols are not salient. This hypothesis seems to emphasize the interfering effects of expectations of disapproval: When group symbols are not in the focus of attention (low salience conditions), expectations concerning the group's reactions to deviations are less likely to occur and hence there would be less resistance to the counternorm communication.

Finally, anticipations of social disapproval might help to explain the relationship between low self-esteem and high persuasibility discussed earlier. We suggested that persons with low self-esteem might be unusually sensitive to *immediate* threats of social disapproval (from the communicator or from the group he represents) and correspondingly less concerned about the more remote threat of *subsequent* disapproval from others (cf. pp. 191 f.). If so, the relative absence of interfering expectations of social disapproval would be one of the factors that accounts for high susceptibility to persuasion among such individuals. On the other hand, the presence of interfering expectations to a marked degree might be an important factor in many cases of low persuasibility. For example, some individuals (e.g., neurotic personalities characterized by obsessional doubts) might prove to be especially resistant to persuasion because of chronic uncertainty about potential disapproval; others (e.g., socially withdrawn, suspicious personalities) might remain unconvinced because of inordinately strong tendencies to respond with expectations of manipulative intent; still others (e.g., persons with high intellectual abilities combined with strong self-assertive motives) might be especially prone to reject persuasive communications as a result of expectations of potential error. Thus, some of the observed relationships between personality factors and persuasibility might be illuminated by investigating the interfering expectations which occur among different types of personalities.

The three different types of expectations which we have delineated are not intended to provide a complete theoretical account of the way in which persuasion is mediated or of the reinforcement mechanisms involved in the acquisition of new opinions. For example, the effects of social rewards and punishments have been taken into account only insofar as they enter into the expectations of the audience at the time of exposure to a communication; we have not considered at all the possible reinforcing effects of direct experiences of social approval or other "external" social rewards. Moreover, in addition to the three we have singled out, there are probably other types of expectations—including those which involve tension-reducing anticipations of averting potential threats—which also mediate acceptance or rejection at the time the communication is received (cf. pp. 61–65).

What the discussion has attempted to do is to indicate how a limited number of theoretical concepts might help to integrate and explain a large number of empirical relationships of the sort which have emerged from the diverse research studies described in this volume. For the present we have formulated these in terms of the expectations (which we consider to be a type of implicit mediating response) that facilitate or interfere with the acceptance of communications. This approach seems to be sufficiently promising to warrant an attempt to develop more refined methods for investigating the expectations elicited during exposure to communication, to supplement the usual measures of opinion change. We believe that a theoretical orientation of this kind applied to the study of communication and persuasion may prove to be extremely effective in uncovering significant motivational mechanisms and thought processes underlying social influence.

References

1. Hovland, C. I. Social communication. *Proc. Amer. Philos. Soc.*, 1948, *92*, 371–375.
2. Hovland, C. I. Changes in attitude through communication. *J. Abnorm. Soc. Psychol.*, 1951, *46*, 424–437.
3. Hovland, C. I. A "communication analysis" of concept learning. *Psychol. Rev.*, 1952, *59*, 461–472.
4. Hovland, C. I., and Mandell, W. An experimental comparison of conclusion-drawing by the communicator and by the audience. *J. Abnorm. Soc. Psychol.*, 1952, *47*, 581–588.
5. Hovland, C. I., and Mandell, W. Is there a law of primacy in persuasion? (In preparation.) Paper, Eastern Psychol. Assn., April 1952.
6. Hovland, C. I., and Sherif, M. Judgmental phenomena and scales of attitude measurement: Item displacement in Thurstone scales. *J. Abnorm. Soc. Psychol.*, 1952, *47*, 822–832.
7. Hovland, C. I., and Weiss, W. The influence of source credibility on communication effectiveness. *Publ. Opin. Quart.*, 1951, *15*, 635–650.
8. Hovland, C. I., and Weiss, W. Transmission of information concerning concepts through positive and negative instances. *J. Exp. Psychol.*, 1953, *45*, 175–182.
9. Janis, I. L. Personality correlates of susceptibility to persuasion. *J. Personal.* 1954. (In press.)
10. Janis, I. L., and Feshbach, S. Effects of fear-arousing communications. *J. Abnorm. Soc. Psychol.*, 1953, *48*, 78–92.
11. Janis, I. L., and Feshbach, S. Personality differences associated with responsiveness to fear-arousing communications. 1953. (In preparation.)
12. Janis, I. L., and Herz, M. The influence of preparatory communications on subsequent reactions to failure. (In preparation.)
13. Janis, I. L., and King, B. T. The influence of role-playing on opinion-change. *J. Abnorm. Soc. Psychol.* (In press.)
14. Janis, I. L., and Milholland, W. The influence of threat appeals on selective learning of the content of a persuasive communication. *J. Psychol.*, 1954, *37*, 75–80.
15. Janis, I. L., Lumsdaine, A. A., and Gladstone, A. I. Effects of preparatory communications on reactions to a subsequent news event. *Publ. Opin. Quart.*, 1951, *15*, 487–518.
16. Kelley, H. H. Salience of membership and resistance to change of group-anchored attitudes. (In preparation.) Abstracted in *Amer. Psychol.*, 1952, *7*, 328–329.
17. Kelley, H. H., and Volkart, E. H. The resistance to change of group-anchored attitudes. *Am. Soc. Rev.*, 1952, *17*, 453–465.

18. Kelley, H. H., and Woodruff, Christine L. Members' reactions to apparent group approval of a counter-norm communication. (In preparation.)
19. Kelley, H. H., Hovland, C. I., Schwartz, M., and Abelson, R. P. The influence of judges' attitudes in three methods of attitude scaling. Paper, Eastern Psychol. Assn., April 1953.
20. Kelman, H. C. Attitude change as a function of response restriction. *Hum. Rel.* 1953, *6*, 185–214.
21. Kelman, H. C., and Hovland, C. I. "Reinstatement" of the communicator in delayed measurement of opinion change. *J. Abnorm. Soc. Psychol.*, 1953, *48*, 327–335.
22. King, B. T., and Janis, I. L. Comparison of the effectiveness of improvised versus non-improvised role playing in producing opinion changes. (In preparation.) Paper, Eastern Psychol. Assn., April 1953.
23. Kurtz, K. H., and Hovland, C. I. The effect of verbalization during observation of stimulus objects upon accuracy of recognition and recall. *J. Exp. Psychol.*, 1953, *45*, 157–164.
24. Lumsdaine, A. A., and Janis, I. L. Resistance to "counterpropaganda" produced by a one-sided versus a two-sided "propaganda" presentation. *Publ. Opin. Quart.* (In press.)
25. Sherif, M. A preliminary study of inter-group relations. In J. H. Rohrer and M. Sherif, eds. *Social psychology at the crossroads.* New York, Harper, 1951, pp. 388–424.
26. Sherif, M., and Hovland, C. I. Judgmental phenomena and scales of attitude measurement: Placement of items with individual choice of number of categories. *J. Abnorm. Soc. Psychol.*, 1953, *48*, 135–141.
27. Sherif, M., Taub, D., and Hovland, C. I. Assimilation and contrast effects of anchoring stimuli on judgments. (In preparation.)
28. Weiss, W. A "sleeper" effect in opinion change. *J. Abnorm. Soc. Psychol.*, 1953, *48*, 173–180.

Index

Abelson, R. P., 285, 302

Ability factors. See Persuasibility, intellectual ability in relation to

Acceptance, and active participation, 215–230, 235–237, 278–280

  analysis of expectations which interfere with, 293–300

  and climax versus anticlimax order of arguments, 112–114, 119–120

  and communicator credibility, 36–39, 40–48, 51–53, 269–270

  contrasted with attention, comprehension and other learning factors, 11, 16–17, 36–38, 59–60, 241, 244, 265, 287–289

  contrasted with superficial conformity to group norms, 144–149, 215

  and "emotional" versus "rational" appeals, 59–60

  and explicit versus implicit presentation of conclusion, 100–105, 272–273

  factors influencing the persistence of, 253–265, 273–275, 280–281, 284

  and fear-arousing appeals, 60–65, 77–89, 92, 94–96, 270–271

  individual differences in, related to critical intellectual abilities, 182–184

    related to personality factors, 184–199, 202–204, 208–212, 277

  and internalization, 281–283

  modification of, through incentives, 10–15

  and one-sided versus two-sided presentation of arguments, 105–112

  of persuasive communications contrasted with formal instruction, 15–17, 290–293

  and primacy versus recency effects, 120–122, 126–130

  and salience of group membership, 155–170, 271–272

  and valuation of group membership, 137–149, 276–277

Active participation, attention effects produced by, 230–231

  effectiveness of different incentives used to elicit, 226–228, 234–237, 279–280

  extraneous rewards involved in, 229–230

  improvisation factor in, 221–228, 233–237, 278–279, 297

  research findings on effects of, 215–228, 231–232

  satisfaction factor in, 222–226, 229–230, 278–279

  selective retention effects produced by, 232–233

Adams, H. F., 115, 132

Aggressiveness, in relation to persuasibility. See Persuasibility, aggressiveness in relation to

Albright, Sue, 211, 213

Alexander, F., 78, 97

Allard, W., 135, 171

Allport, G. W., 53, 54, 250, 267

Anchorage of opinions in group norms. See Group Norms

Annis, A. D., 266, 267

Antecedent communication experiences. *See* Preparatory communications
Anticipations. *See* Expectations
Anticlimax order of presentation. *See* Arguments, order of presentation of
Anxiety and stimulus generalization. *See* Stimulus generalization
Anxiety-arousing appeals. *See* Appeals, fear-arousing
Appeals, bandwagon, 298
  "emotional" vs. "rational," 57–59
  fear-arousing, effects of, 56–96, 270–271, 288
    individual differences in responsiveness to, 83, 93–94, 200–201
Arguments, one-sided presentation contrasted with two-sided, 100, 105–111, 294, 296–297
  order of presentation of, 112–126
    climax compared with anticlimax, 99, 100, 112–120, 290
  refutation of, 99, 106, 129
  rehearsal of, 106, 129
  repetition of, 99, 247
Arnett, C. E., 135, 171
Asch, S. E., 25, 42, 43, 45, 53, 54, 128, 132, 135, 171
"Assimilation" phenomena in judgment, 286
Associative facilitation, 124–125, 131
Associative interference, 117–118, 125, 131
Attention factors, 37, 59–60, 78–79, 84–86, 92, 94, 99, 114–116, 120, 131, 287–290
Attitude, relationship to opinion, 7–8. *See also* Opinion; Opinion change
Attitude toward communicator. *See* Communicator
Attractiveness of a group. *See* Group, attractiveness of
Audience predispositions. *See* Persuasibility; Predispositions
Awareness of group. *See* Group membership, salience of

Back, K. W., 138, 139, 171, 195, 213
Ballard, P. B., 246, 267
Bandwagon appeals. *See* Appeals, bandwagon
Barry, H., Jr., 193, 207, 213
Bartlett, F. C., 250, 267
Bateman, R. M., 126, 132
Bavelas, A., 215, 239
Bell, Elaine, 248, 267
Berelson, B., 23, 50, 55, 209, 214
Berenda, Ruth W., 46, 49, 50, 54
Berlyne, D. E., 250, 267
Bettelheim, B., 82, 97, 149, 171
Birch, H. G., 42, 54
Boomerang effects, 36, 63, 141–143, 164, 286
Bowden, A. O., 22, 54, 135, 171
Brembeck, W. L., 99, 132
Britt, S. H., 19, 55

Brogden, H. E., 177, 207, 213
Brown, J. S., 52, 54, 61, 97
Buros, O. K., 213
Burtt, H. E., 49, 54, 135, 171

Caldwell, F. F., 22, 54, 135, 171
Campbell, D. T., 49, 54
Cantril, H., 53-55, 147, 173
Carr, H. A., 117, 132
Casey, R. D., 12, 18
Chapman, D. W., 135, 171
Charters, W. W., Jr., 156, 171
Chein, I., 169, 171
Chen, W. K. C., 243, 260, 267
Cherrington, B. M., 266, 267
Chowdhry, Kalma, 49, 54
Christiansen, Carole, 211, 213
Clark, K. B., 251, 267
Clausen, J. A., 197, 214
Climax order of presentation. *See* Arguments, organization of
Coch, L., 135, 171, 217, 239
Coffin, T. E., 39, 53, 54
Cohesiveness. *See* Group, cohesiveness of
Commitment, 127-128
Communicator, affection toward, 20
  aggressiveness toward, 63, 79, 86-87, 94-95
  attitude toward, learning of, 20-21
  attributing motives to, 22-24, 42, 73-74, 292, 295-297
  credibility of, 19-53, 269-270, 280
    effects on learning vs. acceptance, 37-39, 270
  expertness, 21-22, 25, 31, 35, 47, 294
    characteristics related to, 21-22, 49-50
  prestige, 13, 257, 298
  trustworthiness, 21-36, 103, 254-259, 296
    characteristics related to, 23-27, 33-34, 73-74, 86-87
  See also Dissociation of source from content; Retention
Compliance. *See* Conformity
Comprehension factors, 37, 59-60, 92, 114, 233-234, 287-290
Concept formation, 285-286
Conclusion drawing, 33, 100-105, 236, 272, 291
Conflict, 148, 283-284. *See also* Internalization; Resistance to influence
Conformity, to group norms. *See* Group Norms, conformity to
  pressures toward, 167-168
  superficial, contrasted with acceptance, 144-149, 215

Content stimuli. *See* Appeals; Arguments
"Contrast effects" in judgment, 286
Controlled experiment. *See* Experimental method
Cooper, Eunice, 100, 103, 132
Coser, Rose L., 194, 213
Counternorm communication, problems in use of, 142–143, 299
  resistance to, 81–82, 108–111, 273–275. *See also* Resistance to influence
Crawford, C. E., 238, 239
Credibility of communicator. *See* Communicator, credibility of
Cromwell, H., 113, 114, 119, 121, 122, 124, 132, 287

Davidson, Helen H., 171
Defense mechanisms in response to fear appeals, 61, 78, 84, 148. *See also* Appeals, fear-arousing
"Defensive identification." *See* Identification
Deutsch, M., 169, 171
Dietze, A. G., 245, 246, 267
Dinerman, Helen, 100, 103, 132
Dissociation of source from content, 30–31, 33, 41–47, 254–259, 280–281, 288
Distortion of communication content, 9, 43, 78, 204, 251, 283–284
Dollard, J., 3, 18, 61, 78, 97
Doob, L. W., 7, 18, 23, 54, 117, 132, 168, 171, 252, 267
Drives. *See* Appeals; Motivational factors; Reinforcement of opinion responses
Duncker, K., 45, 49, 50, 54
Dunlap, K., 100, 132

Ebbinghaus, H., 245
Education level. *See* Persuasibility, intellectual ability in relation to
Edwards, A. L., 251, 252, 267
Ego-involvement, as factor in conclusion drawing, 104, 273
Ehrensberger, R., 116, 132, 246, 267
Emotional adaptation, 76, 93
Emotional appeals. *See* Appeals
Emotional conditioning, 64–65
Emotional innoculation. *See* Preparatory communications
Emphasis devices, 99, 246–247
English, H. B., 248, 267
Evaluations of communications by audience, 25–29, 32, 34–35, 86–87, 269, 286
Ewing, T. N., 25–27, 54
Expectations (facilitating and interfering), of being right or wrong, 292–295
  of communicator's intent, 22–24, 73–74, 292, 295–297
  produced by active participation, 235–237
  produced by threat appeals, 62, 64–65, 95–96
  of social rewards and punishment, 38–39, 150–151, 167–168, 191, 202–203, 292–293, 297–300

Experimental method, contrasted with opinion survey methods, 4
  special problems in use of, 3–6, 58–59, 179–180
Expertness. *See* Communicator, expertness
Explicit vs. implicit conclusions. *See* Conclusion drawing
Eysenck, H. J., 207, 213

Falkenburg, D. R., Jr., 49, 54, 135, 171
Familiarity with content as factor in learning, 128, 287
Farber, I. E., 61, 97
Farnsworth, P. R., 25, 49, 55
Fear-arousing appeals. *See* Appeals, fear-arousing
Fenichel, O., 78, 97, 189, 204, 213
Ferguson, L., 177, 178, 213
Feshbach, S., 63, 68–71, 79–85, 87, 88, 94, 95, 97, 200, 201, 213, 214, 271, 288, 301
Festinger, L., 3, 18, 138, 147, 149, 167, 171, 195, 213
Fiske, D. W., 177, 213
Forgetting. *See* Retention
Frames of reference, 167, 251, 285
French, J. R. P., Jr., 135, 171, 239
French, T. M., 78, 97
Freud, Anna, 147, 148, 171
Freud, S., 3, 61, 97, 147, 171, 195, 213
Furneaux, W. D., 207, 213

Gambrell, Helen, 211, 213
Gaudet, Hazel, 23, 50, 55, 209, 214
Generality of experimental results, 5–6
Generalization. *See* Stimulus generalization
Gladstone, A. I., 75, 97, 261–263, 268, 274, 304
Glover, E., 67, 97
Goodman, C., 105, 133
Gorden, R. L., 168, 171
Granneberg, Audrey G., 57, 84, 98
Grinker, R. R., 67, 97, 189, 213
Group, attractiveness of, 137–139, 147
  cohesiveness of, 139
  power of members within, 150, 169
  power over members, 139, 147, 150
Group membership, motives involved in, 3, 137–138. *See also* Group norms
  salience of, 155–157, 271–272
    and resistance to change, 157–160, 299
    and subsequent retention of opinion change, 161–165
    See also Situational factors
  valuation of, 137–154

Group membership, valuation of (*continued*)
  in relation to resistance to influence, 139–147, 271–272, 298–299. *See also* Resistance
    to influence
Group norms, 136, 154, 271
  conformity to, 134–136, 163–165
    motives underlying. 14, 134, 136–138, 155, 167–168, 276–277
  importance of, 167–168
  knowledge of, 135, 155
  See also Resistance to influence
Guthrie, E. R., 93, 97
Guttman, L., 197, 214

Hadley, J. E., 217, 239
Hall, W., 266, 267
Hanfmann, Eugenia, 84, 97
Harris, R. E., 211, 213
Hartley, E. L., 169, 171, 172, 205, 213, 239
Hartley, Ruth E., 169, 171, 205, 213
Hartmann, G. W., 57–60, 84, 97, 251, 268
Heider, F., 43, 46, 54
Helson, H., 167, 172
Herz, M., 275, 301
Hites, R. W., 49, 54
Hoban, C. F., 243, 267
Hoch, P. H., 97, 212, 213
Hollingworth, H. L., 235, 239, 247, 267
Hostility. *See* Persuasibility, aggressiveness in relation to
Hovland, C. I., 4, 7, 12, 18, 24, 27–35, 37–40, 44, 50, 51, 54, 55, 101–104, 105–108, 117,
    118, 122, 124, 125, 127, 132, 180, 182, 183, 207, 213, 217, 232, 239, 243, 246, 247,
    254–261, 267–269, 272, 278, 280, 281, 285–287, 301, 302
Howell, W. S., 99, 132
Hughes, E. C., 151, 167, 172
Hull, C. L., 3, 18, 51, 54, 93, 97, 119, 132
Hyman, H. H., 135, 169, 171, 172

Identification, with aggressor, 82, 148
  with communicator, 148–149
  See also Internalization
Immediate contrasted with delayed effects of communications, 39–40, 89–91, 108, 161–164,
    241–266
  See also Retention
Implicit mediating responses, 8–9, 95–96, 235–237
  See also Expectations; Opinion change; Overt verbal responses
Implicit vs. explicit conclusions. *See* Conclusion drawing
Improvisation. *See* Active participation

Inattentiveness to fear-arousing communications. *See* Attention factors
Incentives. *See* Acceptance; Active participation; Appeals; Motivational factors
Incidental learning, 250
Inconsistencies in attitudes and behavior, 8–10, 169–170
Individual differences in persuasibility. *See* Persuasibility
Information, in relation to opinion, 4, 103
Initial opinions of audience, 26–27, 41, 103, 106–107, 110, 128–129, 131, 251
Instruction, contrasted with persuasion. *See* Persuasion, contrasted with instruction
Intelligence. *See* Persuasibility, intellectual ability in relation to
Interest in topic as factor in learning, 114–116, 120, 131, 250
Internalization, of group norms in relation to valuation of membership, 144–147
    theories about, 147–149, 281–283

Jahoda, Marie, 169, 171
Janis, I. L., 67–71, 73–76, 79–88, 93–95, 97, 108, 110, 129, 132, 184, 188, 191, 197, 198, 200, 201, 208, 213, 214, 218–225, 228–231, 233–236, 239, 261, 262, 268, 271, 273–275, 277, 278–280, 288, 301, 302
Jersild, A., 116–118, 132, 246, 247, 268
Jones, G. E., 245, 246, 267
Jones, L. V., 35, 55
Judgmental processes, 285–286

Kelley, H. H., 140, 142–144, 146, 152, 153, 157, 159, 162, 166, 167, 171, 172, 271, 276, 283, 285, 301, 302
Kelman, H. C., 31–33, 35, 37, 39, 40, 44, 50, 51, 55, 226–228, 233–236, 239, 256–258, 268, 269, 278–280, 302
Killian, C. D., 248, 267
King, B. T., 219–225, 228–231, 233–236, 239, 278–280, 301, 302
Kitt, Alice S., 3, 18, 135, 172
Klapper, J. T., 16, 18, 105, 131, 132
Klisurich, Dayna, 217, 239
Knower, F. H., 57, 98, 121, 132
Kohler, W., 268
Kris, E., 72, 98
Krueger, W. C. F., 247, 268
Krugman, H. E., 237, 239
Kulp, D. H., II, 22, 25, 51, 55
Kurtz, K. H., 232, 239, 278, 302

Lasswell, H. D., 12, 18, 59, 98, 206, 214
Layman, Emma M., 177, 190, 207, 214
Lazarsfeld, P. F., 16, 18, 23, 49, 55, 172, 197, 209, 214
Learning of communication content, 37–38, 84–86, 99, 114–119, 124–126, 182, 230–231, 246–247, 270

Learning processes in persuasion. *See* Acceptance; Attention factors; Comprehension factors; Motivational factors; Opinion change; Reinforcement of opinion responses
Leites, N., 59, 98
Levine, J. M., 252, 268
Lewin, K., 2, 3, 18, 135, 170, 172, 217, 239
Lewis, H. N., 171
Lewis, Helen B., 25, 42, 43, 46, 49, 55
Linton, Harriet B., 207, 214
Lippitt, R., 169, 172, 215, 239, 240
Lodgen, Pearl, 211, 214
Lucas, D. B., 19, 55
Luchins, A. S., 43, 46, 53, 55
Luh, C. W., 248, 249, 268
Lumsdaine, A. A., 4, 7, 18, 24, 54, 75, 97, 107, 108, 110, 129, 132, 180, 182, 183, 213, 217, 239, 243, 254, 259, 261, 262, 268, 273, 274, 301, 302
Lund, F. H., 121–124, 127, 128, 131, 133, 287

MacCurdy, J. T., 67, 98
Maier, N. R. F., 215, 216, 239
Mandell, W., 33–35, 37, 54, 101–104, 122, 124, 127, 132, 207, 213, 269, 272, 287, 301
Manipulative intent. *See* Communicator; Expectations
McKinnon, Kathern Mae, 190, 207, 214
McNemar, Q., 214
Mediating anticipations. *See* Expectations; Implicit mediating responses
Meier, N. C., 266, 267
Membership. *See* Group membership
Menefee, S. C., 57, 84, 98
Merrill, M. A., 214
Merton, R. K., 3, 18, 23, 24, 49, 55, 98, 135, 154, 172
Milholland, W., 85, 97, 288, 301
Miller, L. W., 266, 267
Miller, N. E., 3, 18, 61, 78, 97, 98
Moreno, J. L., 215, 239
Motivating appeals. *See* Appeals
Motivational factors, 3, 61, 99, 179
   in acceptance, 38–39, 56, 244, 259–260
   in learning and retention, 114–116, 120, 123–124, 131, 249–250
   See also Appeals; Arguments; Expectations; Group membership; Group norms, conformity to
Mowrer, O. H., 3, 18, 61, 98, 147, 148, 172
Murphy, G., 50, 55, 181, 214, 252, 268
Murphy, Lois B., 50, 55, 181, 214
Mussen, P. H., 139, 172, 205, 214
Myers, G. C., 215, 218, 239

Negative adaptation, 116
Net change, definition of, 30, 141
Newcomb, T. M., 3, 18, 49, 50, 54, 55, 135, 151, 152, 156, 171, 172, 181, 194, 210, 212, 214, 239
Nondirective approach, 100, 104, 235–237
Norms. *See* Group norms

One-sided presentation contrasted with two-sided. *See* Arguments, organization of
Opinion, nature of, 6–8
    public and private. *See* Overt verbal conformity; Private versus public conditions of opinion expression
Opinion change, duration of. *See* Retention
    measurement of, 9–10
    theoretical analysis of, 6–10, 25
    See also Persuasion
Order of arguments. *See* Arguments, order of
Overcompensation, as a consequence of prior communication, 164, 263
Overt verbal conformity, 144
    overt response contrasted with implicit responses, 8–9, 14–15
    See also Active participation; Conformity; Public versus private conditions of opinion expression

Participation. *See* Active participation
Persistence of opinion change. *See* Retention
Personality predispositions. *See* Persuasibility; Predispositions
Persuasibility, acute psychoneurotic complaints in relation to, 186, 192, 196–199, 203–204, 277
    aggressiveness in relation to, 63, 74, 188–190, 192–195, 203
    depressive feelings in relation to, 189–190, 208–209
    distrust of others in relation to, 194–195, 199–200
    feelings of personal inadequacy in relation to, 187–190, 208–209
    individual differences in, 177–181, 199–200, 207–208
    intellectual ability in relation to, 102, 103, 107–108, 179, 181–184, 277
    passive-dependent personality tendencies in relation to, 187, 189
    self-esteem in relation to, 187–191, 203, 206–210, 277, 299–300
    social inhibitions in relation to, 187–191
    social withdrawal in relation to, 192, 195–196, 203
Persuasion, contrasted with instruction, 15–17, 290–292
    nature of, 10–12
    See also Acceptance; Opinion change
Peterson, Ruth C., 241, 242, 260, 268
Polansky, N., 169, 172
Popularity, 152
Postman, L., 54, 250, 267

Power of group over members. *See* Group
Practice. *See* Arguments, rehearsal of
Predispositions, related to antiminority group attitudes, 205–206
  related to effectiveness of conclusion drawing, 102–104
  related to group membership. *See* Group membership
  related to learning and retention, 249–253
  related to persuasibility. *See* Persuasibility
  related to primacy effects, 128–129
  related to sleeper effects, 259–260
  topic-free, contrasted with topic-bound, 174–176, 206
  types of, 14, 174–176, 276–277
Preparatory communications, 66
  for failure experiences, 275
  for future events, 76, 91, 273–275, 294–295
  influence of, on reactions to fear-arousing events, 75–77, 261–264
Prestige, 13, 25, 50–51, 254, 257–259
Primacy contrasted with recency, 112, 113, 117, 121–124, 125–130, 287
Private versus public conditions of opinion expression, 127–128, 141–147, 168
Psychotherapy, 78–79, 93, 104, 147, 210–212, 235

Radke, Marian, 217, 239
Rapaport, D., 250, 268
Rational appeals. *See* Appeals, "emotional" vs. "rational"
Razran, G. H. S., 229, 239
Recency. *See* Primacy
Recognition memory. *See* Retention
Redl, F., 50, 55, 147, 172
Reference group, 3, 135–136, 166–167, 285
  comparison and normative functions of, 166
  See also Group; Group norms
Refutation of arguments. *See* Arguments, refutation of
Rehearsal of Arguments. *See* Arguments, rehearsal of
Reinforcement of opinion responses, 10–12, 61–62, 64–66, 77, 147–149, 202–204, 229–230,
    232–237, 300
  See also Acceptance
"Reinstatement" of communicator, 256–259, 280–281
Reminiscence, 246
Remmers, H. H., 126, 132, 266, 268
Repetition of arguments. *See* Arguments, repetition of
Repression, 79, 88–89, 93, 95–96, 250–251
Reproductive facilitation and interference, 125–126, 131, 253
Resistance to influence, as related to group membership, 134–136, 139–147, 157–160,
    163–165, 261
  as related to popularity, 152–154

Restorff, H. von, 246, 268

Retention, of conclusions in contrast to arguments, 248–249

  of informational content, 29–31, 37–38, 44, 84–86, 114–119, 232–233, 241, 244, 245, 246, 251–254, 265

  of opinion change, 15, 241–266, 280

    in relation to communicator, 27, 29–33, 39–40, 51, 254–259, 270. *See also* Communicator

    in relation to salience of group membership, 161–165. *See also* Group membership, salience of

    of pleasant versus unpleasant material, 250–251

    in relation to subsequent experiences, 17, 253, 260–264

    selective recall of fear-arousing communications, 85–86

    of source, 30–31, 44, 254

  types of, 247–249

    recall, 248

    recognition, 248

    relearning, 248

Rewards and punishments. *See* Expectations; Reinforcement of opinion responses

Richards, T. W., 177, 194, 207, 214

Riviere, Joan, 213

Robinson, K. F., 190, 208, 209, 214

Rogers, C. R., 100, 133

Rohrer, J. H., 172, 173, 302

Role-playing. *See* Active participation

Rosen, S., 169, 172

Rosenbaum, G., 52, 55

Saadi, M., 25, 49, 55

Salience of membership. *See* Group membership

Scare propaganda. *See* Appeals, fear-arousing

Schachter, S., 138, 152, 153, 167, 171, 172, 195, 213

Schanck, R. L., 105, 133, 168, 172

Schramm, W., 267

Schwartz, M., 285, 302

Self-consistency, 127–128

Serial position of arguments. *See* Arguments, organization of

Sharp, Agnes Arminda, 251, 268

Sheffield, F. D., 4, 7, 18, 24, 54, 107, 108, 132, 180, 182, 183, 213, 217, 239, 243, 254, 259, 261, 268

Sherif, M., 3, 18, 53, 55, 135, 147, 154, 171, 172, 173, 276, 285, 286, 301, 302

Simons, Marjorie P., 177, 194, 207, 214

Sims, V. M., 266, 268

Situational factors in communication effectiveness, 47, 51–53, 123–124, 131, 287

  related to salience of membership, 155–157, 163–165

Sleeper effect, 243–244, 254–259, 280, 288. *See also* Dissociation of source from content; Retention
Smith, B. L., 12, 18
Smith, F. T., 243, 268
Social rewards and punishments. *See* Expectations of social rewards and punishments
"Sophistication" hypothesis concerning effects of antecedent communication, 128, 263–264
Source of the communication. *See* Communicator; Dissociation of source from content; Retention, of source
Spiegel, J. P., 67, 97, 189, 213
Sponberg, H. A., 112, 113, 133
Stanton, F. N., 55, 172
Star, Shirley A., 197, 214
Status, conferred, 151
    and reference groups, 166–167
    in relation to conformity, 149–154, 195
Stevens, S. S., 98, 132, 267
Stewart, F. A., 49, 55
Stimulus generalization, in relation to anxiety level and communicator effectiveness, 51–53. *See also* Transfer of training
Stouffer, S. A., 168, 173, 197, 214
Subsequent experiences, effects of, on retention, 131, 253, 260–264. *See also* Preparatory communications
Suchman, E. A., 197, 214
Suggestion, direct vs. indirect, 100–105, 235
Susceptibility to persuasion. *See* Persuasibility
Suspicion of the communicator's intentions. *See* Communicator, trustworthiness
Swanson, G. E., 171, 172

Taub, D., 286, 302
Temporal factors. *See* Retention
Tension systems, Lewin's theory of, 170
Thibaut, J., 167, 171
Thomas, W. F., 177, 207, 213
Threat appeals. *See* Appeals, fear-arousing
Thurstone, L. L., 241, 242, 260, 268
Timmons, W. M., 217, 240
Topic-free predispositions. *See* Predispositions
Transfer of training, 17, 91, 131. *See also* Associative facilitation; Associative interference; Stimulus generalization
Trustworthiness of communicator. *See* Communicator, trustworthiness
Two-sided presentation. *See* Arguments, organization of

Underwood, B. J., 126, 133

Valuation of membership. *See* Group membership, valuation of
Van Buskirk, W. L., 246, 268
Van Ormer, E. B., 243, 267
Volkart, E. H., 140, 142, 144, 146, 152, 153, 172, 276, 301
Volkmann, J., 135, 167, 171, 173

Waelder, R., 147, 173
Watson, W. S., 251, 268
Wegrocki, H. J., 181, 182, 183, 214
Weiss, W., 27, 29, 30, 33, 37, 39, 40, 44, 54, 252, 254, 255, 256, 257, 268, 269, 280, 281, 286, 301, 302
Welborn, E. L., 248, 267
West, G. A., 22, 54, 171
Williamson, A. C., 266, 268
Willoughby, R. R., 210, 214
Wilson, M. O., 171
Woodruff, Christine L., 283, 302

Yale Communication Research Program, 2–6

Zander, A., 215, 240
Zeleny, L. D., 217, 240
Zeligs, Rose, 243, 260, 268
Zubin, J., 97, 213